Educated at Stanford University, Dr. Buchanan is Professor of History at the University of California, Santa Barbara. He is the author of *The United States and World War II* (2 volumes) and *David S. Terry: Dueling Judge.* He is also the editor of *The Navy's Air War: A Mission Completed.* His areas of special interest are the recent history of the United States and the history of California.

DATE DUE

OC 30 '07		
OC 16 '07		

#47-0108 Peel Off Pressure Sensitive

The United States and World War II
Military and Diplomatic Documents

The United States
and World War II
Military and
Diplomatic Documents

Edited by

A. RUSSELL BUCHANAN

UNIVERSITY OF SOUTH CAROLINA PRESS
Columbia, South Carolina

68/59

THE UNITED STATES AND WORLD WAR II
MILITARY AND DIPLOMATIC DOCUMENTS

First HARPER PAPERBACK edition published 1972.

This edition published by the UNIVERSITY OF SOUTH CAROLINA PRESS, Columbia, S.C., 1972, by arrangement with HARPER PAPERBACKS, from whom a paperback edition is available.

International Standard Book Number: 0-87249-276-1
Library of Congress Catalog Card Number: 72-7006

Suggested Library of Congress classification furnished by McKissick Memorial Library of the University of South Carolina: D753.B

Manufactured in the United States of America

For
E
B   J
CTL LRJ

Contents

III. War against the Axis

IV. War against Japan

Preface

The written material on World War II is so voluminous that it is impossible to approach full coverage in a single volume. The intent of the editor is to provide a sampling that will be both illustrative and an inducement to further study. These documents concentrate on military and diplomatic phases of the war.

Acknowledgment is made to the many persons who collected the huge documentation from which most of these papers are gleaned, and it is hoped that the more detailed volumes will gain readers as a result of this sampling. Particular thanks go to Dr. Richard B. Morris and Mr. Hugh Van Dusen for their support. I am grateful to Miss Melinda Wright, Mrs. Carl Hehnke, and Mrs. Esther Berger for secretarial and technical assistance. As always, I am indebted to my wife for unfailing encouragement, counsel, and aid.

The United States and World War II
Military and Diplomatic Documents

I
Pre-War and Pearl Harbor

A. Pre-War: United States and the Axis

1. Introduction

When the United States went to war in December, 1941, she did so against two foes, the Axis (Germany and Italy) and Japan, and just as the conflict came to be waged in two great areas, so did the causes of America's entry into war fall into two parts. Although Japan and the Axis joined in a tripartite alliance, each went its own way, with some communication but little or no control by one group over the actions of the other. Consequently, a brief summary of the steps which took the United States into war separates readily into two sections.

The road toward the struggle with the Axis was featured by two conflicting sentiments in the United States. One was a strong feeling of isolationism. Many Americans, including liberals, disillusioned by the aftermath of World War I, arrived at the conclusion that American participation in that conflict had been a mistake, and in an effort to prevent a recurrence, they pushed through legislation designed to prevent the United States from reaching a position as a neutral which might pull it into war. The Johnson Act, passed in 1934, sought to avoid financial involvement by prohibiting further loans to nations already in default on their war debts. Later, the so-called Neutrality Acts, modified by succeeding crises in Europe, limited American trade in an effort to prevent involvement.

In addition, President Franklin D. Roosevelt continued the preceding administration's policy of cooperation with the League of Nations, in the hope that that impotent institution could stave off the coming of war. Roosevelt was a strong believer in personal diplomacy and in his own ability to affect the course of events by top level correspondence and meetings. Before the United States entered the war, he tried writing to world leaders, and he even toyed with the idea of meeting with some of them. After war came, he and Winston Churchill made personal diplomacy an important part of the conduct of the war.

Over against the isolationist mood was the growing feeling of
sympathy for Britain and her allies after war started and the Nazi
forces rolled over Western Europe. Roosevelt shared this feeling
and, in sharp contrast to Woodrow Wilson who earlier had
pleaded for neutrality in thought and deed, on September 3, 1939,
pledged that the nation would remain neutral but added, "I cannot
ask that every American remain neutral in thought as well. Even a
neutral cannot be asked to close his mind on conscience."

When Germany invaded Denmark and Norway, Roosevelt expressed the feelings of many Americans when he declared, "Force
and military aggression are once more on the march against small
nations." Early in May, 1940, the Germans launched their major
thrust against the Dutch, Belgians, French, and the British. Roosevelt made futile diplomatic moves to dissuade Mussolini from
entering the conflict. Importuned by the battered allies to join the
conflict, Roosevelt was sympathetic but cautious; at this time he
did not consider intervening or declaring war. Toward the end of
May, however, the United States Government almost impercep-
tibly and without fanfare or referendum made what has been called
the "great commitment" to give material support to the Allies. On
June 10, 1940, Roosevelt voiced the commitment openly, and at
the same time he denounced Italy for entering the war.

The collapse of France forced the Roosevelt administration to
reexamine its situation. One result was the Ogdensburg Agreement, a defense accord between the United States and Canada.
Another extremely important consequence was the so-called de-
stroyers-for-bases deal of September 2, 1940, in which in exchange
for fifty overage destroyers, Britain granted to the United States
eight bases from Bermuda to British Guiana, either outright or rent-
free for ninety-nine years.

The presidential election of 1940 did not really change the
international picture much, since Wendell Willkie's attitude toward the war was similar to that of Roosevelt. After the election,
on December 20, 1940, Roosevelt tried to arouse the American
people to a sense of the Nazi menace, and in this same "Fireside
Chat," broadcast nationwide by radio, he proclaimed that the
United States would become the "great arsenal of democracy."
Probably the most important step taken toward this objective was
the Lend-Lease Act of March 11, 1941. This act was doubly important; it made possible the financing of the British supply program,

and it gave the United States Government control over the entire field of military supplies.

Meanwhile, as the United States was becoming the economic partner of the Allies, it moved into a state of undeclared war in the Atlantic with German submarines. At the outset of war between Great Britain and Germany, the United States Navy began to patrol the Atlantic coast, and when the Act of Panama proclaimed the existence of a "safety belt" around the Western Hemisphere, the Navy found its duties widely expanded.

At first the Navy's orders were merely to observe and report belligerent craft. As the months passed the directives changed, and long before war was declared, Britain and the United States reached an agreement on a common course of action "should" the United States be drawn into the war. Even before this event, American vessels began to play an increasing role in convoying ships across the Atlantic. At the same time German submarines departed from neutrality and attacked American vessels, such as the Robin Moor. The case of the U.S.S. Greer posed the dilemma of who should fire first; the result was the beginning of de facto war in the Atlantic.

Thus, before December, 1941, the United States and Germany had become fighting enemies, at least on the Atlantic. It took a blow in the Pacific, however, to turn this de facto belligerency into a state of declared war.

2. Correspondence between Roosevelt and Hitler

PRESIDENT ROOSEVELT TO THE GERMAN CHANCELLOR
HITLER*

WASHINGTON, September 26, 1938

The fabric of peace on the continent of Europe, if not throughout the rest of the world, is in immediate danger. The consequences of its rupture are incalculable. Should hostilities break out

SOURCE: Illustrative documents are from U.S. State Department, *Foreign Relations*, 1938, I: 658, 669–672, 684–685.

* Sent simultaneously to the President of Czechoslovakia. By direction of President Roosevelt, the Secretary of State transmitted the signed text to the

the lives of millions of men, women and children in every country involved will most certainly be lost under circumstances of unspeakable horror.

The economic system of every country involved is certain to be shattered. The social structure of every country involved may well be completely wrecked.

The United States has no political entanglements. It is caught in no mesh of hatred. Elements of all Europe have formed its civilization.

The supreme desire of the American people is to live in peace. But in the event of a general war they face the fact that no nation can escape some measure of the consequences of such a world catastrophe.

The traditional policy of the United States has been the furtherance of the settlement of international disputes by pacific means. It is my conviction that all people under the threat of war today pray that peace may be made before, rather than after, war.

It is imperative that peoples everywhere recall that every civilized nation of the world voluntarily assumed the solemn obligations of the Kellogg-Briand Pact of 1928 to solve controversies only by pacific methods. In addition, most nations are parties to other binding treaties obligating them to preserve peace. Furthermore, all countries have today available for such peaceful solution of difficulties which may arise, treaties of arbitration and conciliation to which they are parties.

Whatever may be the differences in the controversies at issue and however difficult of pacific settlement they may be, I am persuaded that there is no problem so difficult or so pressing for solution that it cannot be justly solved by the resort to reason rather than by the resort to force.

During the present crisis the people of the United States and their Government have earnestly hoped that the negotiations for

British Prime Minister and to the President of the French Council of Ministers, who was then in London. The text of the President's appeal was also sent to the Embassy in France as Department's telegram No. 691, September 26, 2 PM, to be transmitted to the Embassy in Germany as Department's No. 164, and at the same time to the Embassies in Poland as No. 41, and Hungary as No. 60, for the information of the Polish and Hungarian Ministers for Foreign Affairs.

the adjustment of the controversy which has now arisen in Europe might reach a successful conclusion.

So long as these negotiations continue so long will there remain the hope that reason and the spirit of equity may prevail and that the world may thereby escape the madness of a new resort to war.

On behalf of the 130 millions of people of the United States of America and for the sake of humanity everywhere I most earnestly appeal to you not to break off negotiations looking to a peaceful, fair, and constructive settlement of the questions at issue.

I earnestly repeat that so long as negotiations continue differences may be reconciled. Once they are broken off reason is banished and force asserts itself.

And force produces no solution for the future good of humanity.

FRANKLIN D. ROOSEVELT

THE GERMAN CHANCELLOR HITLER TO PRESIDENT ROOSEVELT

BERLIN, September 27 (?), 1938
Received September 26—9:14 PM

In your telegram received by me on September 26th, Your Excellency addressed to me an appeal in the name of the American people, in the interest of the maintenance of peace not to break off the negotiations regarding the dispute which has arisen in Europe and to strive for a peaceful, honorable and constructive settlement of this question. Be assured that I can fully appreciate the lofty intent on which your remarks are based, and that I share in every respect your opinion regarding the unforeseeable consequences of a European war. Precisely for this reason, however, I can and must refuse all responsibility of the German people and their leaders, if the further development, contrary to all my efforts up to the present should actually lead to the outbreak of hostilities. In order to arrive at a fair judgment regarding the Sudeten-German problem under discussion, it is indispensable to consider the incidents, in which, in the last analysis the origin of this problem and its dangers has its cause. In 1918, the German people laid down their arms, in the firm confidence that by the conclusion of peace with their enemies at that time the principles and ideals would be realized which had been solemnly announced by President Wilson and had been just as solemnly accepted as binding by all the belligerent powers. Never in history has the confidence of a people been more shamefully betrayed, than it was then. The peace conditions imposed on the conquered nations in the Paris suburbs treaties have fulfilled nothing of the promises given. Rather have they created a political regime in Europe which made of the conquered nations world pariahs without rights and which must be recognized in advance by every discerning person as untenable. One of the points, in which the character of the dictates of 1919 was the most openly revealed was the founding of the Czechoslovakian State, and the establishment of its boundaries without any consideration of history and nationality. The Sudeten land was also included therein, although this area had always been German, and although its inhabitants, after the destruction of the Hapsburg monarchy, had unanimously declared their desire for annexation to the German Reich. Thus the right of self-determination, which had been proclaimed by President Wilson as the most important basis of national life, was simply denied to the Sudeten Germans. But that was not enough. In the treaties of 1919, certain obligations, with regard to the German people, which, according to the text were far reaching, were imposed on the Czechoslovakian state. These obligations also were disregarded from the first. The League of Nations has completely failed to guarantee the fulfillment of these obligations in connection with the task assigned to it. Since then the Sudeten land has been engaged in the severest struggle for the maintenance of its Germanism. It was a natural and inevitable development that after the recovery of strength by the German Reich and after the reunion of Austria with it, the urge of the German Sudetens for maintenance of their culture and for closer union with Germany increased. Despite the loyal attitude of the Sudeten German party and its leaders, the difference with the Czechs became ever stronger. From day to day it became ever clearer that the Government in Prague was not disposed really to consider seriously the most elementary rights of the Sudeten Germans. Rather did it attempt with ever more violent methods the Czechization of the Sudeten land. It was inevitable that this procedure would lead to ever greater and more serious tensions. The German Government at first did not intervene in any way in this development of things, and maintained its calm restraint, even when the Czechoslovakian Government, in May of this year, proceeded to a mobilization of its army, under the purely fictitious pretext of German troop concentrations. The renunciation of military counter measures at that time in Germany, however, only served to strengthen the uncompromising attitude of the Government in Prague. This has been clearly shown by the course of the negotiations of the Sudeten German party with the Government, regarding a peaceful adjustment. These negotiations produced the conclusive proof that the Czechoslovakian Government was far from thoroughly grasping the problem of the Sudeten Germans and bringing about an equitable solution. Consequently conditions in the Czechoslovakian State, as is generally known, have in the last few weeks become utterly intolerable. Political persecution and economic oppression have plunged the Sudeten Germans into extreme misery. To characterize these circumstances it is enough to refer to the following. There are at present 214,000 Sudeten German refugees who had to leave their house and home in their ancestral country and flee across the German border, as they saw therein the last and only possibility to escape from the revolting Czechoslovakian regime of violence and bloodiest terror. Countless dead, thousands of injured, ten thousands of persons arrested and imprisoned, desolated villages are the accusing witnesses before world opinion of an outbreak of hostilities carried out for a long time by the Prague Government which you in your telegram rightly fear. Entirely aside from the German economic life in the Sudeten German territory for 20 years systematically destroyed by the Czech Government, which already shows all the signs of ruin, which you anticipated as the result of an outbreak of war these are the facts which compelled me in my Nuernberg speech of September 13th to state before the whole world that the deprivation of rights of the 3½ millions of Germans in Czechoslovakia must be stopped and that these people if they of themselves cannot find justice and help, must receive both from the German Reich. However, to make a last attempt to reach the goal in a peaceful way, I made concrete proposals for the solution of the problem in a memorandum delivered on September 23rd to the British Premier, which, in the meantime has been made public. Since the Czechoslovakian Government had previously declared itself already to be in agreement with the British and French Governments that the Sudeten German settlement area would be separated from the

Czechoslovakian State and joined to the German Reich, the proposals of the German memorandum contemplate nothing else than to bring about a prompt and equitable fulfillment of that Czechoslovakian promise. It is my conviction that you, Mr. President, when you realize the whole development of the Sudeten German problem from its inception to the present day, will recognize that the German Government has truly not been lacking either in patience or a sincere desire for a peaceful understanding. It is not Germany who is to blame for the fact that there is any Sudeten German problem at all, and that the present unjustifiable circumstances have arisen from it. The terrible fate of the people affected by the problem no longer admits of a further postponement of its solution. The possibilities of arriving at a just settlement by agreement, are therefore exhausted with the proposals of the German memorandum. It does not rest with the German Government, but with the Czechoslovakian Government alone, to decide whether it wants peace or war.

ADOLF HITLER

PRESIDENT ROOSEVELT TO THE GERMAN CHANCELLOR HITLER

WASHINGTON, September 27, 1938—10:18 PM

I desire to acknowledge Your Excellency's reply to my telegram of September 26. I was confident that you would coincide in the opinion I expressed regarding the unforeseeable consequences and the incalculable disaster which would result to the entire world from the outbreak of a European war.

The question before the world today, Mr. Chancellor, is not the question of errors of judgment or of injustices committed in the past. It is the question of the fate of the world today and tomorrow. The world asks of us who at this moment are heads of nations the supreme capacity to achieve the destinies of nations without forcing upon them as a price, the mutilation and death of millions of citizens.

Resort to force in the Great War failed to bring tranquillity. Victory and defeat were alike sterile. That lesson the world should have learned. For that reason above all others I addressed on September 26 my appeal to Your Excellency and to the President of Czechoslovakia and to the Prime Ministers of Great Britain and of France.

The two points I sought to emphasize were, first, that all matters of difference between the German Government and the Czechoslovak Government could and should be settled by pacific methods; and, second, that the threatened alternative of the use of force on a scale likely to result in a general war is as unnecessary as it is unjustifiable. It is, therefore, supremely important that negotiations should continue without interruption until a fair and constructive solution is reached.

My conviction on these two points is deepened because responsible statesmen have officially stated that an agreement in principle has already been reached between the Government of the German Reich and the Government of Czechoslovakia, although the precise time, method and detail of carrying out that agreement remain at issue.

Whatever existing differences may be, and whatever their merits may be—and upon them I do not and need not undertake to pass—my appeal was solely that negotiations be continued until a peaceful settlement is found, and that thereby a resort to force be avoided.

Present negotiations still stand open. They can be continued if you will give the word. Should the need for supplementing them become evident, nothing stands in the way of widening their scope into a conference of all the nations directly interested in the present controversy. Such a meeting to be held immediately—in some neutral spot in Europe—would offer the opportunity for this and correlated questions to be solved in a spirit of justice, of fair dealing, and, in all human probability, with greater permanence.

In my considered judgment, and in the light of the experience of this century, continued negotiations remain the only way by which the immediate problem can be disposed of upon any lasting basis.

Should you agree to a solution in this peaceful manner I am convinced that hundreds of millions throughout the world would recognize your action as an outstanding historic service to all humanity.

Allow me to state my unqualified conviction that history, and the souls of every man, woman, and child whose lives will be lost in the threatened war will hold us and all of us accountable should we omit any appeal for its prevention.

The Government of the United States has no political involvements in Europe, and will assume no obligations in the conduct of the present negotiations. Yet in our own right we recognize our responsibilities as a part of a world of neighbors.

The conscience and the impelling desire of the people of my country demand that the voice of their government be raised again and yet again to avert and to avoid war.

FRANKLIN D. ROOSEVELT

3. Fireside Chat on European War

WASHINGTON, D.C., September 3, 1939

My fellow Americans and my friends:

Tonight my single duty is to speak to the whole of America.

Until four-thirty this morning I had hoped against hope that some miracle would prevent a devastating war in Europe and bring to an end the invasion of Poland by Germany.

For four long years a succession of actual wars and constant crises have shaken the entire world and have threatened in each case to bring on the gigantic conflict which is today unhappily a fact.

It is right that I should recall to your minds the consistent and at times successful efforts of your Government in these crises to throw the full weight of the United States into the cause of peace. In spite of spreading wars I think that we have every right and every reason to maintain as a national policy the fundamental moralities, the teachings of religion and the continuation of efforts to restore peace—for some day, though the time may be distant, we can be of even greater help to a crippled humanity.

It is right, too, to point out that the unfortunate events of these recent years have, without question, been based on the use of force

SOURCE: *The Public Papers and Addresses of Franklin D. Roosevelt* (New York, 1941), VIII: 460–464. Reprinted by permission of Franklin D. Roosevelt Library, Hyde Park, New York.

and the threat of force. And it seems to me clear, even at the outbreak of this great war, that the influence of America should be consistent in seeking for humanity a final peace which will eliminate, as far as it is possible to do so, the continued use of force between nations.

It is, of course, impossible to predict the future. I have my constant stream of information from American representatives and other sources throughout the world. You, the people of this country, are receiving news through your radios and your newspapers at every hour of the day.

You are, I believe, the most enlightened and the best informed people in all the world at this moment. You are subjected to no censorship of news, and I want to add that your Government has no information which it withholds or which it has any thought of withholding from you.

At the same time, as I told my press conference on Friday, it is of the highest importance that the press and the radio use the utmost caution to discriminate between actual verified fact on the one hand, and mere rumor on the other.

I can add to that by saying that I hope the people of this country will also discriminate most carefully between news and rumor. Do not believe of necessity everything you hear or read. Check up on it first.

You must master at the outset a simple but unalterable fact in modern foreign relations between nations. When peace has been broken anywhere, the peace of all countries everywhere is in danger.

It is easy for you and for me to shrug our shoulders and to say that conflicts taking place thousands of miles from the continental United States, and, indeed, thousands of miles from the whole American Hemisphere, do not seriously affect the Americas—and that all the United States has to do is to ignore them and go about its own business. Passionately though we may desire detachment, we are forced to realize that every word that comes through the air, every ship that sails the sea, every battle that is fought, does affect the American future.

Let no man or woman thoughtlessly or falsely talk of America sending its armies to European fields. At this moment there is being prepared a proclamation of American neutrality. This would have been done even if there had been no neutrality statute on the books, for this proclamation is in accordance with international law and in accordance with American policy.

This will be followed by a Proclamation required by the existing Neutrality Act. And I trust that in the days to come our neutrality can be made a true neutrality.

It is of the utmost importance that the people of this country, with the best information in the world, think things through. The most dangerous enemies of American peace are those who, without well-rounded information on the whole broad subject of the past, the present and the future, undertake to speak with assumed authority, to talk in terms of glittering generalities, to give to the nation assurances or prophesies which are of little present or future value.

I myself cannot and do not prophesy the course of events abroad—and the reason is that, because I have of necessity such a complete picture of what is going on in every part of the world, I do not dare to do so. And the other reason is that I think it is honest for me to be honest with the people of the United States.

I cannot prophesy the immediate economic effect of this new war on our nation, but I do say that no American has the moral right to profiteer at the expense either of his fellow citizens or of the men, the women and the children who are living and dying in the midst of war in Europe.

Some things we do know. Most of us in the United States believe in spiritual values. Most of us, regardless of what church we belong to, believe in the spirit of the New Testament—a great teaching which opposes itself to the use of force, of armed force, of marching armies and falling bombs. The overwhelming masses of our people seek peace—peace at home, and the kind of peace in other lands which will not jeopardize our peace at home.

We have certain ideas and certain ideals of national safety, and we must act to preserve that safety today, and to preserve the safety of our children in future years.

That safety is and will be bound up with the safety of the Western Hemisphere and of the seas adjacent thereto. We seek to keep war from our own firesides by keeping war from coming to the Americas. For that we have historic precedent that goes back to the days of the Administration of President George Washington. It is serious enough and tragic enough to every American family in every

State in the Union to live in a world that is torn by wars on other continents. Those wars today affect every American home. It is our national duty to use every effort to keep them out of the Americas.

And at this time let me make the simple plea that partisanship and selfishness be adjourned; and that national unity be the thought that underlies all others.

This nation will remain a neutral nation, but I cannot ask that every American remain neutral in thought as well. Even a neutral has a right to take account of facts. Even a neutral cannot be asked to close his mind or his conscience.

I have said not once, but many times, that I have seen war and that I hate war. I say that again and again.

I hope the United States will keep out of this war. I believe that it will. And I give you assurance and reassurance that every effort of your Government will be directed toward that end.

As long as it remains within my power to prevent, there will be no black-out of peace in the United States.

4. Lend-Lease Act

Further to promote the defense of the United States, and for other purposes

Be it enacted by the Senate and House of Representatives of the United States of America in Congress assembled, That this Act may be cited as "An Act to Promote the Defense of the United States."

SECTION 3.

(a) Notwithstanding the provisions of any other law, the President may, from time to time, when he deems it in the interest of national defense, authorize the Secretary of War, the Secretary of the Navy, or the head of any other department or agency of the Government—

SOURCE: E. R. Stettinius, Jr., *Lend-Lease: Weapon for Victory* (New York, 1944), pp. 335–336. Copyright 1944 by The Macmillan Company. Reprinted by permission of the publisher.

(1) To manufacture in arsenals, factories, and shipyards under their jurisdiction, or otherwise procure, to the extent to which funds are made available therefor, or contracts are authorized from time to time by the Congress, or both, any defense article for the government of any country whose defense the President deems vital to the defense of the United States.

(2) To sell, transfer title to, exchange, lease, lend, or otherwise dispose of, to any such government any defense article, but no defense article not manufactured or procured under paragraph (1) shall in any way be disposed of under this paragraph, except after consultation with the Chief of Staff of the Army or the Chief of Naval Operations of the Navy, or both. The value of defense articles disposed of in any way under authority of this paragraph, and procured from funds heretofore appropriated, shall not exceed $1,300,000,000. The value of such defense articles shall be determined by the head of the department or agency concerned or such other department, agency, or officer as shall be designated in the manner provided in the rules and regulations issued hereunder. Defense articles procured from funds hereafter appropriated to any department or agency of the Government, other than from funds authorized to be appropriated under this Act, shall not be disposed of in any way under authority of this paragraph except to the extent hereafter authorized by the Congress in the Acts appropriating such funds or otherwise.

(3) To test, inspect, prove, repair, outfit, recondition, or otherwise to place in good working order, to the extent to which funds are made available therefor, or contracts are authorized from time to time by the Congress or both, any defense article for any such government, or to procure any or all such services by private contract.

(4) To communicate to any such government any defense information, pertaining to any defense article furnished to such government under paragraph (2) of this subsection.

(5) To release for export any defense article disposed of in any way under this subsection to any such government.

5. Pre-War Correspondence of German Diplomats in United States

THE CHARGÉ D'AFFAIRES IN THE UNITED STATES TO THE FOREIGN MINISTRY

TOP SECRET   WASHINGTON, July 19, 1940—4:51 PM
No. 1482 of July 18   Received July 20—3:00 AM

With reference to your telegram No. 666 and my telegram No. 1345 of July 3.

As I have reported, isolationist Republican Congressmen at the Republican Convention succeeded in affixing firmly to the party platform the language of an isolationist foreign policy that will not let itself become entangled in a European war. Nothing has leaked out about the assistance we rendered in this.

It seemed advisable therefore to undertake similar action during the Democratic Convention in Chicago. The special officer for press relations has seen to it that several reliable isolationist Congressmen went to Chicago in order to exert influence on the delegates with the purpose of including, at least formally, in the Democratic platform as well, a pledge of nonparticipation in a European war.

I have reported by dispatch about the manner in which this was done.

In addition to other means, the Congressmen used for the purpose the tried and proved promotion aid [*Propeller-Hilfsmittel*] on a sensational advertisement in the leading Chicago newspaper. Accordingly, there appeared in the *Chicago Tribune* on the 15th, the opening day of the Convention, an effective full-page advertisement similar to that in the *New York Times* of June 25, on the

SOURCE: [Germany, *Auswärtiges Amt.*], *Documents on German Foreign Policy*, Series D (July 1940, X, 250–251), (October 1940, XI, 243–244), (January 1941, XI, 1117), (February 1941, XII, 60–62), (September 1941, XIII, 474–475), (December 1941, XIII, 950–951).

occasion of the Republican Convention. For travel assistance and cost of the advertisements $4,350 have been disbursed, which please refund to the Embassy. Regarding the accounting I refer to telegraphic instruction No. 749 of July 8.

THOMSEN

THE CHARGÉ D'AFFAIRES IN THE UNITED STATES TO THE FOREIGN MINISTRY

TOP SECRET   WASHINGTON, October 4, 1940—8:22 AM
No. 2141 of October 3   Received October 5—3:00 PM

With reference to your instruction P 187 g. which arrived here August 6 and to your telegram 545 of May 22.

1. For *propaganda* purposes the Embassy in telegram 545 of May 22 was granted $15,000 per month (Information Department), for the period April to September. This amount has been used exclusively for financing the Embassy periodical *Facts in Review*. This was necessary because the number of copies, as a result of constantly growing interest and demand, increased to 80,000 a week, or 360,000 a month, and the number of pages from the original 4 to from 12 to 16 according to the type of propaganda material to be included. Please continue to make this sum available regularly each month. Since owing to the larger circulation the Embassy periodical has been coming out as a publication of the Information Library, the latter has received a tremendous number of inquiries, especially regarding the program of the German short-wave transmitter. Since September 1, therefore, the Information Library has been sending the program to 25,000 interested persons every week, which is extremely valuable for promoting the German short-wave transmitter. This involves expenses amounting to $3,000 a month, which I request be authorized to the Embassy regularly every month starting September 1. This sum also includes the expenses of the monitoring office of the Information Library, which takes down the material of the short-wave transmitter (Lord H[aw] H[aw]) and disseminates it either through F[acts] i[n] R[eview] or in other suitable ways. Thus a total of at least $18,000 a month should be made available for pure propaganda work, all of which is to be turned over by us to the Information Library. This

does not include the funds for the regular budget of the Information Library particularly for purposes of cultural policy.

2. For press purposes besides the usual peace time press fund the Embassy applied for a lump payment of $50,000 for a special press war fund, and was granted it in instruction 379 of April 8. This fund is used for press policy activities, exertion of influence on newspapers, informants, etc. Most of these payments are of such a delicate nature that the method of settlement mentioned in your telegram No. 749 of July 8 is used for them. Furthermore, funds for press policy activities of the consular offices in the United States are taken from here. This fund is already so depleted that I request that it be replenished in the same amount of $50,000, with which I believe I can manage until the end of the fiscal year, to judge from the experiences thus far during the war. This sum would only suffice to maintain the press-policy work so far undertaken by the Embassy.

3. Since the expenses for (1) propaganda, and (2) for press-policy work depend upon political developments and special directives from you, which naturally cannot be anticipated at this time, I must reserve the right as in the past to request in each case special funds for special tasks, to be accounted for as such.

THOMSEN

MEMORANDUM BY THE STATE SECRETARY

BERLIN, January 16, 1941

With reference to the memorandum of Ambassador Dieckhoff of January 9, regarding the handling of the United States of America, and with reference to telegraphic report No. 74 of January 11, from Washington.[1]

1. Both documents proceed from the assumption that the official military participation of the United States on the side of England cannot be considered as being absolutely out of the question. If one were sure of the opposite, the political and journalistic handling of the United States would indeed hardly be a problem.

---

1. This telegram contained speculations about the time necessary to develop America's military potential and about the way in which the United States might carry on the struggle following a military collapse in the British Isles.

2. An official participation of America in the war would in a certain situation have a very important effect on the course of the war, that is, when the resistance of the British Isles collapses. This would be the great hour for the American isolationists. If America should be a belligerent at that time, however, this group would be paralyzed. It could no longer see to it that America would sacrifice England and withdraw from the affair with her own gains.

3. Propagandistically, our aim must in any case be to widen the rift between the isolationists and the interventionists within the United States as well as on the American Continent on the whole. Best suited to this purpose, in my opinion, is the regular coverage of pertinent facts and events, from which the American reader can draw his own conclusions. We have only few possibilities, to be sure, for providing direct, instructive information. Perhaps still more material than heretofore can be circulated via Madrid, via Lisbon, and via Tokyo.

Submitted herewith to the Foreign Minister.

WEIZSÄCKER

THE CHARGÉ D'AFFAIRES IN THE UNITED STATES TO THE FOREIGN MINISTRY

TOP SECRET   WASHINGTON, February 9, 1941—12:02 AM
No. 354 of February 7   Received February 9—12:55 PM

English propaganda is at the present time trying with all conceivable means, both directly and by way of interventionist American organizations and bribed individual agents, to push the quick passage of the law authorizing aid to England. This has required counteraction on our part, concentrating upon promoting the organization of the isolationist opposition, which does exist but is shouted down by the press and terrorized by the Government, and having it exert pressure on congressmen and senators. This is being done both by means of public demonstrations of protest and by having my agents induce as large a number as possible of the American voters to write to the congressmen and senators of their districts letters of protest against passage of the bill. This propaganda method has proved effective in so far as the members of Congress are dependent upon their districts and must listen to the voice of their voters.

The following large-scale propaganda steps have been launched in the last few days:

1. The German-American ethnic group in the Middle West, organized in the "German-American National Alliance," was persuaded by [our] agents to give backing to the "America First Committee" and, in the name of this Committee, to write to their congressmen in Washington. The letters of protest are being sent separately by each member.

2. A well-known anti-Semitic woman writer, who possesses a secret membership list of all anti-Semitic and patriotic organizations and personalities, has likewise been induced to organize a similar flood of letters of protest to members of Congress.

3. A leading woman (group garbled) in New York, who for years has been in touch with all the patriotic women's clubs in America, and is herself the chairman of such an organization, has likewise been induced to organize letters of protest from American women, who are attacking the authorization law from the standpoint of the American mothers concerned about the blood of their sons and husbands.

4. In various cities demonstrations of protest were held through the Peace Mobilization Committee, which is closely allied with us. Such a demonstration took place on February 1 before the Capitol and on February 2 before the White House, on which occasion the Irish freedom fighters, Shaemus and O'Shell, regarding whose activity I reported in No. 259 of January 27, were conspicuous owing to their speeches. In addition, there is being prepared, with our financial support, a women's march on Washington, accompanied by sensational publicity, planned in a way similar to the march of war veterans on the Capitol in 1932. It is being organized under the motto "Mothers' Crusade to defeat H.R. 1776."[1]

5. In connection with points 1 to 4, large quantities of isolationist literature hostile to Roosevelt are being distributed.

Even though it will not be possible to prevent the passage of the bill by means of these propaganda measures, they will nevertheless contribute to lengthening the congressional debate, greatly

1. In English in the original. H.R. 1776 was the bill "To Promote the Defense of the United States and for Other Purposes" commonly known as the Lend-Lease Bill.

strengthening the opposition to the law and the credit agreement, and thereby demonstrate before the world that the credit agreement and interventionist policy is disapproved by certain portions of the people.

I covered the considerable expense incurred for the above-mentioned measures from the War Press Fund.

THOMSEN

THE CHARGÉ D'AFFAIRES IN THE UNITED STATES TO THE FOREIGN MINISTRY

MOST URGENT   WASHINGTON, September 11, 1941—3:17 PM
TOP SECRET   Received September 12—2:00 AM
No. 3125 of September 11

For the State Secretary.

With reference to my telegram No. 3098 of September 9.

On Thursday[1] noon, just a few hours before the Roosevelt address, Senator Nye, as indicated in the above telegraphic report, introduced in the Senate a resolution calling upon the Senate Committee on Naval Affairs to undertake a Congressional investigation of the Greer incident for a clear determination of the facts. The crew and officers of the Greer are to be called to testify and the ship's log is to be examined. Further, the investigating committee is to require production of all orders which the Naval Operations Staff issued to the Greer and other vessels en route between Iceland and U.S. ports, and prepare a report for the Senate. Concurrently, Senator Bennett C. Clark demanded that the Secretary of the Navy produce for the investigating committee the log of the Greer for the two days prior to and following the incident.

Introduction of this resolution was purposely so timed as to cause embarrassment to Roosevelt and give him no time for any countermove.

In addition, immediately following the Roosevelt speech tonight, Lindbergh, as the first isolationist, is to speak from Iowa over the radio network of the Mutual Broadcasting Company against the warmongers.

THOMSEN

1. Sept. 11.

The Chargé d'Affaires in the United States
to the Foreign Ministry

MOST URGENT WASHINGTON, December 4, 1941—4:05 PM
No. 4250 of December 4 Received December 5—2:45 AM

The publication on December 4 in the *Chicago Tribune* and the leading isolationist Washington newspaper, the *Times Herald*, of the secret report of the American High Command to the President about the preparations and prospects for the defeat of Germany and her allies, is causing a sensation here.

This secret report is doubtlessly an authentic war plan drawn up at Roosevelt's request. It probably served as the reason for the special Cabinet meeting about which I reported in my No. 3545, of October 14.

The report confirms in its essentials the known fact that a full commitment of American combat power is not to be expected before July 1943.

The view constantly put forth by Lindbergh, Hoover, and the other leaders of the opposition is now also corroborated by the American High Command; namely that Germany can be conquered neither by dollars, American bombers, nor by American subversive propaganda, but at the most only by an American expeditionary force of several million men; and that activating it, arming and transporting it, would require enormous sums of money and would be attended by a serious shock to the American economy.

The Anglo-American thesis that a war of starvation against Germany would suffice is refuted, and the propaganda theme that Roosevelt merely wanted to do away with the "Nazi regime" in order to bestow upon the German people the blessings of the Four Freedoms is demolished.

Military measures against Japan, in the presentation of the High Command, would be of a defensive character. Japanese policy is thus justified in concluding that America will, in the event of a two-ocean war, make its main offensive effort in the direction of Europe and Africa.

The elimination of the Soviet Union as a fighting power by the summer of 1942 at the latest and the collapse of the British

Empire are soberly included in the calculations of the American General Staff so that the publication of the document will hardly cause any special rejoicing among the allies. To be sure, the High Command characterizes the continued preservation of the British Empire as one of America's most important war aims, an admission which the non-interventionist opposition will not fail to note.

THOMSEN

B. Pre-War: United States and Japan

6. Introduction

Gaining the ascendancy in the Japanese political scene, extremists launched military expansion on the continent of Asia and by early 1932 had virtual control of Manchuria. The United States gave moral support to the League of Nations' inquiry into the matter, and when nothing came of it, Secretary of State Henry L. Stimson openly supported the Open Door Policy and China's territorial and administrative integrity by announcing a policy of non-recognition of forcible changes of government. Japan might have been unhappy about America's attitude, but as long as the United States restricted itself to an attempt to institute moral sanctions, war was unlikely between the two countries.

Tensions increased, however, as Japan moved ahead in July, 1937, to create the puppet states of Inner Mongolia and North China in the so-called "China Affair." In November, 1938, Prince Konoye announced that Japan intended to create a Greater East Asia Co-Prosperity Sphere, consisting of Japan, China, and the puppet state, Manchukuo, lined up against Communism. Chiang Kai-shek, hopeful of aid from the West, rejected the idea.

Roosevelt, sympathetic toward the Chinese, chose not to see that there was a war in progress on the Asiatic continent, and the provisions of the Neutrality Act, which would have hurt China, did not go into effect. Incidents like the firing by Japanese aircraft on the American gunboat Panay on a Chinese river, added to the tension, even though Japan quickly sought to make restitution. The nature of American protest continued to be diplomatic. In the summer of 1938, for example, the United States established a "moral embargo" on the shipment of planes and parts to Japan and urged American manufacturers not to make such shipments. The embargo annoyed but did not hurt Japan, since its crucial needs were for raw materials, not the finished products. In July, 1939, the United States hinted at a threat of embargo by giving the prescribed six-months notice for the abrogation of the Japanese trade agreement.

In 1940, Japan took advantage of Nazi successes in Europe to bring pressure on British and French holdings in the Far East. Japanese forces launched a campaign in South China which conquered the mainland around Hong Kong and the Kowloon Leasehold. In the summer and fall, occupying the Chinese island of Hainan on the way, the Japanese moved against Indo-China and the Burma Road.

American policy reflected the conflict between strong and cautious views in the State Department. On July 25, Roosevelt imposed a licensing system on "petroleum products, tetraethyl lead, and iron and steel scrap." The following day the administration published a note that restricted sharply the items to be licensed. The result was that the new procedure hurt Japan only slightly. Nevertheless, the action showed that the United States was assuming the dominant role against Japan.

In addition to trying to stop the flow of arms to China, Japan sought to deal with the menace of Soviet Russia in the Far East. To this end, in 1936 Japan had joined Germany and Italy in the Anti-Comintern Pact, which although obviously directed at Soviet Russia was not a military agreement. Then with the startling successes of Germany in the Blitzkrieg of 1940, Japan realized that Germany could become a real force in the Far East. However, occupied with war in Europe, Germany was willing to reach an understanding with Japan. The resultant Tripartite Pact of 1940 by Germany, Japan, and Italy was clearly directed at the United States and stated that each ally would aid the other "if attacked by a power at present not involved in the European war or in the Sino-Japanese conflict."

By the beginning of 1941, the Japanese Government had embarked upon two courses of action, one diplomatic and the other military. Japanese diplomats sought to avoid war by gaining concessions from the United States which would facilitate Japan's solution of its "China Question." While the diplomats negotiated, military leaders prepared for war in case the diplomats failed. There was friction within the Japanese Government. Prince Konoye, for example, hoped for a peaceful agreement with the United States. Foreign Minister Yosuke Matsuoka was strongly pro-German and anti-American. Matsuoka lost out but in time Prince Konoye also fell.

The situation became increasingly serious when Japan moved into Indo-China. President Roosevelt decided to shift from moral to economic pressure. On July 26, he issued an Executive Order freezing Japanese assets in the United States. The Japanese countered with a similar move.

By the summer of 1941, Washington officials were being aided, without Japanese knowledge, by intercepted and decoded Japanese messages, through a procedure known as "Magic." Thereafter, the Americans knew as much as did the Japanese diplomats in Washington.

Before losing his office, Prince Konoye, still hopeful for peace, got reluctant permission to seek a meeting with President Roosevelt. At first interested, Roosevelt delayed a response and finally, reacting to State Department advice that such a meeting would be detrimental to the United States, declined the offer. By this time, Japan had launched what has been called its policy of "dual initiative," which set the move toward war in motion, a move which could be stopped only by successful diplomacy. The Prince Konoye Government collapsed and General Hideki Tojo headed a new cabinet, weighted with military members. This government sent Saburo Kurusu, an experienced diplomat, to Washington to assist Ambassador Nomura, who felt out of touch with the new Administration but who was not permitted to resign. It was the thankless task of these two men to conduct the waning efforts of Japanese diplomacy as the military leaders got ready for war.

A Japanese Imperial conference on November 5, 1941, agreed that a last effort would be made for a diplomatic victory. Unsuccessful in persuading Tokyo to moderate its position, the Japanese diplomats in Washington on November 20, presented a proposal known as Proposal B to Secretary Hull. Interpreting the statement as an ultimatum, Hull consulted with Roosevelt and prepared a time-consuming counterproposal or *modus vivendi* which featured a three-months truce. Asked for reactions to the draft document, the Chinese protested violently, and the British were critical of details. By November 26, influenced by these criticisms and perhaps by a feeling that the proposal would be rejected in any case, Roosevelt and Hull discarded the temporizing response and determined on a simple restatement of the American position.

Nomura and Kurusu were "dumbfounded" by the American message when they received it for transmittal, but Hull declined to modify it. On receipt of the proposal, Tokyo notified its ambassadors that negotiations would be "*de facto* ruptured." The message further instructed: "However, I do not wish you to give the impression that the negotiations are broken off. Merely say to them that you are awaiting instructions . . ."

American officials already had been sending war warnings to outlying areas. Curiously, early in 1941 specific war warnings of possible attack had gone to Pearl Harbor, but as war approached there seemed to be no thought that Hawaii would be the object of a sudden blow. Instead, it was felt that the move would be in the Far East and that if any American possession came under attack it would be the Philippines. Thus, the later warnings that went to Hawaii were about the possibility of sudden war but not of surprise attack on Oahu.

During the night of December 6–7, two messages came from Tokyo to the Japanese diplomats in Washington and, through "Magic," to the United States Government. One was a long message, obviously an answer to the American statement, which came through in installments. The fourteenth part charged the United States and Britain with trying to "obstruct Japan's efforts toward the establishment of peace through the creation of a New Order in East Asia" and concluded with a notification that in view of the American attitude the Japanese Government considered it "impossible to reach an agreement through further negotiations."

The other message was shorter: "Will the Ambassador please submit to the United States Government (if possible to the Secretary of State) our reply to the United States at 1:00 PM on the 7th, your time." This message, through "Magic," reached the

White House about 11 AM and was in General George C. Marshall's hand fifteen to thirty minutes later. He sent another war warning, noting the time and stating: "Just what significance the hour set may have we do not know, but be on the alert accordingly." A series of circumstances prevented the message from reaching Hawaii before the attack.

In Washington, the Japanese staff failed to decode the long message in time to meet the prescribed deadline. The diplomats finally arrived in Hull's office a little after 2 PM to deliver the memorandum. By this time Hull had received reports of the Pearl Harbor attack, but not verification. He quickly read through the message, which, thanks to "Magic," he had already seen, and in measured tones he told Nomura and Kurusu that he had never seen a document that "was more crowded with infamous falsehoods and distortions on a scale so huge," and he had "never imagined until today that any Government on this planet was capable of uttering them."

7. Three Power Pact of 1940

GREW, THE AMBASSADOR IN JAPAN,
TO THE SECRETARY OF STATE

TOKYO, September 27, 1940—10 PM
Received September 27—2:15 PM

909. At 9:45 o'clock tonight we were given by the Foreign Office the following four documents in English translation shortly before their release to the press:

1. Summary of the three-power pact between Japan, Germany and Italy signed on September 27, 1940 at Berlin;
2. Radio address by the Minister for Foreign Affairs;
3. Imperial rescript by the Emperor;
4. Message of the Prime Minister.

SOURCE: U.S. State Department, *Japan, 1931–1941,* II: 164–165; [Germany, *Auswärtiges Amt.*], *Documents on German Foreign Policy,* Series D (February 1941, p. 183), (March 1941, pp. 219–220).

In view of the prime importance of these documents in connection with the present critical crisis and being informed that complete texts may not be cabled to the American press, I feel obliged to telegraph documents numbers 2, 3, and 4 in full so that Department may study their tone and substance without delay. The texts follow in three ensuing telegrams. The summary of the pact itself had already been announced on the radio from the United States tonight.

GREW

SUMMARY OF THE THREE-POWER PACT BETWEEN JAPAN, GERMANY, AND ITALY, SIGNED AT BERLIN, SEPTEMBER 27, 1940

The Governments of Japan, Germany and Italy, considering it as the condition precedent of any lasting peace that all nations of the world be given each its own proper place, have decided to stand by and co-operate with one another in regard to their efforts in Greater East Asia and the regions of Europe respectively wherein it is their prime purpose to establish and maintain a new order of things calculated to promote mutual prosperity and welfare of the peoples concerned. Furthermore it is the desire of the three Governments to extend cooperation to such nations in other spheres of the world as may be inclined to put forth endeavours along lines similar to their own, in order that their ultimate aspirations for world peace may thus be realized. Accordingly the Governments of Japan, Germany and Italy have agreed as follows:

ARTICLE 1

Japan recognizes and respects the leadership of Germany and Italy in the establishment of a new order in Europe.

ARTICLE 2

Germany and Italy recognize and respect the leadership of Japan in the establishment of a new order in Greater East Asia.

ARTICLE 3

Japan, Germany and Italy agree to cooperate in their efforts on the aforesaid lines. They further undertake to assist one another with all political, economic and military means when one of the three Contracting Parties is attacked by a power at present not involved in the European War or in the Sino-Japanese Conflict.

No. 119 of February 27   FUSCHL, February 27, 1941
    from Fuschl   Received Berlin, February 27—11:30 PM
No. 232 of February 27
    from the Foreign Ministry   Sent February 27—11:50 PM
RAM 49/R
    Secret for officer in charge.
    For the Ambassador personally.
    I ask you to work with all the means at your command to the end that Japan takes possession of Singapore by surprise as soon as possible. You will learn everything else from the information telegram dispatched today, at the same time.

                                                        RIBBENTROP

DIRECTIVE OF THE HIGH COMMAND OF THE WEHRMACHT

CHEFSACHE   FÜHRER'S HEADQUARTERS, March 5, 1941
High Command of the Wehrmacht
WFSt/Abt. L (I Op.) No. 44282/41 g. K. Chefs.
By officer only

DIRECTIVE No. 24[1]
REGARDING COOPERATION WITH JAPAN

The Führer has ordered the following regarding cooperation with Japan:

1) The *aim* of the cooperation initiated by the Tripartite Pact must be *to bring Japan into active operations in the Far East* as soon as possible. This will tie down strong English forces and the focal point of the interests of the United States of America will be diverted to the Pacific.

In view of the still undeveloped military preparedness of her foes, Japan's prospects of success will be the better, the sooner the

1. Although this was a numbered directive it was issued by the OKW and signed by Keitel rather than by Hitler.

intervention occurs. The *Barbarossa* Operation creates especially favorable political and military conditions for this.

2) For the *preparation* of the cooperation it is necessary to strengthen *Japanese military power* by every means.

To that end, the commanders in chief of the branches of the Wehrmacht will extensively and liberally comply with Japanese requests for the communication of German war and battle experience, and for aid in the field of war economy and of a technical nature. Reciprocity is desirable, but must not impede the negotiations. This naturally concerns in the main such Japanese requests as could have application in military operations within a short time.

With respect to special cases, the Führer reserves his decision.

3) The *coordination of plans of operations* on both sides pertains to the High Command of the Navy.

The following principles apply hereto:

a) The quick defeat of England is to be designated as the common aim in the conduct of the war, thereby keeping the U.S.A. out of the war. Otherwise Germany has neither political, nor military, nor economic interests in the Far East which give occasion to reservations respecting Japanese intentions.

b) The great successes which Germany has achieved in the *war against merchant shipping* make it appear peculiarly appropriate that strong Japanese forces be directed to the same purpose. In addition, every possibility of assistance in Germany's war against merchant shipping is to be exploited.

c) The *situation* of the [Tripartite] Pact Powers with respect to *raw materials* requires that Japan take over those territories which it needs to continue the war, especially if the United States intervenes. Rubber deliveries must take place even after Japan's entry into the war, since they are vital to Germany.

d) *The seizure of Singapore*, England's key position in the Far East, would signify a decisive success for the combined warfare of the three Powers.

Moreover, attacks directed against other bases of the English sea power system—against those of American sea power only if America's entry into the war cannot be prevented—are likely to weaken the power system of the enemy and, just as in the case of attack upon his sea communications, to tie down essential forces of all kinds (Australia).

A date for the beginning of operational conversations can not yet be fixed.

4) In the *military commissions* to be set up under the Tripartite Pact only those subjects should be discussed which concern the *three* Powers in the same fashion. This will primarily include the problems of economic warfare.

Dealing with them in detail is the task of the main commission in concert with the High Command of the Wehrmacht.

5) No hint of the *Barbarossa Operation* must be given to the Japanese.

The Chief of the High Command
of the Wehrmacht
signed in draft: KEITEL

8. Extracts from Henry L. Stimson's Diary

TUESDAY, November 25, 1941

This was a very full day indeed. At 9:30 Knox and I met in Hull's office for our meeting of Three. Hull showed us the proposal for a 3 months' truce, which he was going to lay before the Japanese today or tomorrow. It adequately safeguarded all our interests, I thought as we read it, but I don't think there is any chance of the Japanese accepting it, because it was so drastic. In return for the propositions which they were to do, namely, to at once evacuate and at once to stop all preparations or threats of action, and to take no aggressive action against any of her neighbors, etc., we were to give them open trade in sufficient quantities only for their civilian population. This restriction was particularly applicable to oil. We had a long talk over the general situation.

SOURCE: U.S. Congress, Hearings of the Joint Committee on the Investigation of the Pearl Harbor Attack (Washington, 1946), Part II, pp. 5433–5434, 5438–5439.

Then at 12 o'clock we (viz, General Marshall and I) went to the White House, where we were until nearly half past one. At the meeting were Hull, Knox, Marshall, Stark, and myself. There the President, instead of bringing up the Victory Parade,[1] brought up entirely the relations with the Japanese. He brought up the event that we were likely to be attacked perhaps (as soon as) next Monday, for the Japanese are notorious for making an attack without warning, and the question was what we should do. The question was how we should maneuver them into the position of firing the first shot without allowing too much danger to ourselves. It was a difficult proposition.[2] Hull laid out his general broad propositions on which the thing should be rested—the freedom of the seas and the fact that Japan was in alliance with Hitler and was carrying out his policy of world aggression. The others brought out the fact that any such expedition to the South as the Japanese were likely to take would be an encirclement of our interests in the Philippines and cutting into our vital supplies of rubber from Malaysia. I pointed out to the President that he had already taken the first steps towards an ultimatum in notifying Japan way back last summer that if she crossed the border into Thailand she was violating our safety and that therefore he had only to point out (to Japan) that to follow any such expedition was a violation of a warning we had already given. So Hull is to go to work on preparing that. When I got back to the Department I found news from G-2 that an (a Japanese) expedition had started. Five divisions have come down from Shantung and Shansi to Shanghai and there they had embarked on ships—30, 40, or 50 ships—and have been sighted south of Formosa. I at once called up Hull and told him about it and sent copies to him and to the President of the message from G-2. . . .

I returned to Woodley to lunch and just about 2 o'clock, while I was sitting at lunch, the President called me up on the telephone and in a rather excited voice asked me, "Have you heard the news?" I said, "Well, I have heard the telegrams which have been

1. This was an office nickname for the General Staff strategic plan of national action in case of war in Europe.
2. Our military and naval advisers had warned us that we could not safely allow the Japanese to move against British Malaya or the Dutch East Indies without attempting to prevent it.

coming in about the Japanese advances in the Gulf of Siam." He said, "Oh, no. I don't mean that. They have attacked Hawaii. They are now bombing Hawaii." Well, that was an excitement indeed. The messages which we have been getting through Saturday and yesterday and this morning are messages which are brought by the British patrol south of Indochina, showing that large Japanese forces were moving up into the Gulf of Siam. This itself was enough excitement and that was what we were at work on our papers about. The observer thought these forces were going to land probably either on the eastern side of the Gulf of Siam, where it would be still in Indochina, or on the western side, where it would be the Kra Peninsula, or probably Malay. The British were very much excited about it and our effort this morning in drawing our papers was to see whether or not we should all act together. The British will have to fight if they attack the Kra Peninsula. We three all thought that we must fight if the British fought. But now the Japs have solved the whole thing by attacking us directly in Hawaii.

As soon as I could finish my lunch, I returned to the office and began a long conference which lasted until 6 o'clock. The news coming from Hawaii is very bad. They seem to have sprung a complete surprise upon our fleet and have caught the battleships inside the harbor and bombed them severely with losses. They have also hit our airfields there and have destroyed a great many of our planes, evidently before they got off the ground. It has been staggering to see our people there, who have been warned long ago and were standing on the alert, should have been so caught by surprise. At 4 o'clock McCloy had the chiefs of the arms of the services in his room and I went in there and made them a little pep-up talk about getting right to work in the emergency but most of the time was spent in conference with Marshall, Grenville Clark, Miles, Patterson, McCloy, and their assistants, Lovett and General Gullion, the Provost Marshal General. The main subject that we were talking about was the form of a declaration of war. Grenville Clark had drawn up a copy based largely on the Woodrow Wilson one. We all thought that it was possible we should declare war on Germany at the same time with Japan, but that, of course, is an open question. There will be no doubt about declaring war on Japan now, I think. The President has set a conference at the White House at 8:30 this evening, in which the Cabinet had a conference and then a conference at 9 to which the leaders of the House were coming.

When the news first came that Japan had attacked us, my first feeling was of relief that the indecision was over and that a crisis had come in a way which would unite all our people. This continued to be my dominant feeling in spite of the news of catastrophes which quickly developed. For I feel that this country united has practically nothing to fear; while the apathy and divisions stirred up by unpatriotic men have been hitherto very discouraging.

Our meeting with the President in the evening was in the Oval Room in the White House. He sat behind his desk and we in a semicircle in front of him. He opened by telling us that this was the most serious meeting of the Cabinet that had taken place since 1861 and then he proceeded to enumerate the blows which had fallen upon us at Hawaii. Before he got to that, Knox who sat next to me told me with a rather white face that we had lost seven of the eight battleships in Hawaii. This, however, proved later to be exaggerated. Steve Early sat near the President and dispatches were brought in every few minutes during the meeting. The President had hastily drawn a draft of a message to Congress which he then read to us slowly. It was a very brief message, presenting the same thoughts which he actually presented the following day in his finished message to the Congress.

After the talk with the Cabinet which lasted for at least three-quarters of an hour, the leaders of Congress who had been waiting below came in. I can remember the following as being present: The Vice President, Senators Barkley, Connally, Austin, Hiram Johnson, perhaps George; Representatives: Speaker Rayburn, Sol Bloom, Eaton of New Jersey, Joe Martin; possibly others. The President began by a very frank story of what had happened, including our losses. The effect on the Congressmen was tremendous. They sat in dead silence and even after the recital was over they had very few words. The President asked if they would invite him to appear before the Joint Houses tomorrow and they said they would. He said he could not tell them exactly what he was going to say to them because events were changing so rapidly. We didn't finish until after 11 o'clock, when I returned to the office and stayed there until after 12.

On my return to the office from lunch I had started matters going in all directions to warn against sabotage and to get punch into the defense move. Marshall had sent out word of the attack to all of the corps area commanders and all our people throughout the world, particularly in the Philippines. I ordered all the officers thereafter to appear in uniform and I found that others had ordered the armed guards out over the War Department Building and additional guards over my house. We offered a guard to the White House but it was thought better there to have the FBI. This same activity went on during the intervals of my visit to the White House.

9. The Last Few Days

MEMORANDUM OF A CONVERSATION

WASHINGTON, December 7, 1941

The Japanese Ambassador asked for an appointment to see the Secretary at 1:00 PM,[1] but later telephoned and asked that the appointment be postponed to 1:45 as the Ambassador was not quite ready. The Ambassador and Mr. Kurusu arrived at the Department at 2:05 PM and were received by the Secretary at 2:20.

The Japanese Ambassador stated that he had been instructed to deliver at 1:00 PM the document which he handed the Secretary, but that he was sorry that he had been delayed owing to the need of more time to decode the message. The Secretary asked why he had specified one o'clock. The Ambassador replied that he did not know but that that was his instruction.

SOURCE: U.S. State Department, *Japan, 1931–1941*, II: 786–794; *Pearl Harbor Attack*, Report of the Joint Committee, pp. 41, 44.

1. The Japanese attack on Pearl Harbor, Hawaii, took place on December 7, 1941, at 1:20 PM, Washington time (7:50 AM, Honolulu time), which was December 8, 3:20 AM, Tokyo time. On December 8 at 6 AM, Tokyo time (December 7, 4 PM, Washington time), the Japanese Imperial headquarters announced that war began as of "dawn" on that date.

The Secretary said that anyway he was receiving the message at two o'clock.

After the Secretary had read two or three pages he asked the Ambassador whether this document was presented under instructions of the Japanese Government. The Ambassador replied that it was. The Secretary as soon as he had finished reading the document turned to the Japanese Ambassador and said,

> "I must say that in all my conversations with you (the Japanese Ambassador) during the last nine months I have never uttered one word of untruth. This is borne out absolutely by the record. In all my fifty years of public service I have never seen a document that was more crowded with infamous falsehoods and distortions—infamous falsehoods and distortions on a scale so huge that I never imagined until today that any Government on this planet was capable of uttering them."

The Ambassador and Mr. Kurusu then took their leave without making any comment.

A copy of the paper which was handed to the Secretary by the Japanese Ambassador is attached.

J[OSEPH] W. B[ALLANTINE]

MESSAGE BY PRESIDENT ROOSEVELT TO CONGRESS, DECEMBER 8, 1941

TO THE CONGRESS OF THE UNITED STATES:

Yesterday, December 7, 1941—a date which will live in infamy—the United States of America was suddenly and deliberately attacked by naval and air forces of the Empire of Japan.

The United States was at peace with that Nation and, at the solicitation of Japan, was still in conversation with its Government and its Emperor looking toward the maintenance of peace in the Pacific. Indeed, one hour after Japanese air squadrons had commenced bombing in Oahu, the Japanese Ambassador to the United States and his colleague delivered to the Secretary of State a formal reply to a recent American message. While this reply stated that it seemed useless to continue the existing diplomatic negotiations, it contained no threat or hint of war or armed attack.

It will be recorded that the distance of Hawaii from Japan makes it obvious that the attack was deliberately planned many days or even weeks ago. During the intervening time the Japanese Government has deliberately sought to deceive the United States by false statements and expressions of hope for continued peace.

The attack yesterday on the Hawaiian Islands has caused severe damage to American naval and military forces. Very many American lives have been lost. In addition American ships have been reported torpedoed on the high seas between San Francisco and Honolulu.

Yesterday the Japanese Government also launched an attack against Malaya.

Last night Japanese forces attacked Hong Kong.

Last night Japanese forces attacked Guam.

Last night Japanese forces attacked the Philippine Islands.

Last night the Japanese attacked Wake Island.

This morning the Japanese attacked Midway Island.

Japan has, therefore, undertaken a surprise offensive extending throughout the Pacific area. The facts of yesterday speak for themselves. The people of the United States have already formed their opinions and well understand the implications to the very life and safety of our Nation.

As Commander-in-Chief of the Army and Navy I have directed that all measures be taken for our defense.

Always will we remember the character of the onslaught against us.

No matter how long it may take us to overcome this premeditated invasion, the American people in their righteous might will win through to absolute victory.

I believe I interpret the will of the Congress and of the people when I assert that we will not only defend ourselves to the uttermost but will make very certain that this form of treachery shall never endanger us again.

Hostilities exist. There is no blinking at the fact that our people, our territory, and our interests are in grave danger.

With confidence in our armed forces—with the unbounded determination of our people—we will gain the inevitable triumph —so help us God.

I ask that the Congress declare that since the unprovoked and dastardly attack by Japan on Sunday, December seventh, a state of war has existed between the United States and the Japanese Empire.

FRANKLIN D. ROOSEVELT

THE WHITE HOUSE, December 8, 1941

THE "MAGIC"

With the exercise of the greatest ingenuity and utmost resourcefulness, regarded by the committee as meriting the highest commendation, the War and Navy Departments collaborated in breaking the Japanese diplomatic codes. Through the exploitation of intercepted and decoded messages between Japan and her diplomatic establishments, the so-called Magic, a wealth of intelligence concerning the purposes of the Japanese was available in Washington.[1]

Both the Army and Navy maintained several stations throughout the United States and in the Pacific for the purpose of intercepting Japanese radio communications. These stations operated under instructions emanating from Washington and forwarded the intercepted traffic to Washington without themselves endeavoring to decode or translate the material. The only exception to this procedure was in the case of the Corregidor station which had been provided with facilities for exploiting many of the Japanese diplomatic messages in view of its advantageous location from the standpoint of intercepting Tokyo traffic.[2]

Insofar as the commanding officers in Hawaii were concerned they received none of the Magic save as it was supplied them by the War and Navy Departments in the original, paraphrased, or captioned form or, operationally, through instructions predicated on this source of intelligence. While the highest military officials in

SOURCE: *Pearl Harbor Attack*, Report of the Joint Committee, pp. 179–181.

1. For a discussion of Magic and its great significance to the prosecution of the war see letters dated September 25 and 27, 1944, from General Marshall to Governor Dewey. Committee record, pp. 2979–2989.

2. For a discussion of the mechanics of the Magic, see testimony of Admiral Noyes and Capts. L. F. Safford and A. D. Kramer of the Navy, and Cols. Otis K. Sadtler and Rufus Bratton of the Army before the committee.

Washington did not know the precise nature of radio intelligence activities in Hawaii, it is clear that those charged with handling the Magic did not rely upon either the Army or Navy in Hawaii being able to decode the diplomatic messages which were decoded in Washington. However, both Admirals Stark and Turner testified that they were under the impression that Japanese diplomatic messages were being decoded by the Navy in Hawaii. No justification for this impression existed in fact apart from the failure of these officers to inform themselves adequately concerning Navy establishments.[3] Under arrangements existing during 1941 between the Army and the Navy in Washington the decoding and translating of Magic was divided between the Army Signal Intelligence Service under the direction of the Chief Signal Officer and a unit in the Navy, known as OP-20-G, under the control of the Director of Naval Communications. The responsibility for decoding and translating messages was allocated between the two services on the basis of the dates of the messages with each service ordinarily handling all messages originated on alternate days, the Army being responsible for even dates and the Navy, for odd dates. This procedure was flexible in that it was departed from in order to expedite the handling of material as the occasion demanded or in the case of any unusual situation that might prevail in one or the other of the services.

Policy With Respect to Dissemination of Magic

The Magic intelligence was regarded as preeminently confidential and the policy with respect to its restricted distribution was dictated by a desire to safeguard the secret that the Japanese diplo-

---

3. Admiral Stark testified: "I inquired on two or three occasions as to whether or not Kimmel could read certain dispatches when they came up and which we were interpreting and sending our own messages and I was told that he could. However, *I want to make it plain that that did not influence me in the slightest regarding what I sent.* I felt it my responsibility to keep the commanders in the field and to see to it that they were kept informed of the main trends and of information which (would) be of high interest to them. Regardless of what dispatches I might have seen, they may have formed background for me but I saw that affirmative action was taken from the Chief of Naval Operations to the commanders in the field on matters which I thought they should have."

matic codes were being broken.[4] Delivery of the English texts of the intercepted messages was limited, within the War Department, to the Secretary of War, the Chief of Staff, the Chief of the War Plans Division, and the Chief of the Military Intelligence Division; within the Navy, to the Secretary of Navy, the Chief of Naval Operations, the Chief of the War Plans Division, and the Director of Naval Intelligence; to the State Department; and to the President's naval aide for transmittal to the President. By agreement between the Army and Navy in Washington, the Army was responsible for distribution of Magic within the War Department and to the State Department; the Navy, for distribution within the Navy Department and to the White House. Any disclosure of the fact that the Japanese messages were being decoded or any disclosure of information obtainable only from that source would inevitably have resulted in Japan's changing her codes with attendant loss completely of the vital Magic. This fact was responsible for the translated material being closely held among a few key individuals, in addition necessarily to those who processed the messages.

The policy generally prevailed in the days before Pearl Harbor that the Magic materials were not ordinarily to be disseminated to field commanders. This policy was prescribed for the reason that (1) the Japanese might conceivably intercept the relayed Magic intelligence and learn of our success in decrypting Japanese codes; (2) the volume of intercepted traffic was so great that its transmission, particularly during the critical period of diplomatic negotia-

4. During the course of his testimony, General Miles was asked: "Who made the decision that these messages should not be sent to Hawaii as they were intercepted and translated as far as the Army is concerned?" He replied: "That followed from the general policy laid down by the Chief of Staff that these messages and the fact of the existence of these messages or our ability to decode them should be confined to the least possible number of persons; no distribution should be made outside of Washington.

"The value of that secret, the secret that we could and did decode Japanese messages, in their best code, was of incalculable value to us, both in the period when war threatened and most definitely during our waging of that war. That was the basic reason for the limitation on the distribution of those messages and of the constantly increasing closing in, as I might express it, on any possible leaks in that secret."

tions, would have overtaxed communication facilities; and (3) responsibility for evaluation of this material which was largely diplomatic in nature was properly in Washington, where the Magic could be considered along with other pertinent diplomatic information obtained from the State Department and other sources. There was no inflexible rule, however, which precluded sending to theater commanders in proper instances, either in its original form as paraphrased or in the form of estimates, conclusions, or orders based wholly or in part upon Magic. Important information derived therefrom was from time to time sent to the Hawaiian commanders by the Navy Department in paraphrased form or in the form of estimates. The War Department, on the other hand, did not send the Magic to the field, for the reason that the Army code was not believed to be as secure as that of the Navy.

For purposes of the investigation Magic fell generally into two categories: first, messages relating to diplomatic matters of the Japanese Government; and second, messages relating to espionage activities by Japanese diplomatic representatives, particularly with respect to American military installations and establishments.

The decision not to endeavor to supply field commanders all of the Magic intelligence as such was a reasonable one under the circumstances. However, *it is incumbent to determine whether responsible commanding officers were otherwise supplied the equivalent of intelligence obtained from the Magic materials.*

Excerpts from "Magic"

From: Washington (Nomura)
To: Tokyo
July 30, 1941
Purple
#609   (Secret)
Today I knew from the hard looks on their faces that they meant business and I could see that if we do not answer to suit them that they are going to take some drastic steps.

Source: *Pearl Harbor Attack*, Part 12, pp. 8, 116–117, 165, 195, 215.

During my first conversation with Roosevelt after I took office the President, referring to the Panay incident, said that at the time he cooperated with the Secretary of State and succeeded in restraining popular opinion but that in case such a thing happened a second time, it would probably be quite impossible to again calm the storm. The latest incident brought all this back to me and I can see just how gravely they are regarding it. Think of it! Popular demand for the freezing of Japanese funds was subsiding and now this had to happen. I must tell you it certainly occurred at an inopportune moment.

Things being as they are, need I point out to you gentlemen that in my opinion it is necessary to take without one moment's hesitation some appeasement measures. Please wire me back at the earliest possible moment.

From: Tokyo (Foreign Minister)
To: Washington
July 31, 1941
Purple (CA) K9
(Secret)
#433 (Part 1 of 4) (Message to Berlin #708)

From time to time you have been sending us your various opinions about what we ought to do to help Germany who desires our assistance now that she is at war with Russia. After a conference with the military, at the risk of a certain amount of repetition which may cause you some ennui, I am wiring you the Imperial Government's policy and views. Hereafter, will you please act accordingly.

1. In a cabinet meeting during the forenoon of July 2, the broad outlines of our decision concerning our future policy were drawn. You were informed of it by Circular #1390. Ever since then the Government has been and is devoting every effort to bring about the materialization of that policy.

2. The China incident has already extended over a period of four years, and the Imperial Government's general trend, particularly its military trend, has hitherto been to expend the greater part of its energies in an endeavor to bring a conclusion to the incident, and now a new situation faces us from the north and from the

south. In order to meet it, there is more reason than ever before for us to arm ourselves to the teeth for all-out war.

From: Tokyo
To: Washington
November 11, 1941
(Purple—CA)
#762 (Secret)

Judging from the progress of the conversations, there seem to be indications that the United States is still not fully aware of the exceedingly criticalness of the situation here. The fact remains that the date set forth in my message #736 is absolutely immovable under present conditions. It is a definite dead-line and therefore it is essential that a settlement be reached by about that time. The session of Parliament opens on the 15th (work will start on (the following day?)) according to the schedule. The government must have a clear picture of things to come, in presenting its case at the session. You can see, therefore, that the situation is nearing a climax, and that time is indeed becoming short.

I appreciate the fact that you are making strenuous efforts, but in view of the above mentioned situation, will you redouble them. When talking to the Secretary of State and others, drive the points home to them. Do everything in your power to get a clear picture of the U.S. attitude in the minimum amount of time. At the same time do everything in your power to have them give their speedy approval to our final proposal.

We would appreciate being advised of your opinions on whether or not they will accept our final proposal A.

From: Tokyo
To: Washington
November 22, 1941
Purple CA (Urgent)
#812 (Secret)

To both you Ambassadors.

It is awfully hard for us to consider changing the date we set in my #736. You should know this, however, I know you are working hard. Stick to our fixed policy and do your very best. Spare no efforts and try to bring about the solution we desire. There are reasons beyond your ability to guess why we wanted to settle Japanese-American relations by the 25th, but if within the next three or four days you can finish your conversations with the Americans; if the signing can be completed by the 29th, (let me write it out for you—twenty ninth); if the pertinent notes can be exchanged; if we can get an understanding with Great Britain and the Netherlands; and in short if everything can be finished, we have decided to wait until that date. This time we mean it, that the deadline absolutely cannot be changed. After that things are automatically going to happen. Please take this into your careful consideration and work harder than you ever have before. This, for the present, is for the information of you two Ambassadors alone.

From: Tokyo
To: Washington
November 28, 1941
Purple (CA)
#844   (Secret)
Well, you two Ambassadors have exerted superhuman efforts but, in spite of this, the United States has gone ahead and presented this humiliating proposal. This was quite unexpected and extremely regrettable. The Imperial Government can by no means use it as a basis for negotiations. Therefore, with a report of the views of the Imperial Government on this American proposal which I will send you in two or three days, the negotiations will be de facto ruptured. This is inevitable. However, I do not wish you to give the impression that the negotiations are broken off. Merely say to them that you are awaiting instructions and that, although the opinions of your Government are not yet clear to you, to your own way of thinking the Imperial Government has always made just claims and has borne great sacrifices for the sake of peace in the Pacific. Say that we have always demonstrated a long-suffering and conciliatory attitude, but that, on the other hand, the United States has been unbending, making it impossible for Japan to establish negotiations. Since things have come to this pass, I contacted the man you told me to in your #1180 and he said that under the present circumstances what you suggest is entirely unsuitable. From now on do the best you can.

From: Tokyo (Togo)
To: Washington
December 2, 1941
Purple
#867   (Strictly Secret)

1. Among the telegraphic codes with which your office is equipped burn all but those now used with the machine and one copy each of "O" code (Oite) and abbreviating code (L). (Burn also the various other codes which you have in your custody.)

2. Stop at once using one code machine unit and destroy it completely.

3. When you have finished this, wire me back the one word "haruna."

4. At the time and in the manner you deem most proper dispose of all files of messages coming and going and all other secret documents.

5. Burn all the codes which Telegraphic Official KOSAKA brought you. (Hence, the necessity of getting in contact with Mexico mentioned in my #860 is no longer recognized.)

From: Tokyo (Togo)
To: Havana
December 2, 1941
J 19–K 9
Circular #2445   (Strictly secret)

Take great pains that this does not leak out.

You are to take the following measures immediately:

1. With the exception of one copy of the O and L code, you are to burn all telegraph codes (this includes the code books for communication between the three departments and the code books for Army and Navy communication).

2. As soon as you have completed this operation, wire the one word Haruna.

3. Burn all secret documents and the work sheets on this message.

4. Be especially careful not to arouse the suspicion of those on the outside. Confidential documents are all to be given the same handling.

The above is preparatory to an emergency situation and is for your information alone. Remain calm ——— ——— ———.

"One O'Clock" and Final Code Destruction Messages

Two messages intercepted on the morning of December 7 have received paramount consideration—the celebrated "one o'clock" message specifying the time for delivery of the Japanese 14-part memorandum to the Government of the United States and the message setting forth final instructions to the Japanese Embassy concerning the destruction of codes and secret papers. The latter was as follows:

After deciphering part 14 of my #902 and also #907, #908, and #909, please destroy at once the remaining cipher machine and all machine codes. Dispose in like manner also secret documents.

This message was intercepted shortly after the one o'clock message but from the evidence it appears that both these intercepts were distributed at approximately the same time. The "one o'clock" message read as follows:

Will the Ambassador please submit to the United States Government (if possible to the Secretary of State) our reply to the United States at 1:00 PM on the 7th, your time.

This dispatch was filed by the Japanese at 4:18 AM December 7, and intercepted by a Navy monitoring station at 4:37 a.m. It was decrypted and available in the Navy Department at approximately 7 AM thereupon being sent to the Army for translation inasmuch as there was no translator on duty in the Navy Department at that time. Translated copies of the "one o'clock" message appear to have been returned to the Navy at approximately 9 AM Captain Kramer testified that upon his return to the Navy Department at 10:20 AM he found the "one o'clock" message and thereafter, between 10:30 and 10:35 AM, delivered it to the office of the Chief of Naval Operations, where a meeting was in progress. Delivery was then made within approximately 10 minutes to an aide to Secretary Hull at the State Department and thereafter within roughly another 10 minutes, to a Presidential aide at the White House. In the course of delivery to the office of the Chief of Naval Operations and to Secretary Hull's aide mention was made of the fact that 1 PM, Washington time, was about dawn at Honolulu and about the middle of the night in the Far East. *No mention was made that the time indicated an attack at Pearl Harbor.*

Delivery of the "one o'clock" message within the War Department was made at some time between 9 and 10 AM. General

SOURCE: *Pearl Harbor Attack*, Report of the Joint Committee, pp. 222 226.

Marshall, after being advised at his quarters that an important message had been received, arrived at this office at some time between 11:15 and 11:30 AM where he saw for the first time the 14-part memorandum, General Gerow, General Miles, and Colonel Bratton, among others, being present. After completion of his reading of the memorandum, General Marshall came to the "one o'clock" message and appears to have attached immediate significance to it. He testified that he and the officers present in his office were certain the hour fixed in the "one o'clock" message had "some definite significance"; that "something was going to happen at 1 o'clock"; that "when they specified a day, that of course had significance, but not comparable to an hour"; and, again, that it was "a new item of information of a peculiar character." At 11:30 or 11:40 AM General Marshall telephoned Admiral Stark and, upon learning the latter had read the message, proposed that a warning be sent immediately to all theaters concerned. It should be noted that the exact time of Admiral Stark's arrival at the Navy Department is not definitely established although it is known that he was there by 10:30 AM on the morning of December 7, at the very latest. Admiral Stark hesitated because he regarded the theater commanders as already alerted and he was afraid of confusing them further. General Marshall nevertheless wrote in longhand the draft of a warning message to the Western Defense Command, the Panama Command, the Hawaiian Command, and the Philippine Command, as follows:

> The Japanese are presenting at 1 PM Eastern Standard Time, to-day, what amounts to an ultimatum. Also they are under orders to destroy their code machine immediately. Just what significance the hour set may have we do not know, but be on alert accordingly.

He instructed Colonel Bratton to take the foregoing message immediately to the message center to be dispatched by radio but as Colonel Bratton was leaving the room, Admiral Stark called to request that there be placed on the dispatch the "usual expression to inform the naval officer." The following was therefore added in handwriting by General Marshall, "Inform naval authorities of this communication."

EVENTS ATTENDING TRANSMITTAL OF THE DECEMBER 7 DISPATCH

By 11:50 AM the handwritten warning had been delivered by Colonel Bratton to Colonel French, in charge of the message center. When Colonel Bratton returned, General Marshall inquired as to how much time would be required to encipher and dispatch the message. Not understanding the explanation, he instructed both Colonels Bratton and Bundy to obtain a clearer picture from the message center. These two officers upon returning advised that the message would be in the hands of the recipients within thirty minutes. Still not being satisfied, General Marshall is indicated to have sent the two officers back again and their report upon returning was regarded as satisfactory; that is, he felt assured from what he was told that the warning would be received by the pertinent commanders before 1:00 PM.

After receiving the message Colonel French personally took charge of its dispatch. Learning that the War Department radio had been out of contact with Honolulu since approximately 10:20 AM he thereupon immediately decided that the most expeditious manner of getting the message to Hawaii was by commercial facilities; that is, Western Union to San Francisco, thence by commercial radio to Honolulu. The message was filed at the Army signal center at 12:01 PM (6:31 AM, Hawaii); teletype transmission to Western Union completed at 12:17 PM (6:47 AM, Hawaii); received by RCA Honolulu 1:03 PM (7:33 AM, Hawaii); received by signal office, Fort Shafter, Hawaii, at approximately 5:15 PM (11:45 AM, Hawaii) after the attack. It appears that the teletype arrangement between RCA in Honolulu and Fort Shafter was not operating at the particular hour the message was received with the result that it was dispatched by a messenger on a bicycle who was diverted from completing delivery by the first bombing.

CHOICE OF FACILITIES

Colonel French testified that important messages to be transmitted immediately had previously been sent by commercial means when there was interference on the Army circuit between Honolulu and the War Department; that on the morning of December 7 Honolulu appeared to be in touch with San Francisco; that he had a teletype connection from his office to the Western Union office in Washington and knew Western Union had a tube connecting with RCA across the street in San Francisco; that RCA had 40 kilowatts of power whereas his set had 10 kilowatts; and that he concluded the fastest means of transmission would be via Western Union and RCA. He stated that he acted within his authority in deciding to send the message by commercial means and did not tell General Marshall how the message was going.

Colonel French stated further that he had not considered using the telephone; that the telephone was never used by the signal center; that it was unsuitable for a classified message; and that, in any event, "if they wanted to use the telephone that was up to the individuals themselves, Chief of Staff, or whoever the individual concerned."

According to General Marshall, the telephone was not considered as a means of transmission, or that it may have been considered but would not have been used, he was quite certain, certainly not to Hawaii first; that if he had thought he could put a telephone call through, he would have called General MacArthur first, and then would have called the Panama Canal. He observed that it was important to send the message in code because it was not known what "one o'clock meant" and that it might have meant only a termination of diplomatic relations or some action in southeast Asia. General Marshall pointed out that there was no secrecy in the telephone and that he was trying to gain time and yet had to be careful not to "precipitate the whole business" or do anything which could be construed as an act of war; that it was important not to disclose to the Japanese our reading of their codes.

With respect to the matter of using Navy radio facilities, Colonel French stated that the Navy used more power than did the Army and occasionally the Army asked the Navy to communicate messages but that in practice they did not use the Navy for expediting traffic to Honolulu. He considered the possible use of Navy transmission of the warning message but decided against it since it would have required time to determine whether the Navy was also having trouble getting through to Hawaii and the message would have had to be delivered from the Navy at Pearl Harbor to Fort Shafter.

General Marshall had no knowledge on the morning of December 7 that the Army radio could not establish contact with Hawaii nor that the Navy had a more powerful radio to Honolulu. It is to be noted that the message got through to addresses other than Hawaii prior to the attack.

After the event it is easy to find other means of communication which General Marshall might have employed. This will always be the case. It is clear from the record, however, that he selected a secure means dictated by the contents of the message and was assured after two or three requests for verification that the message would get through in adequate time. It did not reach Hawaii because of a failure in communications concerning which he could not have known and concerning which he was not advised. It was the failure of communications and not the selection of an improper channel that occasioned the delay.

While it is not regarded as contributing to the disaster, for reasons hereinafter to appear, it is considered extremely regrettable that Colonel French did not advise the Chief of Staff upon his inability to employ the Army's radio, the anticipated means of communication, particularly when he realized the great importance of the message and the personal concern of the Chief of Staff for its expeditious transmittal.

C. Pearl Harbor and War

10. Investigations of Pearl Harbor Attack

In the United States there have been eight investigations of the Pearl Harbor attack, and their documents and findings fill many volumes. The documents presented here can at best be considered briefly illustrative and suggestive of further study.

SOURCE: A. R. Buchanan, *The United States and World War II* (New York, 1964) I: 77.

Following is a summary of the investigations held:

The Roberts Commission, organized under Executive Order dated December 18, 1941. The inquiry lasted from December 18, 1941, to January 23, 1942, and was headed by Justice Owen J. Roberts.

The Hart Inquiry, initiated by Secretary of the Navy Frank Knox, lasted from February 12 to June 15, 1944.

The Army Pearl Harbor Board, appointed pursuant to provisions of Public Law 339, approved June 13, 1944, was initiated by an order of the Adjutant General, War Department, dated July 8, 1944. Its investigation lasted from July 20 to October 20, 1944.

The Navy Court of Inquiry also originated from Public Law 339 and came into being as a result of an order by Secretary of the Navy James Forrestal dated July 13, 1944. It held sessions from July 24 to October 19, 1944.

The Clarke Inquiry, conducted by Colonel Carter W. Clarke, "regarding the manner in which certain Top Secret communications were handled," resulted from oral instructions from General George C. Marshall. This inquiry was held from September 14 to 16, 1944, and July 13 to August 4, 1945.

The Clausen Investigation came from an order by Secretary of War Henry L. Stimson and extended from November 23, 1944, to September 12, 1945. It was conducted by Major Henry C. Clausen, JAGD.

The Hewitt Inquiry, conducted by Admiral H. Kent Hewitt, came from an order of Secretary of the Navy James Forrestal and lasted from May 14 to July 11, 1945.

The Joint Congressional Committee on the Investigation of the Pearl Harbor Attack came into being as a result of Senate Resolution No. 27 (as extended). It held its first hearings November 15, 1945, and submitted its report July 20, 1946. This committee published not only its own hearings and supporting exhibits but also the records of the other investigating agencies in 39 volumes.

No clear-cut findings have emerged. The Congressional Committee, for example, published a majority and a minority report. While critical of many persons and actions, the majority report tended to absolve the Washington administration of responsibility and to place the blame on those in command in Hawaii. The minority report put the blame on officials in both Washington and Hawaii.

11. American War Plans

RAINBOW PLANS

The five specific situations forming the basis of the five RAINBOW plans were defined by the Joint Board as follows:

RAINBOW 1 assumed the United States to be at war without major allies. United States forces would act jointly to prevent the violation of the Monroe Doctrine by protecting the territory of the Western Hemisphere north of latitude 10° south, from which the vital tasks of the United States might be threatened. The joint tasks of the Army and Navy included protection of the United States, its possessions and its seaborne trade. A strategic defensive was to be maintained in the Pacific, from behind the line Alaska-Hawaii-Panama, until developments for offensive action against Japan.

RAINBOW 2 assumed that the United States, Great Britain, and France would be acting in concert, with limited participation of U.S. forces in continental Europe and in the Atlantic. The United States could, therefore, undertake immediate offensive operations across the Pacific to sustain the interests of democratic powers by the defeat of enemy forces.

RAINBOW 3 assumed the United States to be at war without major allies. Hemisphere defense was to be assured, as in RAINBOW 1, but with early projection of U.S. forces from Hawaii into the western Pacific.

RAINBOW 4 assumed the United States to be at war without major allies, employing its forces in defense of the whole of the Western Hemisphere, but also with provision for United States Army forces to be sent to the southern part of South America, and to be used in joint operations in eastern Atlantic areas. A strategic defensive, as in RAINBOW 1, was to be maintained in the Pacific until the situation in the Atlantic permitted transfer of major naval forces for an offensive against Japan.

RAINBOW 5 assumed the United States, Great Britain, and France to be acting in concert; hemisphere defense was to be assured as in RAINBOW 1, with early projection of U.S. forces to the eastern At-

SOURCE: Quoted in Louis Morton, *Strategy and Command: The First Two Years* (Washington, 1962), pp. 71–72. Reprinted by permission of the Department of the Army.

lantic, and to either or both the African and European continents;
offensive operations were to be conducted, in concert with British
and allied forces, to effect the defeat of Germany and Italy. A strategic defensive was to be maintained in the Pacific until success
against European Axis Powers permitted transfer of major forces to
the Pacific for an offensive against Japan.

AMERICAN-DUTCH-BRITISH CONVERSATIONS, APRIL 1941

MOST SECRET

[Singapore]

VI – PLAN FOR THE EMPLOYMENT
OF NAVAL FORCES

Definition of Phase I and Phase II

40. Phase I is regarded as existing from the outbreak of hostilities with Japan until the arrival of the British Far Eastern Fleet in
the Eastern Theatre.

Phase II refers to operations subsequent to this.

OPERATIONS AGAINST JAPAN IN THE PACIFIC
AND INDIAN OCEANS
DURING PHASE I

41. The basic principle of the strategy of the Associated Powers
is that the Atlantic and Europe are the decisive theatre of war. It
follows that the forces employed in other theatres must be reduced
to a minimum so as not to impair our main effort in the decisive
theatre.

Nevertheless, it is necessary to allot large forces to other theatres,
and such forces should be used whenever possible, to inflict the
maximum loss on our enemies.

The chief example of this is the United States Pacific Fleet,
which it is essential to maintain in strength at least equal to the
Japanese fleet, in order to hold our position in the Pacific and to act
offensively against Japanese forces and bases in order to counter the

SOURCE: *Pearl Harbor Attack*, Part 15, 1568–1569.

certain Japanese offensive against the position of the Associated Powers in the Eastern Theatre.

The remaining naval forces of the Associated Powers in the Eastern Theatre are so weak that they will inevitably find themselves very largely occupied with the local defence of bases and the protection of vital sea communications. Nevertheless, whenever and wherever they can, they should assume the offensive against Japanese naval forces and sea communications.

United States Pacific Fleet.

42. As stated in the Report of the Washington Conversations, the United States Pacific Fleet at Hawaii will operate offensively against the Japanese Mandated Islands and against Japanese sea communications in the Pacific. The support to be afforded to British forces south of the equator between 155° East and 180° cannot be defined until further information is received from the Commander in Chief, United States Pacific Fleet, as to his intentions.

As the United States Pacific Fleet is responsible for operations, including the protection of sea communications, to the Eastward of 180°, it will be necessary for Australia and New Zealand to cooperate direct with the Commander in Chief of the United States Pacific Fleet.

United States Asiatic Fleet.

43. Based on Manila initially. Should movements of Japanese naval and air forces become threatening, it is proposed to despatch the submarine, destroyer and large patrol plane tenders and the tankers to Singapore before the commencement of hostilities. If hostilities start before these auxiliaries are safely disposed, the combatant vessels will escort them. It is estimated that Japan's most probable course of action will be to:

(a) contain the Asiatic Fleet in Manila Bay with the object of destroying it by air and torpedo attacks and failing in this, to

(b) locate the fleet at the earliest possible moment and endeavor to destroy it by air, submarine or surface vessel attacks.

44. The submarine, naval air and naval local defence forces will be employed in support of the Army in its defence of Luzon, conducting reconnaissance and such offensive operations against

Japanese sea communications and naval forces as are consistent with that mission. Hong Kong will be available as a base for these operations.

45. The cruisers with attached aviation units and destroyers will, when ordered by C in C Asiatic Fleet, proceed towards Singapore reporting to Commander in Chief China, to operate under his strategic direction.

46. Upon the "Ultimate Defence Area" (which includes Corregidor at the entrance to Manila Bay) becoming untenable, all remaining naval and naval air forces retaining combat value will, when released by Commander in Chief, Asiatic Fleet, retire southward passing under the strategic direction of Commander in Chief China.

British Naval Forces.

47. Apart from the local defence of bases, British naval forces will be employed on the defence of our vital sea communications, and the attack on Japanese sea communications. It is clear that the forces available are quite inadequate for the introduction of general convoy system and that evasive routing or sailings under cover must therefore form the main defence for trade.

Dutch Naval Forces.

48. These will be employed primarily for the defence of the Netherlands East Indies and of the narrow passages between the islands.

12. Pearl Harbor Attack:
Interrogation of Japanese Personnel

Subject: Pearl Harbor Attack.

Personnel Interrogated: Captain Minoru Genda; Air Operations officer on staff of Admiral Nagumo during attack on Pearl Harbor. He was with Admiral Nagumo aboard his Flagship Akagi. Captain Genda was given the responsibility of planning the attack.

Source: *Pearl Harbor Attack*, Part 13, pp. 426–427.

Interrogators: Captain Robinson and Captain Payton Harrison, USNR.

Interpreter: Douglas Wada.

Summary:

The idea of the surprise attack originated with Admiral Yamamoto during a conversation with Admiral Onishi of the 11th Carrier Division about February 1, 1941. Captain Genda was present at this meeting and remembers Yamamoto saying, "If we have war with the United States we will have no hope of winning unless the U. S. Fleet in Hawaiian waters can be destroyed." After some further discussion Yamamoto directed Onishi to draw up a plan for a surprise attack. Captain Genda was later called in by Onishi to draw up broad outlines for such a plan and determine its feasibility and possibility of success.

About September 1st map games were begun at the War College in Tokyo, to test the plan on the game board and work out all details connected therewith. The following Naval officers were the only ones who had knowledge of the plan and who worked on it at the War College at this time; Admirals Yamamoto, Ugiki, Naguno, Yamagushi, Okusaka; Captains Onishi, Genda, Kuroshima; Commanders Sasaki, Ono; following members of the Navy General staff: Admiral Fukudome, Captains Sanagi and Tonioka, Commander Miyo.

On about November 15th Admiral Yamamoto finally approved the plan and gave it to Admiral Naguno with orders covering the manner of its final execution. On November 22nd the striking force rendezvoused at Etorofu and departed on its mission at 0600 hours Nov. 26th. A speed of from 12 to 14 knots was maintained and the Task Force fueled at sea whenever the weather permitted, in order to keep full tanks. The weather was stormy and refueling difficult. It was, however, because of the weather conditions prevailing in this part of the Pacific at this time of year that the northern route was chosen. They didn't expect to meet any shipping, and fog and stormy weather would impair visibility conditions, anyway. Twice after departure information was received from Naval General Headquarters in Tokyo giving the dispositions of the U. S. Fleet in Pearl Harbor. The second despatch on this subject was received three days before the attack, or December 5th.

[2] The green light to execute the attack was sent by Admiral Yamamoto from his Flagship the Yamato on December 2nd. The message was "NIITA KAYAMA NOBORE" and means climb mount NIITAKA. This was the code phrase meaning "proceed with attack." There was an additional part to the message specifying X-Day as December 8th at the time this message was received, the striking force was near the 180th meridian at latitude 42.

In the early morning of December 7th the Force was 700 miles north of Lanai, at which time it turned south and commenced the dash in at a speed of 26 knots.

The following was the composition of the striking force:

> 6 Carriers with Akagi Flagship of Admiral Naguno.
> 2 Battleships; Hiei and Kiroshima.
> 2 Heavy Cruisers; Tone and Chikuma.
> 9 Destroyers with light cruiser Abukuma as flagship.
> 3 Submarines; I–19, I–21, and I–23.

Following is the number and type of planes used in the attack:

Fighters	81
Dive bombers	145
Horizontal bombers	104
Torpedo planes	40
Total	370

Of the fighters, 39 were kept around the Carriers as intercepters, in case the U. S. planes got in the air and made an attack. They went out in two waves about one half hour apart. At time of launching position of striking force was about 200 miles north of western tip of Lanai.

Several planes were sent early which got over Pearl about daylight and reported that the Fleet was in.

Surprise was expected, but if the U. S. Forces were on the alert and the attack discovered, all attacking planes were to drive home the attack regardless.

A very close watch was kept on Hawaiian broadcasts by Commander Ono, Staff Communication officer. Admiral Naguno and his staff felt that they could sense from these broadcasts whether or not the Forces on Oahu had an inkling of the impending attack. They felt they could judge the tenseness of the situation by these broadcasts. Since KGU and KGMB were going along in their normal manner, Naguno felt that our forces were still oblivious to developments.

For several days prior to the attack the Jap Force had been intercepting messages from our patrol planes. They had not broken the code, but they had been able to plot in their positions with radio bearings and knew the number of our patrol planes in the air at all times and that they were patrolling entirely in the south western sector from Oahu.

[3] The three submarines were placed in a line 100 miles ahead of the carriers for the final dash southward. Surface speed of these submarines was 23 knots. If they sighted any planes or shipping they were to submerge, get clear and radio the striking force as soon as it was safe to surface.

Everything went off according to plan. Total Japanese losses were 29 planes.

13. Pearl Harbor: Use of Radar

Top Secret

1 April 1941
From: OPNAV
Action: Com all Nav Districts NY Wash Governors of Guam and Samoa
Info:
Ø12358

Personnel of your Naval Intelligence Service should be advised that because of the fact that from past experience shows the Axis powers often begin activities in a particular field on Saturdays and Sundays or on national holidays of the country concerned, they should take steps on such days to see that proper watches and precautions are in effect.

Two instances occurred early on the morning of December 7th, which, if interpreted differently at the time, might have had a very great result upon the action that followed.

SOURCE: *Pearl Harbor Attack,* Part 14, pp. 1395–1396; Part 18, pp. 2966–2968.

About 7:15 AM a two-man submarine entered Pearl Harbor and was destroyed by ships on duty. Had the Naval authorities foreseen this as a possible forerunner of an air attack and notified the army, time would have been available for the dispersion of the planes. However, the naval authorities did not connect this submarine attack with a possible general attack. The army was not notified until after the attack at 8:00.

After the Air Craft Warning Service Information Center was closed at 7:00 AM, December 7th, the OPANA station remained in operation for further practice. At 7:20 AM a very significant event occurred, as shown by the following affidavits—
Exhibit "8":
"FORT SHAFTER, T. H.
Territory of Hawaii, 88:
Personally appeared before me, the undersigned, authority for administering oaths of this nature, one Grover C. White, Jr. O–396182, 2nd Lieut., Signal Corps, Signal Company, Aircraft Warning, Hawaii, who after being duly sworn according to law deposes and sayeth:

1. At the request of the Control Officer and Naval Liaison Officer the AWS agreed to operate its detectors beyond the daily period of two hours before until one hour after dawn. The first schedule required operation of all stations from 4 AM to 6 PM. This schedule was modified to the hours of 4 AM to 4 PM. A temporary schedule was next devised which required all stations to operate from 4 AM to 11 AM and to have "staggered" operation, i.e., 3 stations from 11 AM to 1 PM, the remaining 3 stations from 1 PM to 4 PM. On Saturday, December 6, 1941, I contacted the Control Officer to request authority to have all stations operate from 4 AM to 7 AM only on Sunday, December 7, 1941; this was agreed to by the Control Officer.

2. Staff Sergeant Stanley J. Wichas, SCAWH, acting RDF Officer, reports that he saw nothing that could be construed as suspicious in the information received by the AWS Information Center from 4 AM to [7 AM] Sunday, December 7, 1941. This is verified by Lt. Kermit A. Tyler, Air Corps, who was the only officer in the Information Center from 4 AM to 7 AM.

3. At approximately 7:20 AM a report was received from a Detector station at Opena that a large number of planes was

approaching Oahu on a course North 3 degrees East at a distance of approximately 192 miles. This information was immediately transmitted by the switchboard operator, Pfc. Joseph McDonald to Lt. Tyler, who talked to Opana about the flight. The statement of Pfc. Joseph McDonald, SCAWH, the switchboard operator is attached.

4. The Navy Liaison Officer's position within the Information Center was not manned when I reached the Information Center at about 8:30 AM. This position was manned shortly thereafter by Technical Sergeant Merle E. Stouffer, SCAWH, who remained on the position until approximately 4:30 PM when the position was taken over by Naval Officers.

Further the deponent sayeth not.

GROVER C. WHITE, JR.
2nd Lieut., Signal Corps, Signal Company, Aircraft Warning, Hawaii

Subscribed and sworn to before me this 9th day of Dec. AD 1941, at Fort Shafter, T. H.

(Signed)   ADAM R. HUGGINS,
2nd Lt., Signal Corps,
Summary Court.

"FORT SHAFTER, T. H.,
88:
Territory of Hawaii,

Personally appeared before me, the undersigned authority for administering oaths of this nature, one Joseph P. McDonald, 13006145, Pvt. 1cl, Signal Company Aircraft Warning, Hawaii, who after being duly sworn according to law deposes and sayeth:

I was on duty as telephone operator at the AWS Information Center on Sunday morning, December 7, 1941. I received a telephone call from Opana at 7:20 A. M. stating that a large number of planes were heading towards Oahu from North 3 points east. I gave the information to Lt. Kermit A. Tyler, Air Corps, 78th Pursuit Squadron, Wheeler Field, T. H., and the Lieutenant talked with private Lockhard at the Opana station. Lt. Tyler said that it wasn't anything of importance. At that time the planes were 132 miles out. I asked if we shouldn't advise Corporal Beatty and have the plotters come back. The Opana Unit stressed the fact that it was a very large number of planes and they seemed excited. Lt.

Tyler said that it was not necessary to call the plotters or get in touch with anyone. Further the deponent sayeth not.

(Signed) Joseph P. McDonald,

JOSEPH P. McDONALD,

Sig Co., *Aircraft Warning, Hawaii*

Subscribed and sworn to before me this 9th day of December A. D. 1941 at Fort Shafter, T. H.

(Signed) Adam R. Huggins,

ADAM R. HUGGINS,

2nd Lieut., Signal Corps,

Summary Court.

STATEMENT OF LIEUT. KERMIT A. TYLER

20 DECEMBER 1941

On Wednesday, 3 December 1941, I was first detailed to learn the operation of the plotting board in the Interception Control Center. I reported for duty at 1210, just as the crew on duty was leaving. I spoke with Lt. White, Signal Corps, a few minutes and he showed me the operating positions for Navy, Bombardment, Antiaircraft, Controller's position and Aircraft Warning Service. I remained on duty until 1600. Only a telephone operator was on duty with me.

On Sunday, 7 December 1941, I was on duty from 0400 to 0800 as Pursuit Officer at the Interceptor Control Center. From 0400 until approximately 0610 there were no plots indicated on the interception board. From that time until 0700 a number of plots appeared on the control board at various points surrounding the Island of Oahu, I particularly remember at least one plot South of Kauai and I believe there was one South of Molokai. There were two plots at some distance north of Oahu and which I remember seeing on the historical record. At the time, I questioned the plotter of the historical record who stated that he makes a record of all plots as they come in. There were a number of plots over and around the Island of Oahu. Having seen the plotters work once before with about the same general layout, this did not seem irregular to me. At 0700 all of the men except the telephone operator folded up their equipment and left. At about 0700 the operator at the OPANA RDF Station called me and said that the instrument indicated a large number of planes at 132 miles to the North. Thinking it must be a returning naval patrol, a flight of Hickam bombing planes, or possibly a flight of B–17 planes from the coast, I dismissed it as nothing unusual. (It is common knowledge that when Honolulu radio stations are testing by playing Hawaiian music throughout the night that coincidentally B–17s are apt to come in using the station for radio direction finding. The radio station was testing on the morning of 7 December, 0230–0400). At about 0750 I heard some airplanes outside and looking toward Pearl Harbor saw what I thought to be the navy practicing dive bombing runs. At a little after 0800, Sergeant Eugene Starry, A. C., Wheeler Field, called me to tell me that Wheeler Field had been attacked. I immediately had the telephone operator call all men back to duty. Most of the men had returned to duty by 0820 when Major L. N. Tindal arrived and took charge of the Control Center. I remained on duty assisting Major K. P. Bergquist and Major L. N. Tindal as Pursuit Control Officer until about 1615, 8 December 1941, with the exception of rest periods from 2000 to 2400, 7 December, and 0600 to 1000, 8 December.

(Signed) Kermit A. Tyler,

KERMIT A. TYLER,

1st Lieut., Air Corps.

Had Lieut. Tyler alerted the Hawaiian Air Force instead of deciding that the planes were friendly, there would have been time to disperse the planes but not to get them in the air as they were not warmed up. Dispersion, in all probability, would have decreased the loss in planes, but would not have prevented the attack on Pearl Harbor.

14. Pearl Harbor Attack: Japanese Account

THE SOUTHERN CROSS
by
KURAMOTI, Iki

An account written in flowery language of the experience of KU-RAMOTI, Iki in the attack on Pearl Harbor and in various other operations in the South Seas in 1942. The author has not been identified but was probably an enlisted man. Interspersed in the account will be found information of military interest from an historical point of view.

CONFIDENTIAL

HAWAII OPERATION

8 December

At the time of year when green leaves turn suddenly to red in the cool winds of approaching autumn, and one begins to feel the piercing breath of the North Wind—that is to say, on 18 November 1941—we left KURE harbor and sailed for the distant northern seas. The purpose of this operation was unknown to us.

We had taken on board warm clothing, materials for protecting the guns against the cold, and a great quantity of sea nets, but we understood nothing of this.

Day after day and night after night the ships carried out target practice.

In the newspapers that we had on board it was said that we were to attack DUTCH HARBOR, but we did not believe it.

Why did we not believe it? Consider the moderate course of Japanese diplomacy up to that time. It seemed unlikely that Japan meant at this time to lift up her hand against Britain and America. Indeed, was there not at that moment a conference in progress at Washington between America and Japan?

SOURCE: Reprinted in *Pearl Harbor Attack*, Part 13, pp. 513, 516–518.

Our hopes were betrayed. We learned this when we went into port to refuel. Then we learnt for the first time how grave the situation was. Within the bay in that island of the bitterly cold North Pacific the air fleet was gathered. The crews, who every day were busy at conferences and discussions, were in an excited state of mind.

Finally, the Navigation Officer, Liet. Comdr. YANO, told us we were to make a surprise attack on HAWAII. At last Japan would be at war with Britain and the U.S.A.!

An air attack on HAWAII! A dream come true. What will the people at home think when they hear the news? Won't they be excited! I can see them clapping their hands and shouting with joy. These were our feelings. We would teach the arrogant Anglo-Saxon scoundrels a lesson!

We must be inflexible in our course . . . We could not expect to return alive . . . Thinking that, for all we knew, we might now be eating and drinking for the last time, we gorged ourselves on wine and cakes from the canteen.

Finally, early in the morning of 26 November, our magnificent air fleet set out through the thick fog and stormy waves. Following a pre-arranged course it continued on its way toward PEARL HARBOR expecting to destroy the enemy's Pacific Fleet.

The weather grows worse, a gale blows, the seas rage, a dense fog descends. In this bitter weather, a show of actual force, a test by the gods, though tossed about in their struggle with the elements, the ships continue on their glorious way.

In the several days of danger when flags were blown away, and men washed overboard, throughout the storm, the target practice went on ceaselessly.

Every man was completely exhausted by continuous watches without sleep, and by the silent struggle with Nature; but our spirits were buoyed up by the thought that we were to strike the very first blow in this greatest of all wars.

Behind us there were a hundred million people, amongst them our own families, who had limitless faith in us. Imagine the joy of these people on the morning when we should successfully carry out this operation!

Soon the fleet crossed the 180° date-line into the Eastern Hemisphere. About this time we received a report that a steamship was proceeding on the same course as ourselves, from SAN FRAN-CISCO to RUSSIA.

It was most important now to keep a good watch. There could be no doubt of our success, provided that this operation was not discovered by the enemy. Thereafter the whole crew kept watch for sight or sound of this ship; but fortunately even when near 0 point we had caught no sight of it. Considering the dense fog, we seemed to be under divine protection.

Finally, on the long-awaited X-Day, 8 December 1941, at 0130, we reached a point 300 miles to the north of HAWAII. Then the Imperial decree on the great battle was made public.

On this day there appeared in the clear sky a dense white cloud as if it were blessing our passage. Then from the decks of the aircraft carriers, plane after plane rose, flashing their silver wings in the sunlight, and soon there were a hundred and more aircraft in the sky.

Our Sea Eagles were now moving into a great formation. Our ten years and more of intensive training, during which we had endured many hardships in anticipation of this day—would they now bear fruit? At this thought a thousand emotions filled our hearts as, close to tears, we watched this magnificent sight. One and all, in our hearts, we sent our pleas to the gods, and putting our hands together, we prayed.

Meanwhile, our Sea Eagles, with the drone of their engines resounding across the heavens like a triumphal song, turned their course toward PEARL HARBOR on the island of OAHU and set forth on their splendid enterprise.

About thirty minutes later the fleet received the first report that the raid had been successful.

The second wave of the air attack force, in a large formation composed of some two hundred planes, took off in the same way an hour later.

Reports come in one after another: "Enemy anti-aircraft fire is becoming more and more intense—we are now attacking against the main force of the enemy—we are bombing enemy airfields, the damage is enormous—"

In this moment we are repaid for all our painstaking labors. The gods themselves will bear witness to the glory of our great enter-prise!

The deck is now transformed into a whirlpool of excitement. As the glorious battle results are announced one after another by the pipes of the hurrying orderlies, shouts of joy are raised on all sides, and all gloom is completely swept away.

Meanwhile the fleet moves swiftly onward at a high speed of 26 knots.

About 0900 the welcome shapes of the returning raiders begin to appear through the clouds. One by one, like fledglings longing for their nest, they came to rest on the decks of the carriers.

Well done! But have they all come back? At this moment, my most earnest hope is that our losses may be small.

Within an hour, all the planes were brought aboard. We had lost only 29 planes. It was an incredibly small number when compared with our glorious battle results; nevertheless, when their heroic end was announced, the hearts of the crew were filled with sorrow for those men, and for the fate of our special submarines.

Suddenly the anti-aircraft defense signal was sounded. An enemy plane, above the clouds, was insolently following in the trail of our aircraft. Intending to shoot it down with one blast from our ship, we manned our battle stations, but in a moment the enemy got away.

It was also reported that the enemy fleet was on our trail; but this was only a false alarm, and all the ships withdrew towards 0 point.

Thus, having inflicted upon America a loss which cannot be wiped out in a lifetime, we finally set out upon our homeward journey.

On the way, the 2nd Cardiv and the 8th Cardiv were detached and headed for WAKE Island as an attack force.

On a morning near the end of the year—25 December—we entered the harbor at KURE, which we had long been yearning to see again.

On thinking back, it was a long journey. The heroic men who took part in it, the public excitement at home of which we learned by radio, and the wild waves of the stormy North Pacific, are all etched upon my heart like a vivid dream.

Ah, memorable day—8 December 1941!

(This concludes my recollections of the Hawaii Operation)

15. Pearl Harbor Attack: Summary

Review by Admiral R. B. Inglis

Phase I: 7:55–8:25 AM—Combined Torpedo Plane and Dive Bomber Attacks

The beginning of the attack coincided with the hoisting of the preparatory signal for 8 o'clock colors. At this time (namely, 7:55 AM) Japanese dive bombers appeared over Ford Island, and within the next few seconds enemy torpedo planes and dive bombers swung in from various sectors to concentrate their attack on the heavy ships moored in Pearl Harbor. It is estimated that nine planes engaged in the attack on the naval air station on Ford Island and concentrated on the planes parked in the vicinity of hangar No. 6.

At the time of the attack Navy planes (patrol flying boats, float planes, and scout bombers, carrier type) were lined up on the field. These planes caught fire and exploded. Machine-gun emplacements were set up hastily and manned, although the return fire from shore on Ford Island was pitifully weak. Then, as suddenly as they had appeared, the Japanese planes vanished. No further attack on this air station was made during the day. Except for a direct hit on hangar No. 6 resulting from a bomb which was apparently aimed at the battleship *California* and which fell short, the damage to the station itself was comparatively slight. However, 33 of the Navy's best planes out of a total of 70 planes of all types were destroyed or damaged.

As soon as the attack began, the commander of patrol wing 2 broadcasted from Ford Island the warning: "Air raid, Pearl Harbor. This is *not* drill." This warning was followed a few minutes later by a similar message from the commander in chief, United States Fleet.

At approximately the same time that the Japanese dive bombers appeared over Ford Island, other low-flying planes struck at the

SOURCE: *Pearl Harbor Attack*, Report of the Joint Committee, pp. 58–62.

Kaneohe Naval Air Station on the other side of the island. The attack was well executed, with the planes coming down in shallow dives and inflicting severe casualties on the seaplanes moored in the water. Machine guns and rifles were brought out, and men dispersed to fire at will at the low-flying planes. After a period of 10 to 15 minutes, the attacking planes drew off to the north at a low altitude and disappeared from sight. Several other contingents of bombers passed over, but none dropped bombs on Kaneohe Bay.

About 25 minutes after the first attack, another squadron of planes, similar to one of the Navy's light bomber types, appeared over Kaneohe and commenced bombing and strafing. No. 3 hangar received a direct hit during this attack, and four planes in the hangar were destroyed. The majority of the casualties suffered at Kaneohe resulted from this attack. Most of the injured personnel were in the squadrons attempting either to launch their planes or to save those planes not as yet damaged. When the enemy withdrew, some 10 to 15 minutes later, salvage operations were commenced, but it was too late to save No. 1 hangar, which burned until only its steel structural work was left. Only 9 out of the 36 planes at Kaneohe escaped destruction in this attack; 6 of these were damaged, and 3 were in the air on patrol south of Oahu.

Meanwhile, the Marine air base at Ewa was undergoing similar attack. Apparently the attack on Ewa preceded that at Pearl Harbor by about 2 minutes. It was delivered by 2 squadrons of 18 to 24 single-seater fighter planes using machinegun strafing tactics, which came in from the northwest at an altitude of approximately 1,000 feet. These enemy planes would descend to within 20 to 25 feet of the ground, attacking single planes with short bursts of gunfire. Then they would pull over the treetops, reverse their course, and attack from the opposite direction. Within less than 15 minutes, all the Marine tactical aircraft had been shot up or set on fire. Then the guns of the enemy fighters were turned upon Navy utility aircraft, upon planes that had been disassembled for repair, and upon the marines themselves.

Effective defense measures were impossible until after the first raid had subsided. Pilots aching to strike at the enemy in the air viewed the wreckage which until a few minutes before had been a strong air group of Marine fighters and bombers. Altogether 33 out of the 49 planes at Ewa had gone up in smoke. Some marines, unable to find anything more effective, had tried to oppose fighter planes with pistols, since the remaining 16 planes were too badly damaged to fly.

Although in phase I of the attack on the ships at Pearl Harbor Japanese dive bombers were effective, *the torpedo planes did the most damage.* They adhered strictly to a carefully laid plan and directed their attacks from those sectors which afforded the best avenues of approach for torpedo attack against selected heavy ship objectives. Thus they indicated accurate knowledge of harbor and channel depths and the berths ordinarily occupied by the major combatant units of the fleet. At least in the great majority of cases, the depth of water in Pearl Harbor did not prevent the successful execution of this form of attack. Shallow dives of the torpedoes upon launching were assured by the use of specially constructed wooden fins, remnants of which were discovered on enemy torpedoes salvaged after the attack.

Four separate torpedo plane attacks were made during phase I. The major attack was made by 12 planes, which swung in generally from the southeast over the tank farm and the vicinity of Merry Point. After splitting, they launched their torpedoes at very low altitudes (within 50 to 100 feet of the water), and from very short distances, aiming for the battleships berthed on the southeast side of Ford Island. All the outboard battleships (namely, the *Nevada, Arizona, West Virginia, Oklahoma,* and *California*) were effectively hit by one or more torpedoes. Strafing was simultaneously conducted from the rear cockpits. A recovered unexploded torpedo carried an explosive charge of 1,000 pounds.

During the second of these attacks, the *Oklahoma* was struck by three torpedoes on the port side and heeled rapidly to port, impeding the efforts of her defenders to beat off the attackers.

The third attack was made by one torpedo plane which appeared from the west and was directed against the light cruiser *Helena* and the minelayer *Oglala,* both of which were temporarily occupying the berth previously assigned to the battleship *Pennsylvania,* flagship of the Pacific Fleet. One torpedo passed under the *Oglala* and exploded against the side of the *Helena.* The blast stove in the side plates of the *Oglala.* Submersible pumps for the *Oglala* were obtained from the *Helena* but could not be used since no power was available because of damage to the ship's engineering plant.

The fourth wave of five planes came in from the northwest and attacked the seaplane tender *Tangier*, the target ship *Utah*, and the light cruisers *Raleigh* and *Detroit*. The *Raleigh* was struck by one torpedo, and the *Utah* received two hits in succession, capsizing at 8:13 AM. At first it was feared that the *Raleigh* would capsize. Orders were thereupon given for all men not at the guns to jettison all topside weights and put both airplanes in the water. Extra manila and wire lines were also run to the quays to help keep the ship from capsizing.

The *Utah*, an old battleship converted into a target ship, had recently returned from serving as a target for practice aerial bombardment. As soon as she received her torpedo hits, she began listing rapidly to port. After she had listed to about 40 degrees, the order was given to abandon ship. This order was executed with some difficulty, as the attacking planes strafed the crew as they went over the side. Remnants of the crew had reached Ford Island safely. Later knocking was heard within the hull of the *Utah*. With cutting tools obtained from the *Raleigh* a volunteer crew succeeded in cutting through the hull and rescuing a fireman, second class, who had been entrapped in the void space underneath the dynamo room.

An interesting sidelight on Japanese intentions and advance knowledge is suggested by the fact that berths F–10 and F–11 in which the *Utah* and *Raleigh* were placed, were designated carrier berths and that a carrier was frequently moored in nearby F–9.

The *Detroit* and *Tangier* escaped torpedo damage, one torpedo passing just astern of the *Detroit* and burying itself in the mud. Another torpedo passed between the *Tangier* and the *Utah*.

It is estimated that the total number of torpedo planes engaged in these 4 attacks was 21.

In the eight dive-bomber attacks occurring during phase I, three types of bombs were employed—light, medium, and incendiary.

During the second of these attacks, a bomb hit exploded the forward 14-inch powder magazine on the battleship *Arizona* and caused a ravaging oil fire, which sent up a great cloud of smoke, thereby interfering with antiaircraft fire. The battleship *Tennessee* in the adjacent berth was endangered seriously by the oil fire.

The *West Virginia* was hit during the third of these attacks by two heavy bombs as well as by torpedoes. Like the *California*, she had to be abandoned after a large fire broke out amidships. Her executive officer, the senior survivor, dove overboard and swam to the *Tennessee*, where he organized a party of *West Virginia* survivors to help extinguish the fire in the rubbish, trash, and oil which covered the water between the *Tennessee* and Ford Island.

The total number of dive bombers engaged in this phase is estimated at 30. While a few fighters were reported among the attackers in the various phases, they were no doubt confused with light bombers and accordingly are not treated as a distinct type.

Although the major attack by high-altitude horizontal bombers did not occur until phase III, 15 planes of this type operating in 4 groups were active during phase I.

Most of the torpedo damage to the fleet had occurred by 8:25 AM. All outboard battleships had been hit by one or more torpedoes; all the battleships had been hit by one or more bombs with the exception of the *Oklahoma*, which took four torpedoes before it capsized, and the *Pennsylvania*, which received a bomb hit later. By the end of the first phase, the *West Virginia* was in sinking condition; the *California* was down by the stern; the *Arizona* was a flaming ruin; the other battleships were all damaged to a greater or lesser degree.

Although the initial attack of the Japanese came as a surprise, defensive action on the part of the fleet was prompt. All ships immediately went to general quarters. Battleship ready machine guns likewise opened fire at once, and within an estimated average time of less than 5 minutes, practically all battleship and antiaircraft batteries were firing. The cruisers were firing all antiaircraft batteries within an average time of about 4 minutes. The destroyers, although opening up with machine guns almost immediately, averaged 7 minutes in bringing all antiaircraft guns into action.

During this phase of the battle there was no movement of ships within the harbor proper. The destroyer *Helm*, which had gotten under way just prior to the attack, was just outside the harbor entrance when, at 8:17 AM, a submarine conning tower was sighted to the right of the entrance channel and northward of buoy No. 1. The submarine immediately submerged. The *Helm* opened fire at 8:19 AM, when the submarine again surfaced temporarily. No hits were observed.

Phase II: 8:25–8:40 AM—Lull in Attacks

This phase is described as a lull only by way of comparison. Air activity continued, although somewhat abated, with sporadic attacks by dive and horizontal bombers. During this phase an estimated total of 15 dive bombers participated in 5 attacks upon the ships in the navy yard, the battleships *Maryland*, *Oklahoma*, *Nevada*, and *Pennsylvania*, and various light cruisers and destroyers.

Although three attacks by horizontal bombers occurred during the lull, these appear to have overlapped into phase III and are considered under that heading.

At 8.32 AM the battleship *Oklahoma* took a heavy list to starboard and capsized.

During phase II there was still relatively little ship movement within the harbor. The ready-duty destroyer *Monaghan* had received orders at 7:51 AM (Pearl Harbor time) to "proceed immediately and contact the *Ward* in defensive sea area." At about 8:37, observing an enemy submarine just west of Ford Island under fire from both the *Curtiss* and *Tangier*, the *Monaghan* proceeded at high speed and at about 8:43 rammed the submarine. As the enemy vessel had submerged, the shock was slight. The *Monaghan* thereupon reversed engines and dropped two depth charges.

The *Curtiss* had previously scored two direct hits on the conning tower. This submarine was later salvaged for inspection and disposal. The *Monaghan* then proceeded down the channel and continued her sortie. At the same time that the *Monaghan* got under way, the destroyer *Henley* slipped her chain from buoy X–11 and sortied, following the *Monaghan* down the channel.

Phase III: 8:40–9:15 AM—Horizontal Bomber Attacks

The so-called "lull" in the air raid was terminated by the appearance over the fleet of eight groups of high-altitude horizontal bombers which crossed and recrossed their targets from various directions, inflicting serious damage. Some of the bombs dropped were converted 15- or 16-inch shells of somewhat less explosive quality, marked by very little flame. According to some observers, many bombs dropped by high-altitude horizontal bombers either failed to explode or landed outside the harbor area.

During the second attack (at 9:06 AM) the *Pennsylvania* was hit by a heavy bomb which passed through the main deck amidships and detonated, causing a fire, which was extinguished with some difficulty.

The third group of planes followed very closely the line of battleship moorings. It was probably one of these planes that hit the *California* with what is believed to have been a 15-inch projectile equipped with tail vanes which penetrated to the second deck and exploded. As a result of the explosion, the armored hatch to the machine shop was badly sprung and could not be closed, resulting in the spreading of a serious fire.

Altogether, 30 horizontal bombers, including 9 planes which had participated in earlier attacks, are estimated to have engaged in phase III. Once more it was the heavy combatant ships, the battleships and cruisers, which bore the brunt of these attacks.

Although phase III was largely devoted to horizontal bombing, approximately 18 dive bombers organized in 5 groups also participated.

It was probably the second of these groups which did considerable damage to the *Nevada*, then proceeding down the South Channel, and also to the *Shaw*, *Cassin*, and *Downes*, all three of which were set afire.

During the fifth attack, a Japanese dive bomber succeeded in dropping 1 bomb on the seaplane tender *Curtiss* which detonated on the main deck level, killing 20 men, wounding 58, and leaving 1 other unaccounted for.

During this same phase, the *Curtiss* took under fire one of these bombers, which was pulling out of a dive over the naval air station. Hit squarely by the *Curtiss'* gunfire, the plane crashed on the ship, spattering burning gasoline and starting fires so menacing that one of the guns had to be temporarily abandoned.

Considerable ship movement took place during phase III. At 8:40 AM the *Nevada* cleared berth F–8 without assistance and proceeded down the South Channel. As soon as the Japanese became aware that a battleship was trying to reach open water, they sent dive bomber after dive bomber down after her and registered several hits. In spite of the damage she had sustained in the vicinity of floating drydock No. 2, and although her bridge and forestructure were ablaze, the ship continued to fight effectively. At

9:10, however, while she was attempting to make a turn in the channel, the *Nevada* ran aground in the vicinity of buoy No. 19.

Meanwhile the repair ship *Vestal*, also without assistance, had gotten under way at about 8:40, had cleared the burning *Arizona*, and at about 9:40 anchored well clear northeast of Ford Island.

Soon after the *Nevada* and *Vestal* had cleared their berths, tugs began to move the *Oglala* to a position astern of the *Helena* at 10-10 dock. The *Oglala* was finally secured in her berth at about 9, but shortly thereafter she capsized.

At 8:42, the oiler *Neosho* cleared berth F-4 unaided and stood toward Merry Point in order to reduce fire hazard to her cargo and to clear the way for a possible sortie by the battleship *Maryland*.

Phase IV: 9:15–9:45—Dive Bomber Attacks

During phase IV an estimated 27 dive bombers conducted 9 strafing attacks directed against ships throughout the entire harbor area. In all probability the planes were the same ones that had conducted previous attacks. These attacks overlapped by about 10 minutes the horizontal bomber attacks described in phase III.

Phase V: 9:45—Waning of Attacks and Completion of Raid

By 9:45 all enemy planes had retired. Evading Navy aerial searches, both shore-based and from carriers at sea, the Japanese striking force retired to its home waters without being contacted by any American units.

An outline review of the Japanese attack on Army planes and installations is as follows:

Hickam Field

(Army planes at the time of the attack were lined up on the warming-up aprons three or four abreast with approximately 10 feet between wing tips, and approximately 135 feet from the tail of one plane to the nose of another.)

First attack (lasting about 10 minutes): At about 7:55 AM nine dive bombers attacked the Hawaiian Air Depot buildings and three additional planes attacked the same objectives from the northwest. Several minutes later nine additional bombers bombed Hickam Field hangar line from the southeast. Immediately thereafter, seven more dive bombers attacked the hangar line from the east.

Second attack (lasting between 10 and 15 minutes): At about 8:25 AM between six and nine planes attacked the No. 1 Aqua System, the technical buildings, and the consolidated barracks. During and immediately after this bombing attack, Army planes on the parking apron were attacked with gunfire. About 8:26 AM a formation of five or six planes bombed the baseball diamond from a high altitude, possibly believing the gasoline storage system to be in that area.

Third attack (lasting about 8 minutes): At 9 AM from six to nine planes attacked with machine gun fire the technical buildings behind the hangar lines and certain planes which by then were dispersed. At about the same time from seven to nine planes bombed the consolidated barracks, the parade ground and the post exchange.

Wheeler Field

(Army planes were parked in the space between the aprons in front of the hangars, generally in a series of parallel lines approximately wing tip to wing tip, the lines varying from 15 to 20 feet apart.)

First attack (lasting approximately 15 minutes): At 8:02 AM 25 planes divebombed the hangar lines; machine-gun fire was also employed during the attack.

Second attack (lasting less than 5 minutes): At 9 AM seven planes machine-gunned Army planes being taxied to the airdrome.

Bellows Field

(The P–40s were parked in line at 10 to 15 feet intervals; the reconnaissance planes were also parked in a line at slightly greater intervals.)

First attack: At 8:30 a single Japanese fighter machine-gunned the tent area.

Second attack (lasting about 15 minutes): At about 9 AM nine fighters machine-gunned the Army planes.

Haleiwa Field was not attacked and after 9:45 AM there were no further attacks on Army installations. The evidence indicates that a maximum of 105 planes participated in the attacks on the airfields, it being noted that some of the planes included in this number may have taken part in more than one attack.

16. Pearl Harbor and War: Reaction
of David E. Lilienthal

DECEMBER 11, 1941
THURSDAY, 11:20 AM

I am writing this in the visitors' gallery of the Senate Chamber. In about a half-hour a messenger will appear at the door down there, and be announced as bearing a message from the President of the United States. The Clerk will read that message; it will say that a state of war exists between Germany and Italy and the United States, and will ask that we recognize that state of war. And the Senate, without dissent, will vote to put us into war with Germany.

There are thousands of people lined up outside trying to get a place to see this ceremony. Above us are the strange, rather ominous-looking girders, iron bridge effects, to support the roof of the Senate Chamber. The Senate needs some support, God help us all, for at the moment I feel very doubtful whether such an institution will survive if we do, or if it does that we can survive. The seats below are spotted with white papers that give it all, in the dim light, a weird, funeral-parlor look.

We were sitting in the office when we heard "Extras" being shouted in the street. Usually that means nothing, but at ten o'clock in the morning it might these days. We sent out for a copy: "Germany and Italy declare war on the United States." And a few minutes later Miss Owen learned that the Democratic Clerk would arrange for us to attend the noon session, and away we went.

Now it is twelve. The Chaplain drones through a prayer and the stenographers take it down busily so the Lord can read it in the Record tomorrow. There is Norris, who saw this happen before,

SOURCE: David E. Lilienthal, *The Journals of David E. Lilienthal: The TVA Years 1939–1945* (New York, 1964), I, 414–415. Copyright © 1964 by David E. Lilienthal. Reprinted by permission of Harper & Row, Publishers, Inc.

the only one and next to him Bob La Follette, looking quite young. I wonder if he is thinking about his father. And Nye—he probably thinks the German declaration is another piece of British propaganda.

After some delay, the mild little man whom I used to deal with occasionally in the President's office appeared in the doorway, with a large manila envelope; Mr. Biffle, the Senate Majority Clerk, took the envelope, handed it to the Vice President. It is slit open on the desk of the Vice President, and the Clerk begins to read the message. The Clerk is white-haired, with a long coat that reminds you of an itinerant preacher. Into the reading he puts a good deal of feeling and expression.

Senator Connally, chairman of the Foreign Relations Committee, is recognized, and is about to send to the desk a joint resolution declaring war. In the middle aisle appears an excited little man with a bald spot and heavy pince-nez, Sol Bloom, chairman of the House Foreign Affairs Committee. He can't get the attention of the tall Texan, and Senator David Walsh has to stop him for Sol. The Texan isn't upset. He says slowly, "Will the Senate be at ease a moment." And there is a conference between the two—such a contrast, too, such as you see everywhere in this country—and they are off again, and then the vote—unanimous. An expectant ripple through the place when Nye's name is called. Wheeler is away because of a sick brother, but it is announced that he would have voted "Yea." When the resolution against Italy was introduced, I thought I heard a yawn; Senators broke up into knots. And then a resolution authorizing drafted soldiers to be sent outside the United States—Senator Hiram Johnson dramatically withdraws his objection.

17. Pearl Harbor and War: German Reactions

THE CHARGÉ D'AFFAIRES IN THE UNITED STATES
TO THE FOREIGN MINISTRY

MOST URGENT   WASHINGTON, December 7, 1941—8:36 PM
No. 4293 of December 7   Received December 9—8:55 AM

The Japanese attack on Hawaii and the Philippines struck the American Government and the American people like a bolt of lightning. The first reports came from the White House and were soon supplemented by the broadcasting companies' own news reports which immediately interrupted all programs. As we see from the statement of Hull, which follows verbatim in No. 4292, in which he in an excess of fury and anger virtually calls Ambassador Nomura a (1 group apparently missing) and swindler, the Japanese attack came as a complete surprise and caused the greatest consternation among leading American statesmen. The reaction in London seems to be similar, according to reports received so far. The measures, reported in detail by the DNB in New York, which have in the meantime been taken also reflect a state of extreme nervousness. They include, for example, police protection for Japanese Consulates, out of fear of riots, mobilizing the Federal Bureau of Investigation [Bundes-Geheimpolizei] for surveillance of Japanese nationals, orders to guard all vital war plants, apprehension of all Japanese in the Panama Canal Zone, enforcement of the Espionage Law of 1917, which is tantamount to instituting censorship, especially of the isolationist press. These all reflect extreme nervousness. All the American war plans which, as was demonstrated by the recent article in the Chicago Tribune, were oriented toward Europe and calculated to gain time for at least another year or two, have suddenly been scuttled. A war in the Pacific 2 to 3 years before the completion of the two-ocean navies, at a time when one's own army has not been equipped and the

SOURCE: [Germany, Auswärtiges Amt.] Documents on German Foreign Policy, Series D, XIII, 968–969, 980.

great armament industry has only just been started up, must come at an extremely inopportune time for the American Government.

They [the Americans] had thought that they themselves could choose their enemy and the time to begin the war and in the meantime let other peoples fight for American imperialism. They now see that they have been terribly deceived in this calculation which had been based on Japan's willingness to yield, and her fear of America. The last thing that had been expected was a Japanese surprise attack which, as the first reports of heavy losses and great material damage in Hawaii indicate, deprived the Americans of military initiative. It is significant that the bombastic prophesies that a war against Japan would be a "promenade" have now been silenced. Senator George, in one of the first statements which we have here from Congress, speaks of the possibility of a war against Japan lasting 2 to 3 years.

THOMSEN

THE CHARGÉ D'AFFAIRES IN THE UNITED STATES TO THE FOREIGN MINISTRY

MOST URGENT   WASHINGTON, December 8, 1941—9:19 PM
No. 4294 of December 7   Received December 9—3:10 PM

With reference to my telegram No. 4293 of December 7.

In the message to Congress which Roosevelt has just drafted the President will ask Congress to declare the existence of a state of war with Japan and Congress will immediately comply. While the American people were not as yet ripe for war on European soil, Roosevelt can count on the solid backing of the nation in a war against Japan. This is also confirmed by statements from the isolationist camp by such Senators as Wheeler, Taft, and Vandenberg. The nature of Japan's surprise action which is of course termed here a "brutal act of aggression against a peace-loving country," will undoubtedly produce a tremendous upsurge of patriotism and thus render unnecessary any further propaganda on the part of Roosevelt to rally the nation behind him. Roosevelt will utilize this opportunity to obtain from Congress the full grant of authority he needs for carrying on a total war and effecting a total mobilization of industry. It may be expected that all war powers legislation of

1917 and 1918, will again become effective inasmuch as the conditions for enacting such legislation originally, that is "immediate danger of war" and "state of war" are present.

Whether Roosevelt will at the same time ask that a state of war be declared with Germany and Italy is uncertain. From the standpoint of the American conduct of war against Japan it would seem logical to avoid a war on two fronts with all the consequences so often described. However, Roosevelt may attempt at least in this regard to anticipate the decisions of Germany and Italy, if only to make up for some of the loss of prestige throughout the whole world and particularly in South America resulting from the inadequate preparations against the Japanese operation.

War with Japan means re-direction of all efforts to the country's own rearmament, a corresponding reduction in lend-lease assistance, shift of all activity to the Pacific, so far as the garrisoning of Iceland permits this, organization of convoys in the Pacific, closing of Vladivostok as far as shipments to the Soviets are concerned, jeopardizing the supply of raw materials, especially rubber.

THOMSEN

Correspondence with the United States

THE FOREIGN MINISTER TO THE EMBASSY IN THE UNITED STATES

MOST URGENT   BERLIN, December 10, 1941
TOP SECRET   RAM 257.
Priority Handling
No. 2391

For the Chargé d'Affaires personally.

On December 11, at 3:30 PM, German summer time, please deliver to Mr. Hull or, in case he cannot be reached, to his representative, a copy of the following note which I shall deliver an hour earlier to the American Chargé d'Affaires here:

"Mr. Chargé d'Affaires: The Government of the United States of America having violated in the most flagrant manner and in ever increasing measure all rules of neutrality in favor of the adversaries

SOURCE: [Germany, Auswärtiges Amt.] German Foreign Policy, XIII, 999–1000.

of Germany and having continually been guilty of the most severe provocations toward Germany ever since the outbreak of the European War, provoked by the British declaration of war against Germany on September 3, 1939, has finally resorted to open military acts of aggression.

"On September 11, 1941, the President of the United States of America publicly declared that he had ordered the American Navy and Air Force to shoot on sight at any German war vessel. In his speech of October 27, 1941, he once more expressly affirmed that this order was in force.

"Acting under this order, vessels of the American Navy, since early September 1941, have systematically attacked German naval forces. Thus, American destroyers, as for instance the *Greer*, the *Kearney* and the *Reuben James*, have opened fire on German submarines according to plan. The Secretary of the American Navy, Mr. Knox, himself confirmed that American destroyers attacked German submarines.

"Furthermore, the naval forces of the United States of America under order of their Government and contrary to international law have treated and seized German merchant vessels on the high seas as enemy ships.

"The German Government therefore establishes the following facts:

"Although Germany on her part has strictly adhered to the rules of international law in her relations with the United States of America during every period of the present war, the Government of the United States of America from initial violations of neutrality has finally proceeded to open acts of war against Germany. It has thereby virtually created a state of war.

"The Government of the Reich consequently discontinues diplomatic relations with the United States of America and declares that in these circumstances brought about by President Roosevelt Germany too, as from today, considers herself as being in a state of war with the United States of America.

"Accept Mr. Chargé d'Affaires, the expression of my high consideration. RIBBENTROP."

Following this, please ask for your passports and request proper repatriation to Europe for Embassy personnel and include as many press and other representatives as possible. Please entrust the protection of German interests to the Swiss Minister in Washington who will receive appropriate instruction from his Government.

Please ensure that, before carrying out the foregoing instruction there is no contact whatsoever between the Embassy and the State Department. For that reason no official communication from the State Department must be accepted before your démarche is made.

Immediate acknowledgment of receipt of this order is requested. The secret transmitter is to be destroyed beyond recognition, the entire cipher material at your post is to be destroyed and its destruction is to be reported to us.

RIBBENTROP

German Generals and the Outbreak of War

We did not even know why, immediately afterwards, Hitler and his entourage, including Generals Keitel and Jodl, took the train for Berlin. The reason was soon clear. During the afternoon of 11 December he appeared before the Reichstag and, in the full glare of publicity, declared war on the United States of America. This produced the following memorable telephone conversation:

> Jodl, calling me from Berlin (I was just finishing lunch and discussing this latest development with certain officers of the staff): 'You have heard that the Führer has just declared war on America?'
> Myself: 'Yes and we couldn't be more surprised.'
> Jodl: 'The staff must now examine where the United States is most likely to employ the bulk of her forces initially, the Far East or Europe. We cannot take further decisions until that has been clarified.'
> Myself: 'Agreed; this examination is obviously necessary, but so far we have never even considered a war against the United States and so have no data on which to base this examination; we can therefore hardly undertake this job just like that.'
> Jodl: 'See what you can do. When we get back tomorrow we will talk about this in more detail.'

This and no more was the beginning for our headquarters of German strategy against America which was to reach its end on the banks of the Elbe in May 1945.

SOURCE: W. Warlimont, *Inside Hitler's Headquarters* (London, [c 1964]), p. 208. Reprinted by permission of Bernard & Graefe Verlag.

II
War-Time Diplomacy

18. Introduction

During World War II the Allied leaders met in a series of conferences. There were two basic themes. One, dominant at the outset, was military planning for successful prosecution of the war. To attend the first of these meetings, called the Arcadia Conference, Churchill went to Washington with his entourage of military and diplomatic advisers. On the American side, military and personal advisers like Harry Hopkins overshadowed the State Department. From the start Roosevelt and Churchill took active roles in the conferences as they put into operation the personal diplomacy which they both so enthusiastically espoused.

The second theme, planning for peace and the immediate postwar period, naturally was in a secondary position early in 1942; yet an important start was made by the Declaration of the United Nations, the roster of which later became a basis for entry into the United Nations organization. As an example of top level influence, one might note that it was Roosevelt's insistence that made China one of the "Big Four" powers. The conference concentrated on military matters and established agencies for controlling military logistics and strategy. From the start, the Americans strongly advocated opening a second front in Europe, while the British preferred to wait until the enemy became weaker. From Soviet Russia came insistent and continued demands for a second front to relieve German pressure on Russia.

In early 1943, Churchill and Roosevelt met again, this time at Casablanca. The main concern still centered on military matters: the Battle of the Atlantic, the decision to invade Sicily after conclusion of the North African campaign, and agreement to select a chief planner for the invasion of western Europe. During the course of the conference, Roosevelt enunciated the principle of "unconditional surrender."

The next major conference was held in Quebec in August, 1943. The British and American leaders approved revision of the so-called "Cossac" plan for invasion of France. Roosevelt was not satisfied with a meeting of only the British and Americans; so he worked hard to persuade the Russians to join. Finally, after a preliminary meeting of ministers in Moscow, Roosevelt, Churchill and Stalin met at Teheran (also spelled Tehran) in late November, 1943. Stalin's refusal to meet also with Chiang Kai-shek, on the ground that Russia was not at war with Japan, led to two meetings in Cairo by British, American and Chinese leaders before and after the Teheran Conference. The principal result of the Teheran Conference was a firm decision for a major assault on Normandy and a minor one on southern France, starting in May, 1944. During the meeting the Big Three discussed matters of international organization, but reached no agreement.

In the Teheran and Cairo Conferences military strategy was set, and in subsequent high-level conferences interest shifted to ending the war and planning for an international organization. Also, as victory appeared certain the Allies began to pull apart; it was easier to agree on how to win the war than on how to establish a post-war world. Churchill had always been suspicious of the Russians, and his suspicions were returned by them. The Americans were less inclined to question the motives of their allies, but there were increasing signs of disaffection on their side as the war moved toward its conclusion in Europe.

In a second conference held in Quebec, September, 1944, the mood was victory. The "Morgenthau Plan" to reduce Germany to agrarian status met with support by Churchill and Roosevelt at the conference, but sober second thought urged on them by their advisers caused them to reverse their position. Until the Quebec meeting, American military leaders had had largely a free hand in planning the war in the Pacific. At Quebec, the British pledged themselves to continue fighting after Germany's collapse. Although American military leaders were reluctant to share strategic planning, President Roosevelt accepted Churchill's offer of aid in the Far East.

The Dumbarton Oaks Conference in Washington, September, 1944, was not attended by the Big Three, but it brought together their representatives to plan for the establishment of the new international body which was to be called the United Nations.

Churchill, Roosevelt and Stalin met once more, at Yalta in February, 1945. On the way, Churchill and Roosevelt stopped at Malta for important military discussions concerning the continued attack on Germany. At Yalta, Roosevelt and Stalin cemented the agreement made at Teheran that Soviet Russia would enter the war against Japan after Germany fell. Some of the conditions for Russian entry, to which Roosevelt agreed, infringed upon China's sovereignty in Port Arthur and Manchuria. The Big Three also discussed the end of the war in Europe and the treatment to be accorded Germany. A protocol defined three zones of occupation under an Allied Control Council and a special zone for Berlin. The Allied leaders in addition agreed on such matters as destruction of the Nazi Party and German militarism and referred other questions to their chief ministers. Agreement in principle was reached on reparations. Looking to the future, the Big Three decided on a meeting of the United Nations organization in San Francisco, April 25, 1945. Roosevelt later brought embarrassment for himself by trying to negotiate a trade on subsidiary votes in the United Nations to balance those sought by Russia for its satellites. The question of Poland was also an important issue at the conference.

One of Roosevelt's mistakes had been failure to keep his Vice President informed of international matters; so when Roosevelt died on April 12, 1945, Truman succeeded him completely uninstructed. James F. Byrnes, who would soon become Secretary of State and who had been at Yalta, was one of a number of high ranking officials who quickly briefed the new President.

To the great dissatisfaction of the American leaders, Stalin announced that he would not send his Foreign Minister, V. M. Molotov, to the San Francisco Conference. Ambassador Harriman, after Roosevelt's death, was able to convince Stalin of the importance of sending his chief emissary to the meeting.

When the San Francisco Conference met, its first and most important task was to decide on new members. When Molotov failed in his attempt to bargain separately for the admission of Poland, he went directly to the General Assembly and consumed a great deal of time in an unsuccessful debate to gain his objective. Later he was able to obtain the admission of the Ukraine and White Russia, as agreed upon at Yalta.

The course of the meeting at San Francisco soon became clear: debate would reach an impasse until the Big Three agreed on a solution. One of the most serious issues was on voting procedures;

President Truman was able to break this deadlock by sending Harry Hopkins to Russia to appeal directly to Stalin.

Careful selection of the members of the American delegation to the United Nations conference made certain approval by the Senate, for Senate members in the delegation could lead the fight for approval of the Charter.

While the Senate considered the Charter, Truman attended the last great conference of the war at Potsdam. Accompanied by Byrnes, he and Stalin met first with Churchill and then, when the Prime Minister lost his election, with Prime Minister Clement Attlee. The leaders established a Council of Ministers, whose duties included preparing drafts of treaties with the defeated powers, discussing the Polish issue and recommending rules for the political conduct of occupation forces. The Potsdam Conference worked on reparations and reached an agreement on this, as well as on Poland's western borders. Most of the decisions were temporary in nature.

It was when he was at Potsdam that Truman heard of the successful atomic bomb test in New Mexico and decided to use the bomb against Japan. Before dropping the bomb, however, Truman and the other Allied leaders issued the Potsdam Proclamation to Japan. Unfortunately, the Japanese leaders intentionally or unintentionally missed its significance.

In these various wartime conferences, the Allies successfully planned the conduct of the war and for immediate post-war settlements. Perhaps understandably they dealt less effectively with the problems of permanent peace.

19. Pre-Teheran Correspondence

MARSHAL STALIN TO PRESIDENT ROOSEVELT AND PRIME
MINISTER CHURCHILL

PERSONAL AND SECRET   Moscow, August 24, 1943

From Premier Stalin to Prime Minister Mr. W. Churchill and
President Mr. F. D. Roosevelt.

I have received your joint message of August 19th.

I entirely share your opinion and that of Roosevelt about the
importance of a meeting between the three of us. In this connection
I beg you most earnestly to understand my position at this moment, when our armies are carrying on the struggle against the
main forces of Hitler with the utmost strain and when Hitler not
only does not withdraw a single division from our front but on the
contrary has already succeeded in transporting, and continues to
transport fresh divisions to Soviet-German front. At such a moment, in the opinion of all my colleagues, I cannot without
detriment to our military operations leave the front for so distant a
point as Fairbanks although if the situation on our front were
different Fairbanks undoubtedly would be very convenient as a
place for our meeting as I said before.

As regards a meeting of representatives of our states and in particular of representatives in charge of Foreign Affairs, I share your
opinion about the expediency of such a meeting in the near future.
This meeting however ought not to have a purely exploratory
character but a practicable and preparatory character in order that
after that meeting has taken place our Governments are able to
take definite decisions and thus that delay in the taking of decisions on urgent questions can be avoided. Therefore I consider it
indispensable to revert to my proposal that it is necessary in
advance to define the scope of questions for discussion by repre-

SOURCE: U.S. State Department, *Foreign Relations, The Conferences at Cairo and Tehran* (1943), pp. 22, 67–68, 71, 72; *Diplomatic Papers* (1942), I: 25–26.

sentatives of the Three Powers and to draft the proposals which ought to be discussed by them and presented to our Governments for final decision.

MARSHAL STALIN TO PRESIDENT ROOSEVELT

Moscow, November 5, 1943

Personal and confidential from Premier J. V. Stalin to President Franklin D. Roosevelt

Mr. Hull has transmitted to me on October 25, your latest message and I had a chance to talk with him regarding it. My reply has been delayed because I was sure that Mr. Hull had transmitted to you the contents of the eventuated talk and my views regarding my meeting with you and Mr. Churchill.

I cannot but give consideration to the arguments you gave regarding the circumstances hindering you from travelling to Teheran. Of course, the decision of w[h]ether you are able to travel to Teheran remains entirely with yourself.

On my part, I have to say that I do not see any other more suitable place for a meeting, than the aforementioned city.

I have been charged with the duties of Supreme Commander of the Soviet troops and this obliges me to carry out daily direction of military operations at our front. This is especially important at the present time, when the uninterrupted four-months summer campaign is overgrowing into a winter campaign and the military operations are continuing to develop on nearly all the fronts, stretching along 2600 kilometers.

Under such conditions for myself as Supreme Commander the possibility of travelling farther than Teheran is excluded. My colleagues in the Government consider, in general, that my travelling beyond the borders of the U. S. S. R. at the present time is impossible due to great complexity of the situation at the front.

That is why an idea occurred to me about which I already talked to Mr. Hull. I could be successfully substituted at this meeting by Mr. V. M. Molotov, my first deputy in the Government, who at negotiations will enjoy, according to our Constitution, all powers of the head of the Soviet Government. In this case the difficulties regarding the choice of the place of meeting would drop off. I hope that this suggestion could be acceptable to us at the present time.

NOVEMBER 5, 1943

PRESIDENT ROOSEVELT TO MARSHAL STALIN

SECRET WASHINGTON, 8 November 1943
PRIORITY

Personal and secret from the President to Marshal Stalin.

Thank you for your message of November fifth which Mr. Gromyko was good enough to deliver.

I hope to leave here in a few days and to arrive in Cairo by the twenty-second of November.

You will be glad to know that I have worked out a method so that if I get word that a bill requiring my veto has been passed by the Congress and forwarded to me, I will fly to Tunis to meet it and then return to the Conference.

Therefore, I have decided to go to Teheran and this makes me especially happy.

As I have told you, I regard it as of vital importance that you and Mr. Churchill and I should meet. The psychology of the present excellent feeling really demands it even if our meeting last only two days. Therefore, it is my thought that the Staffs begin their work in Cairo on November twenty-second, and I hope Mr. Molotov and your military representative, who I hope can speak English, will come there at that time.

Then we can all go to Teheran on the twenty-sixth and meet with you there on the twenty-seventh, twenty-eighth, twenty-ninth or thirtieth, for as long as you feel you can be away. Then Churchill and I and the top Staff people can return to Cairo to complete the details.

The whole world is watching for this meeting of the three of us. And even if we make no announcements as vital as those announced at the recent highly successful meeting in Moscow, the fact that you and Churchill and I have got to know each other personally will have far-reaching effect on the good opinion within our three nations and will assist in the further disturbance of Nazi morale.

I am greatly looking forward to a good talk with you.

ROOSEVELT

DECLARATION BY UNITED NATIONS

A JOINT DECLARATION BY THE UNITED STATES OF AMERICA, THE UNITED KINGDOM OF GREAT BRITAIN AND NORTHERN IRELAND, THE UNION OF SOVIET SOCIALIST REPUBLICS, CHINA, AUSTRALIA, BELGIUM, CANADA, COSTA RICA, CUBA, CZECHOSLOVAKIA, DOMINICAN REPUBLIC, EL SALVADOR, GREECE, GUATEMALA, HAITI, HONDURAS, INDIA, LUXEMBOURG, NETHERLANDS, NEW ZEALAND, NICARAGUA, NORWAY, PANAMA, POLAND, SOUTH AFRICA, YUGOSLAVIA

The Governments signatory hereto,

Having subscribed to a common program of purposes and principles embodied in the Joint Declaration of the President of the United States of America and the Prime Minister of the United Kingdom of Great Britain and Northern Ireland dated August 14, 1941, known as the Atlantic Charter.

Being convinced that complete victory over their enemies is essential to defend life, liberty, independence and religious freedom, and to preserve human rights and justice in their own lands as well as in other lands, and that they are now engaged in a common struggle against savage and brutal forces seeking to subjugate the world, DECLARE:

(1) Each Government pledges itself to employ its full resources, military or economic, against those members of the Tripartite Pact and its adherents with which such government is at war.

(2) Each Government pledges itself to cooperate with the Governments signatory hereto and not to make a separate armistice or peace with the enemies.

The foregoing declaration may be adhered to by other nations which are, or which may be, rendering material assistance and contributions in the struggle for victory over Hitlerism.

Done at WASHINGTON

January First, 1942

20. Cairo Conferences

First Cairo Conference Communique

President Roosevelt, Generalissimo Chiang Kai-Shek and Prime Minister Churchill, together with their respective military and diplomatic advisers, have completed a conference in North Africa. The following general statement was issued:

"The several military missions have agreed upon future military operations against Japan. The three great Allies expressed their resolve to bring unrelenting pressure against their brutal enemies by sea, land and air. This pressure is already rising.

"The three great Allies are fighting this war to restrain and punish the aggression of Japan. They covet no gain for themselves and have no thought of territorial expansion. It is their purpose that Japan shall be stripped of all the islands in the Pacific which she has seized or occupied since the beginning of the first World War in 1914, and that all the territories Japan has stolen from the Chinese, such as Manchuria, Formosa, and the Pescadores, shall be restored to the Republic of China. Japan will also be expelled from all other territories which she has taken by violence and greed. The aforesaid three great powers, mindful of the enslavement of the people of Korea, are determined that in due course Korea shall become free and independent.

"With these objects in view the three Allies, in harmony with those of the United Nations at war with Japan, will continue to persevere in the serious and prolonged operations necessary to procure the unconditional surrender of Japan."

SOURCE: *Foreign Relations, Conferences at Cairo and Tehran 1943*, pp. 448–449.

Second Cairo Conference: Operations Plan Against Japan

MEMORANDUM BY THE UNITED STATES CHIEFS OF STAFF

SECRET   CAIRO, 3 December 1943

C. C. S. 397 (Revised)

SPECIFIC OPERATIONS FOR THE DEFEAT OF JAPAN, 1944
References: a. CCS 242/6
b. CCS 319/5
c. CCS 417

1. We are agreed that every effort should be exerted to bring the U. S. S. R. into the war against Japan at the earliest practicable date, and that plans should be prepared in that event.

2. We are agreed that plans should be prepared for operations in the event that Germany is defeated earlier than the fall of 1944.

3. A schedule of proposed operations and projected target dates for planning purposes is given in the appendix to the enclosure. The operations envisaged are based on a concept of obtaining strategic objectives and bases from which to conduct further operations to force the unconditional surrender of Japan at the earliest practicable date. The operations are in consonance with the over-all objective and over-all strategic concept agreed upon at QUADRANT and reaffirmed by the Combined Chiefs of Staff in C. C. S. 380/2, and with the provisions of C. C. S. 417 (Over-all Plan for the Defeat of Japan).

4. *General.* In addition to the specific objectives hereinafter indicated, supporting operations should be conducted. Both the specific and supporting operations will be designed to destroy the Japanese Fleet at an early date; to secure maximum attrition of enemy air forces; to intensify air, submarine, and mining operations against enemy shipping and lines of communication; to establish air and sea blockade of the main Japanese islands; to continue efforts to keep China in the war; and to enable us to launch land and carrier-based air operations against Japan.

5. *North Pacific.* Plans for the North Pacific involve the augmentation of base facilities and defensive installations in the

SOURCE: *Foreign Relations, Conferences at Cairo and Tehran 1943*, pp. 779–781.

Aleutians in preparation for entry into the Kuriles and Soviet territory in the event of Russian collaboration. Naval surface and submarine action, including raids on the Japanese fishing fleet will be carried out. Preparations will be made for executing very long range strategic bombing against the Kuriles and northern Japan.

6. *Central, South and Southwest Pacific.* The advance along the New Guinea-N.E.I.-Philippine axis will proceed concurrently with operations for the capture of the Mandated Islands. A strategic bombing force will be established in Guam, Tinian, and Saipan for strategic bombing of Japan proper. Air bombardment of targets in the N. E. I.-Philippine Area and the aerial neutralization of Rabaul will be intensified.

7. *China.* Our efforts in the China area should have as their objective the intensification of land and air operations in and from China and the build-up of the U. S. A. A. F. and the Chinese army and air forces. It shall include also the establishing, without materially affecting other approved operations, of a very long range strategic bombing force at Calcutta, with advanced bases at Chengtu to attack vital targets in the Japanese "inner zone."

8. *Southeast Asia.* In the Southeast Asia Area operations should be carried out for the capture of Upper Burma in order to improve the air route and establish overland communications with China. Operation BUCCANEER will be conducted. Within the means available additional offensive operations including carrier borne raids should be conducted by sea, air, and ground forces for the purpose of maintaining pressure on the enemy, inducing dispersion of his forces, and attaining the maximum attrition practicable on [of?] his air and naval forces and shipping. The preparation of the bases in India required for approved operations in the S. E. A. and China Theaters should continue.

9. As more carriers become available, the operations set forth should be supplemented, between scheduled operational dates as practicable, with massed carrier task force strikes against selected vital targets.

10. The completion of these operations will place the United Nations in positions from which to use most advantageously the great air, ground, and naval resources which will be at our disposal after Germany is defeated.

Conference on Policy in China

December 6, 1943, at Alexander Kirk's home, Cairo. After Te-heran.

Present: Roosevelt, H.H. [Harry Hopkins], J.W.S. [Joseph W. Stilwell]

F.D.R. Well, Joe, what do you think of the bad news?

J.W.S. I haven't heard yet how bad it is.

F.D.R. We're in an impasse. I've been stubborn as a mule for four days but we can't get anywhere, and it won't do for a con-ference to end that way. The British just won't do the op-eration, and I can't get them to agree to it.

J.W.S. I am interested to know how this affects our policy in China.

F.D.R. Well, now, we've been friends with China for a gr-e-e-at many years. I ascribe a large part of this feeling to the mis-sionaries. You know *I* have a China history. My grandfather went out there, to Swatow and Canton, in 1829, and even went up to Hankow. He did what was every American's am-bition in those days—he made a million dollars, and when he came back he put it into western railroads. And in eight years he lost every dollar. Ha! Ha! Ha! Then in 1856 he went out again and *stayed there all through the Civil War*, and made another million. This time he put it into coal mines, and they didn't pay a dividend until two years after he died. Ha! Ha! Ha!

J.W.S. I take it that it is our policy to build China up.

F.D.R. Yes. Yes. Build her up. After this war there will be a great need of our help. They will want loans. Madame Chiang and the G-mo wanted to get a loan now of a billion dollars, but I told them it would be difficult to get Congress to agree to it. Now, I'm not a financial expert (!!) but I have a plan to take fifty or a hundred million dollars and buy up Chinese paper dollars on the black market. It wouldn't take much.

SOURCE: Joseph W. Stilwell, *The Stilwell Papers* (New York, 1948), pp. 251–252. Copyright © 1948 by Winifred A. Stilwell. Reprinted by permission of William Morrow and Company, Inc.

(!!) When the Chinese found out that these notes were being bought up, they would tend to hold them and the rate would come down. We might beat the inflation that way. And I'd share the profit with the Chinese government—I'd put the notes in escrow and when they were needed I'd sell them to the Chinese for what I paid for them.

21. Teheran Conference

FIRST PLENARY MEETING, NOVEMBER 28, 1943, 4 PM

Bohlen Minutes

SECRET

THE PRESIDENT said as the youngest of the three present he ventured to welcome his elders. He said he wished to welcome the new members to the family circle and tell them that meetings of this character were conducted as between friends with complete frankness on all sides with nothing that was said to be made public. He added that he was confident that this meeting would be successful and that our three great nations would not only work in close cooperation for the prosecution of the war but would also remain in close touch for generations to come.

THE PRIME MINISTER then pointed out that this was the greatest concentration of power that the world had ever seen. In our hands here is the possible certainty of shortening the war, the much greater certainty of victories, but the absolute certainty that we held the happy future of mankind. He added that he prayed that we might be worthy of this God-given opportunity.

MARSHAL STALIN welcomed the representatives of Great Britain and the United States. He then said that history had given to us here a great opportunity and it was up to the representatives here to use wisely the power which their respective peoples had given to them and to take full advantage of this fraternal meeting.

SOURCE: *Foreign Relations, Conferences at Cairo and Tehran 1943*, p. 487.

TRIPARTITE DINNER MEETING, NOVEMBER 29, 1943

Bohlen Minutes

SECRET

The most notable feature of the dinner was the attitude of Marshal Stalin toward the Prime Minister. Marshal Stalin lost no opportunity to get in a dig at Mr. Churchill. Almost every remark that he addressed to the Prime Minister contained some sharp edge, although the Marshal's manner was entirely friendly. He apparently desired to put and keep the Prime Minister on the defensive. At one occasion he told the Prime Minister that just because Russians are simple people, it was a mistake to believe that they were blind and could not see what was before their eyes.

In the discussion in regard to future treatment of Germans, Marshal Stalin strongly implied on several occasions that Mr. Churchill nursed a secret affection for Germany and desired to see a soft peace.

Marshal Stalin was obviously teasing the Prime Minister for the latter's attitude at the afternoon session of the Conference, he was also making known in a friendly fashion his displeasure at the British attitude on the question of OVERLORD.

Following Mr. Hopkins' toast to the Red Army, MARSHAL STALIN spoke with great frankness in regard to the past and present capacity of the Red Army. He said that in the winter war against Finland, the Soviet Army had shown itself to be very poorly organized and had done very badly; that as a result of the Finnish War, the entire Soviet Army had been re-organized; but even so, when the Germans attacked in 1941, it could not be said that the Red Army was a first class fighting force. That during the war with Germany, the Red Army had become steadily better from [the] point of view of operations, tactics, etc., and now he felt that it was genuinely a good army. He added that the general opinion in regard to the Red Army had been wrong, because it was not believed that the Soviet Army could reorganize and improve itself during time of war.

SOURCE: *Foreign Relations, Conferences at Cairo and Tehran 1943*, pp. 552–555.

In regard to the future treatment of Germany, MARSHAL STALIN developed the thesis that he had previously expressed, namely, that really effective measures to control Germany must be evolved, otherwise Germany would rise again within 15 or 20 years to plunge the world into another war. He said that two conditions must be met:

(1) At least 50,000 and perhaps 100,000 of the German Commanding Staff must be physically liquidated.

(2) The victorious Allies must retain possession of the important strategic points in the world so that if Germany moved a muscle she could be rapidly stopped.

MARSHAL STALIN added that similar strong points now in the hands of Japan should remain in the hands of the Allies.

THE PRESIDENT jokingly said that he would put the figure of the German Commanding Staff which should be executed at 49,000 or more.

THE PRIME MINISTER took strong exception to what he termed the cold blooded execution of soldiers who had fought for their country. He said that war criminals must pay for their crimes and individuals who had committed barbarous acts, and in accordance with the Moscow Document, which he himself had written, they must stand trial at the places where the crimes were committed. He objected vigorously, however, to executions for political purposes.

MARSHAL STALIN, during this part of the conversation, continuously referred to Mr. Churchill's secret liking for the Germans.

With reference to the occupation of bases and strong points in the vicinity of Germany and Japan, THE PRESIDENT said those bases must be held under trusteeship.

MARSHAL STALIN agreed with the President.

THE PRIME MINISTER stated that as far as Britain was concerned, they do not desire to acquire any new territory or bases, but intended to hold on to what they had. He said that nothing would be taken away from England without a war. He mentioned specifically, Singapore and Hong Kong. He said a portion of the British Empire might eventually be released but that this would be done entirely by Great Britain herself, in accordance with her own moral precepts. He said that Great Britain, if asked to do so, might occupy certain bases under trusteeship, provided others would help pay the cost of such occupation.

MARSHAL STALIN replied that England had fought well in the war and he, personally, favored an increase in the British Empire, particularly the area around Gibraltar. He also suggested that Great Britain and the United States install more suitable government[s] in Spain and Portugal, since he was convinced that Franco was no friend of Great Britain or the United States. In reply to the Prime Minister's inquiry as to what territorial interests the Soviet Union had, MARSHAL STALIN replied, "there is no need to speak at the present time about any Soviet desires, but when the time comes, we will speak."

Although the discussion between Marshal Stalin and the Prime Minister remained friendly, the arguments were lively and Stalin did not let up on the Prime Minister throughout the entire evening.

ROOSEVELT-STALIN MEETING, DECEMBER 1, 1943

PRESENT

UNITED STATES	SOVIET UNION
President Roosevelt	Marshal Stalin
Mr. Harriman	Foreign Commissar Molotov
Mr. Bohlen	Mr. Pavlov

Bohlen Minutes

SECRET

THE PRESIDENT said he had asked Marshal Stalin to come to see him as he wished to discuss a matter briefly and frankly. He said it referred to internal American politics.

He said that we had an election in 1944 and that while personally he did not wish to run again, if the war was still in progress, he might have to.

He added that there were in the United States from six to seven million Americans of Polish extraction, and as a practical man, he did not wish to lose their vote. He said personally he agreed with

SOURCE: *Foreign Relations, Conferences at Cairo and Tehran 1943*, p. 594.

the views of Marshal Stalin as to the necessity of the restoration of a Polish state but would like to see the Eastern border moved further to the west and the Western border moved even to the River Oder. He hoped, however, that the Marshal would understand that for political reasons outlined above, he could not participate in any decision here in Tehran or even next winter on this subject and that he could not publicly take part in any such arrangement at the present time.

MARSHAL STALIN replied that now the President explained, he had understood.

THE PRESIDENT went on to say that there were a number of persons of Lithuanian, Latvian, and Estonian origin, in that order, in the United States. He said that he fully realized the three Baltic Republics had in history and again more recently been a part of Russia and added jokingly that when the Soviet armies re-occupied these areas, he did not intend to go to war with the Soviet Union on this point.

DECLARATION OF THE THREE POWERS

December 6, 1943

WE—The President of the United States, The Prime Minister of Great Britain, and the Premier of the Soviet Union, have met these four days past in this, the capital of our ally, Iran, and have shaped and confirmed our common policy.

We express our determination that our nations shall work together in war and in the peace that will follow.

As to war—Our military staffs have joined in our round table discussions, and we have concerted our plans for the destruction of the German forces. We have reached complete agreement as to the scope and timing of the operations which will be undertaken from the East, West and South.

The common understanding which we have here reached guarantees that victory will be ours.

And as to peace—we are sure that our concord will make it an enduring peace. We recognize fully the supreme responsibility

SOURCE: *Foreign Relations, Conferences at Cairo and Tehran 1943*, pp. 640–641.

resting upon us and all the United Nations to make a peace which will command the good will of the overwhelming mass of the peoples of the world, and banish the scourge and terror of war for many generations.

With our diplomatic advisers we have surveyed the problems of the future. We shall seek the cooperation and the active participation of all nations, large and small, whose peoples in heart and mind are dedicated, as are our own peoples, to the elimination of tyranny and slavery, oppression and intolerance. We will welcome them, as they may choose to come, into a world family of democratic nations.

No power on earth can prevent our destroying the German armies by land, their U-boats by sea, and their war plants from the air.

Our attack will be relentless and increasing.

Emerging from these friendly conferences we look with confidence to the day when all peoples of the world may live free lives, untouched by tyranny, and according to their varying desires and their own consciences.

We came here with hope and determination. We leave here, friends in fact, in spirit and in purpose.

Signed at Teheran, December 1, 1943.

ROOSEVELT
STALIN
CHURCHILL

MILITARY CONCLUSIONS OF THE TEHERAN CONFERENCE

(1) Agreed that the Partisans in Yugoslavia should be supported by supplies and equipment to the greatest possible extent, and also by commando operations.

(2) Agreed that, from the military point of view, it was most desirable that Turkey should come into the war on the side of the Allies before the end of the year.

(3) Took note of Marshal Stalin's statement that if Turkey found herself at war with Germany, and as a result Bulgaria declared war on Turkey or attacked her, the Soviet would immedi-

SOURCE: *Foreign Relations, Conferences at Cairo and Tehran 1943*, p. 652.

ately be at war with Bulgaria. The Conference further took note that this fact could be explicitly stated in the forthcoming negotiations to bring Turkey into the war.

(4) Took note that Operation OVERLORD would be launched during May 1944, in conjunction with an operation against Southern France. The latter operation would be undertaken in as great a strength as availability of landing-craft permitted. The Conference further took note of Marshal Stalin's statement that the Soviet forces would launch an offensive at about the same time with the object of preventing the German forces from transferring from the Eastern to the Western Front.

(5) Agreed that the military staffs of the three Powers should henceforward keep in close touch with each other in regard to the impending operations in Europe. In particular it was agreed that a cover plan to mystify and mislead the enemy as regards these operations should be concerted between the staffs concerned.

F. D. R.
[Stalin] H. C.
W. S. C.

TEHERAN, December 1, 1943

22. Yalta Conference

TRIPARTITE DINNER MEETING, FEBRUARY 8, 1945, 9 PM
YUSUPOV PALACE

Bohlen Minutes

TOP SECRET

Subject: General Conversation.

The atmosphere of the dinner was most cordial, and forty-five toasts in all were drunk. Marshal Stalin was in an excellent humor and even in high spirits. Most of the toasts were routine—to the armed forces of the representative countries and the military leaders and the continuing friendship of the three great powers.

MARSHAL STALIN proposed a toast to the health of the Prime

SOURCE: *Foreign Relations, The Conferences at Malta and Yalta 1945,* pp. 797–799.

Minister, who he characterized as the bravest governmental figure in the world. He said that due in large measure to Mr. Churchill's courage and staunchness, England, when she stood alone, had divided the might of Hitlerite Germany at a time when the rest of Europe was falling flat on its face before Hitler. He said that Great Britain, under Mr. Churchill's leadership, had carried on the fight alone irrespective of existing or potential allies. The Marshal concluded that he knew of few examples in history where the courage of one man had been so important to the future history of the world. He drank a toast to Mr. Churchill, his fighting friend and a brave man.

THE PRIME MINISTER, in his reply, toasted Marshal Stalin as the mighty leader of a mighty country, which had taken the full shock of the German war machine, had broken its back and had driven the tyrants from her soil. He said he knew that in peace no less than in war Marshal Stalin would continue to lead his people from success to success.

MARSHAL STALIN then proposed the health of the President of the United States. He said that he and Mr. Churchill in their respective countries had had relatively simple decisions. They had been fighting for their very existence against Hitlerite Germany but there was a third man whose country had not been seriously threatened with invasion, but who had had perhaps a broader conception of national interest and even though his country was not directly imperilled had been the chief forger of the instruments which had led to the mobilization of the world against Hitler. He mentioned in this connection Lend-Lease as one of the President's most remarkable and vital achievements in the formation of the Anti-Hitler combination and in keeping the Allies in the field against Hitler.

THE PRESIDENT, in reply to this toast, said he felt the atmosphere at this dinner was as that of a family, and it was in those words that he liked to characterize the relations that existed between our three countries. He said that great changes had occurred in the world during the last three years, and even greater changes were to come. He said that each of the leaders represented here were working in their own way for the interests of their people. He said that fifty years ago there were vast areas of the world where people had little opportunity and no hope, but much had been accomplished, although there were still great areas where people had little opportunity and little hope, and their objectives here were to give to every man, woman and child on this earth the possibility of security and wellbeing.

In a subsequent toast to the alliance between the three great powers, MARSHAL STALIN remarked that it was not so difficult to keep unity in time of war since there was a joint aim to defeat the common enemy which was clear to everyone. He said the difficult task came after the war when diverse interests tended to divide the allies. He said he was confident that the present alliance would meet this test also and that it was our duty to see that it would, and that our relations in peacetime should be as strong as they had been in war.

THE PRIME MINISTER then said he felt we were all standing on the crest of a hill with the glories of future possibilities stretching before us. He said that in the modern world the function of leadership was to lead the people out from the forests into the broad sunlit plains of peace and happiness. He felt this prize was nearer our grasp than anytime before in history and it would be a tragedy for which history would never forgive us if we let this prize slip from our grasp through inertia or carelessness.

JUSTICE BYRNES proposed a toast to the common man all over the world. He said there had been many toasts to leaders and officials and while we all shared these sentiments we should never forget the common man or woman who lives on this earth.

MISS HARRIMAN, replying for the three ladies present, then proposed a toast to those who had worked so hard in the Crimea for our comfort, and having seen the destruction wrought by the Germans here she had fully realized what had been accomplished.

TEHERAN CONFERENCE: MILITARY CONCLUSIONS

Agreement Regarding Entry of the Soviet Union into the War against Japan

TOP SECRET

The leaders of the three Great Powers—the Soviet Union, the United States of America and Great Britain—have agreed that in

SOURCE: *Foreign Relations, Conferences at Malta and Yalta 1945,* p. 984.

two or three months after Germany has surrendered and the war in Europe has terminated the Soviet Union shall enter into the war against Japan on the side of the Allies on condition that:

1. The *status quo* in Outer-Mongolia (The Mongolian People's Republic) shall be preserved;

2. The former rights of Russia violated by the treacherous attack of Japan in 1904 shall be restored, viz:

(a) the southern part of Sakhalin as well as all the islands adjacent to it shall be returned to the Soviet Union,

(b) the commercial port of Dairen shall be internationalized, the preeminent interests of the Soviet Union in this port being safeguarded and the lease of Port Arthur as a naval base of the USSR restored,

(c) the Chinese-Eastern Railroad and the South-Manchurian Railroad which provides an outlet to Dairen shall be jointly operated by the establishment of a joint Soviet-Chinese Company it being understood that the preeminent interests of the Soviet Union shall be safeguarded and that China shall retain full sovereignty in Manchuria;

3. The Kuril islands shall be handed over to the Soviet Union.

It is understood, that the agreement concerning Outer-Mongolia and the ports and railroads referred to above will require concurrence of Generalissimo Chiang Kai-Shek. The President will take measures in order to obtain this concurrence on advice from Marshal Stalin.

The Heads of the three Great Powers have agreed that these claims of the Soviet Union shall be unquestionably fulfilled after Japan has been defeated.

For its part the Soviet Union expresses its readiness to conclude with the National Government of China a pact of friendship and alliance between the USSR and China in order to render assistance to China with its armed forces for the purpose of liberating China from the Japanese yoke.

H. Стајінн [I. Stalin]
Franklin D. Roosevelt
Winston S. Churchill

February 11, 1945

23. Potsdam Conference

THE ASSISTANT TO THE SECRETARY OF STATE BOHLEN TO THE PRESIDENT

BABELSBERG, July 24, 1945

The following, as near as I can remember it, is the Prime Minister's toast to you yesterday evening, your reply, and Marshal Stalin's additions:

THE PRIME MINISTER said they had already drunk to the President as Head of.State, but he wished now to propose a toast to the President as a man. He said that he had not had the pleasure of meeting Mr. Truman until this Conference, but he was sure that everyone present had been as impressed as he had with the firm, decisive and business-like direction of their deliberations. He said that they had all been struck also with the President's sincerity, frankness and powers of decision. The President, Mr. Churchill continued, reflected in his character and abilities the best qualities of the great republic which he headed. He said he knew he was speaking for Marshal Stalin when he said they were glad to welcome the President into association and friendship and he wished to raise his glass to a man who was sincere in purpose, clear in speech, and true in deed.

THE PRESIDENT, in reply to this toast, expressed his deep appreciation for the kind words of the Prime Minister and said that he was naturally a timid man and that when the Prime Minister had suggested and Marshal Stalin had supported the proposal that he be made presiding officer over this Conference he had been literally overwhelmed. He said he would continue to do his utmost for the success of the Conference and for the future peace and well-being of the world, and he wished to say what a great pleasure and privilege it was for him, a country boy from Missouri, to be associated with two such great figures as the Prime Minister and Marshal Stalin.

SOURCE: *Foreign Relations, The Conference of Berlin (The Potsdam Conference) 1945*, II: 320–321.

MARSHAL STALIN then arose to say that in his opinion modesty such as the President's was a great source of strength and a real indication of character; he added that this was particularly true when it was coupled, as in the case of President Truman, with real strength and character and honesty of purpose. He concluded that he wished to associate himself fully with the remarks of the Prime Minister and was delighted to welcome President Truman into their midst.

CHARLES E. BOHLEN

24. United Nations Conference

Preliminaries

GENERAL GEORGE C. MARSHALL, CHIEF OF STAFF
OF THE UNITED STATES ARMY,
TO THE SECRETARY OF STATE

WASHINGTON, 3 August, 1944

MY DEAR MR. SECRETARY: It is quite possible that in the coming discussions with the other principal United Nations, concerning the proposed General International Organization, questions will arise directly or indirectly related to the subject of postwar territorial settlements, as for example the question of "Territorial Trusteeships."

It is noted that the Table of Contents of the United States Tentative Proposals for a General International Organization dated 18 July 1944, (which have been furnished the other governments concerned), indicates that Section IX deals with "Arrangements for Territorial Trusteeships" and that the "documents on this subject will be available later."

It appears to the Joint Chiefs of Staff after examining the 6th July draft of Section IX, that this subject of Territorial Trusteeships is closely related to the broader subject of territorial settlements and that the question as to whether either subject should be

SOURCE: *Foreign Relations* (1944), I: 699–703.

discussed at this time is directly related to two basic military considerations. These military considerations are:

a. The incalculable importance to the United States of the early entry of Russia into the war against Japan, and

b. The very profound changes that will be found in the relative military strengths of the major powers of the world upon the conclusion of the present war.

In order that our representatives at forthcoming discussions may be informed of the views of the Joint Chiefs of Staff concerning these military considerations, the accompanying memorandum expressive of these views is enclosed.

Sincerely yours,

For the Joint Chiefs of Staff:

G. C. MARSHALL

[Enclosure]

MEMORANDUM BY THE JOINT CHIEFS OF STAFF TO THE SECRETARY OF STATE

Subject: Fundamental Military Factors in Relation to Discussions Concerning Territorial Trusteeships and Settlements

1. Discussions are to be held in the near future with representatives of the three other principal United Nations concerning the proposed future international organization. While these discussions are intended to be exploratory only, it is possible that directly or indirectly, questions concerning territorial settlements may arise. Should this be the case, it appears certain that on some questions of this nature, Russian aspirations will be found in conflict with those of the British on the one hand, and with those of China on the other. The interests of the United States would undoubtedly be involved, particularly as to the future status of the Japanese Mandated Islands, and British and Chinese interests could be expected to come in conflict, especially as to Hong Kong.

2. The question of whether the subject of territorial settlements should be discussed during these conversations—either specifically as to certain areas, or in general terms as to the trusteeship or other status of such areas under the General International Organization—is an important matter of policy which should be determined only after thorough examination of all factors involved. Among the

basic factors which must be given full weight in determining the United States policy in this regard is the over-all military situation as it can be foreseen both before and after the defeat of Japan.

3. While the war with Germany is well advanced toward a final conclusion, the defeat of Japan is not yet in sight. The defeat of Germany will leave Russia in a position of assured military dominance in eastern Europe and in the Middle East. While it is true that on the fall of Germany the United States and Britain will occupy and control western Europe, their strength in that area will thereafter progressively decline with the withdrawal of all but their occupational and enforcement forces, for employment against Japan, or for demobilization.

4. At present, the war against Japan is being carried on almost entirely by the United States. Notwithstanding British commitments, this will continue to be substantially true after the defeat of Germany, unless Russia effectively enters the war against Japan. In this connection it must be borne in mind that whether or not Russia enters the war, the fall of Japan will leave Russia in a dominant position on continental Northeast Asia in so far as military power is concerned.

5. The land forces of Russia can provide a major contribution by being brought to bear directly against the most powerful element of Japanese military strength—her Army. The air forces of Russia or of the United States, operating from Siberian or Korean bases, would provide the most effective short range land-based air attack against the heart of Japan. Should Russia promptly and effectively enter the war after the fall of Germany, she would bring her great land and air forces into action directly against Japan, thereby materially shortening the war and effecting vast savings in American lives and treasure. Should Russia abstain from such action, due to our untimely pressing the subject of territorial settlement—or any other avoidable cause—we must be prepared to accept responsibility for a longer war. In other words, it should be clearly recognized by those guiding these prospective discussions that there is an important connection between the timeliness of discussing territorial trusteeships or other forms of territorial settlements and the earliest and least costly defeat of Japan and therefore that discussion of these controversial subjects should be delayed until that end is achieved.

6. In all discussions of post-war international arrangements it will be of great importance that our representatives keep clearly in mind the essential facts of the future world-wide military situation, which, in the last analysis, not only will largely determine the eventual territorial settlements, but which must be recognized and accepted if we are to create a post-war world structure on the basis of that reality without which it cannot be expected to endure. When Germany and Japan are defeated and disarmed, and assuming they are prevented from re-building their military power, the facts of the post-war military situation will be those briefly stated in the following paragraphs.

7. The successful termination of the war against our present enemies will find a world profoundly changed in respect of relative national military strengths, a change more comparable indeed with that occasioned by the fall of Rome than with any other change occurring during the succeeding fifteen hundred years. This is a fact of fundamental importance in its bearing upon future international political settlements and all discussions leading thereto. Aside from the elimination of Germany and Japan as military powers, and developments in the relative economic power of principal nations, there are technical and material factors which have contributed greatly to this change. Among these are the development of aviation, the general mechanization of warfare and the marked shift in the munitioning potentials of the great powers.

8. After the defeat of Japan, the United States and Russia will be the strongest military powers in the world. This is due in each case primarily to a combination of geographical position and extent, manpower, and vast munitioning potential. While the United States can project its military power into many areas overseas, it is nevertheless true that the relative strength and geographic positions of these two powers are such as to preclude the military defeat of one of these powers by the other, even if that power were allied with the British Empire.

9. As a military power, the British Empire in the post-war era will be in a lower category than the United States and Russia. The primacy of the British Empire in the century before World War I, and her second-to-none position until World War II, have built up a traditional concept of British military power. It is important that as regards British military power, we clearly recognize the substan-

tial change that' has taken place. Except for the elimination of Germany as a threat and rival, nearly all the essential factors of national power in the post-war era will have altered, to the disadvantage of the British Empire. Both in an absolute sense and relative to the United States and Russia, the British Empire will emerge from the war having lost ground both economically and militarily. In addition to the broad effect of such losses on the military power of the Empire there are two factors which directly depreciate the military power of the United Kingdom. These are the inroads of aviation and submarine developments on the former security of her sea lanes, and the relative decline in her munitioning capacity during the past seventy years, from about fifty per cent to approximately eight per cent of world totals. A future world conflict may be expected to find British military resources so strained in the defense of her essential sea lanes, so involved in maintaining the integrity of her Empire, that little, if any, of these resources will be available for offensive action against a land power.

10. Notwithstanding her vast population and area, China possesses at present but little military strength. This condition will not be improved prior to her extensive industrialization, which in turn is dependent on the firm establishment of political unity and a stable government. Her ultimate munitioning potential, while it may be considerable, will not be developed for a long time and cannot be expected to be of the order of magnitude of either Russia or the United States because of the smaller size of her reserves of iron ore.

11. As a military power, France will be found in a category below the British Empire. Nevertheless, France after her recovery will be in a position to exert a greater effort than Britain in land operations on the European continent, because of her high degree of economic self-sufficiency and the very considerable munitioning capacity she will eventually possess after the re-acquisition of the Lorraine ore fields and the reconstruction of her industry.

12. In spite of her resources in manpower, Italy, because of her very notable deficiencies in essential mineral reserves, must remain a relatively minor military power, largely dependent upon others for her munitioning needs.

13. To summarize:

a. From the military point of view, it is highly desirable that discussions concerning the related subjects of territorial trusteeship and territorial settlements, particularly as they may adversely affect our relations with Russia, be delayed until after the defeat of Japan.

b. Concerning the post-war era, such discussions should give due weight to the facts that:

(1) As regards their military power, the United States and Russia are dominant in their respective areas.

(2) The relative strength and geographic positions of the United States and Russia are such as to preclude the military defeat of one of these powers by the other, even if that power were allied with the British Empire.

(3) The relative military power of the British Empire has declined and will continue to be considerably less than that of Russia or the United States, but superior to that of any nation other than those two powers.

(4) The military power of China at present and for many years to come will be very small.

(5) Assuming the effective disarmament of Germany and Japan, nations other than United States, Russia, and the British Empire, may be potential sources of breaches of the international peace and security, as conceived by the General International Organization, but even collectively they will not possess sufficient military power to involve the world in a global war against the concerted will of the three great powers.

Hopkins Mission to Moscow

THE AMBASSADOR IN THE SOVIET UNION HARRIMAN TO THE SECRETARY OF STATE

Moscow, April 13, 1945—11 PM
Received April 13—7:50 PM

This evening I called on Marshal Stalin. Stalin was obviously deeply distressed at the death of President Roosevelt. He asked many questions about the situation in the US resulting from his death. He assured me that it was his desire to work with President Truman as he had with President Roosevelt in the past. I will report in more detail in a later telegram on this aspect of the conversation. I proposed to Stalin that the most effective way to

SOURCE: *Foreign Relations* (1945), I: 289–290.

assure the American public and the world of the desire of the Soviet Government to continue collaboration with us and the other United Nations would be for Mr. Molotov to go to the US at this time. I suggested that he might stop at Washington to see the President and then proceed to San Francisco, even though he might be able to remain there only a few days. If it would assist I felt sure that arrangements could be made to place one of our latest planes at his disposal such as the one used by President Roosevelt.

Stalin inquired whether I was expressing my personal views. I made it clear that I was, but added that I felt completely confident that I was expressing the views of the President and yourself and that you would be ready to confirm this.

After a brief discussion between Molotov and Stalin the latter stated categorically that Molotov's trip to the US, although difficult at this time, would be arranged. He made it clear, however, that this decision was based on my assurance that you would authorize me with the approval of the President to renew the hope that it would be possible for Mr. Molotov to come to Washington and San Francisco as you considered his presence there at this time of real importance.

I hope that you will send me immediately instructions so that I may confirm without delay what I said to Stalin this evening.

I hope also you will bear in mind that I have promised a suitably equipped C–54 to take him to the US via the North Atlantic Scandinavian route if he so desires.

HARRIMAN

U.S. Delegation to United Nations

UNITED STATES DELEGATION

February 13, 1945

The President announced on February 13 that he will invite the following to be the members of the United States Delegation to the United Nations Conference on April 25, 1945 at San Francisco: Secretary of State Stettinius, Chairman; the Honorable Cordell Hull; Senator Connally; Senator Vandenberg; Representa-

SOURCE: *Foreign Relations* (1945), I: 70, 116–118.

tive Bloom; Representative Eaton; Commander Harold Stassen; Dean Virginia Gildersleeve.

Mr. Hull also will serve as senior adviser to the United States Delegation.

Minutes of the First Meeting of the United States Delegation, Held at Washington, Tuesday, March 13, 1945, 11 AM

[Here follows list of names of persons (15) present (6 delegates and 9 Departmental officers) and preliminary announcements by the Secretary on arrangements for delegation meetings and for the Conference.]

THE SECRETARY said that he had outlined to the President the question of the publicity policy for the Conference. He had explained the need of a liberal and progressive policy in this respect, to which the President had agreed. THE SECRETARY suggested a formula along the following lines:

(1) The plenary sessions of the Conference would be open to the public, including the press, radio, and newsreels;

(2) The meetings of commissions would likewise be open to the public;

(3) The Chairman of the Conference would hold a press conference every day at noon to keep the press fully posted on developments;

(4) All other matters would be private. This would include meetings of subcommittees, the executive committee, and the steering committee.

THE SECRETARY said that an arrangement along these lines had worked well at Mexico City, and that at his press conference here yesterday the correspondents had passed a resolution expressing approval of the Mexican arrangements and expressing the hope that similar arrangements could be made at San Francisco.

SENATOR CONNALLY questioned having the meetings of Commissions open to the public on the ground that this would lengthen the Conference. COMMANDER STASSEN thought that while it might lengthen the Conference the price might be worth the benefits resulting from such a policy.

At this point as a result of a question concerning the commissions, MR. HISS explained briefly the tentative organization charts. He said that there probably would be five commissions as follows:

(1) General Structure, (2) Security Problems, (3) Economic and Social Problems, (4) Judicial Organization and Legal Problems, (5) Trusteeship Arrangements. He pointed out that in addition there would be an executive committee consisting of the chairmen of the various delegations, a steering committee, and subcommittees of the various commissions.

REPRESENTATIVE BLOOM asked what was meant by "trusteeship." It was explained that this had reference to the treatment of certain dependent territories, including the League mandates. He inquired whether the people would be satisfied with such a title for this subject. Representative Eaton inquired whether "trusteeship" would include the treatment of colonial problems.

THE SECRETARY explained that at the San Francisco Conference it would be possible only to deal with arrangements for handling former League mandates and certain areas to be detached from the enemy powers. It would not be possible to deal with particular areas and there would be no consideration of the allocation or treatment of specific territories.

SENATOR VANDENBERG said that this suggested one important matter which ought to be cleared up in the minds of the public; that is at San Francisco we would be dealing only with the creation of an organization—we would not be dealing with specific problems of the peace settlement, such as territorial dispositions. SENATOR CONNALLY agreed with this and said that there was considerable confusion in the public mind as to the purpose of the Conference. There was general agreement that it was important to clarify the purpose of the Conference whenever opportunity offered.

Returning to the question of trusteeship, REPRESENTATIVE BLOOM inquired whether the proposals under consideration contemplated taking over the League mandates. MR. HISS said that this was so, but not as to the disposition to be made of specific mandated areas.

COMMANDER STASSEN expressed his approval of the use of the word "trusteeship," and there was general agreement with this view. REPRESENTATIVE BLOOM said that he had only brought the question up for the purposes of clarification.

REPRESENTATIVE EATON inquired what this meant as to the disposition of the League of Nations. THE SECRETARY pointed out that the League's Supervisory Commission had at a meeting in

December appointed a committee of three members to negotiate with the new organization with respect to the disposition of the League's property and functions. MR. PASVOLSKY said that the members of the League present at San Francisco might pass a resolution providing for the liquidation of the League. SENATOR CONNALLY remarked that it was self-evident that we could not have two general organizations in being at the same time.

THE SECRETARY said that the President had told him that he did not want alternates to the Delegates. The President had had some fifty or more suggestions for additions to the Delegation. He did not want to appoint any additional delegates or any alternates. This met with general approval.

At this point the meeting was adjourned to enable the Delegates to go to the White House.

III

War against the Axis

25. Introduction

As indicated in the section on diplomacy, the main decision under-
lying military strategy was that this was to be a coalition war. In
some ways coalition warfare was difficult with Soviet Russia fighting its own war with Germany and not in conflict with America's
enemy in the Far East until the last days of the struggle. Cooperation with the British came earlier and was more continuous.
Meeting from January 29 to March 27, 1941, British and American
military representatives agreed that if the United States got into
the war, "The broad strategic objectives of the Associated Powers
will be the defeat of Germany and her Allies."

Although they agreed on this objective, the British and the
Americans disagreed on the means. British leaders wanted to use
naval and air strength to force the Axis to its knees before making
an assault on the continent. The Americans, on the other hand,
wanted to invade Europe as soon as possible.

The first military action against Germany came in North Africa,
over the initial protests of the American military leaders, who felt
that the move would delay the assault on Europe. President
Roosevelt, however, was convinced that the invasion of North
Africa was the right move, and he and Prime Minister Churchill
made the key decision. Once the decision had been made, the
American military leaders worked with their British counterparts
on plans for an Anglo-American invasion, in which the Americans
would have the larger share partly as a symbol of American military
involvement and partly in the hope that French in North Africa
would be more receptive to the Americans than they might be to a
British-led expedition.

The landings in North Africa went ahead on schedule in
November, 1942. The Germans reacted quickly and poured reinforcements into Tunisia, and the Allied move to counter this
German action bogged down in rainy weather and mud. The
winter stalemate and the subsequent fighting in North Africa
became a testing ground for American men and officers. Generals
Eisenhower, Bradley and Patton were among those who got their
battle training in North Africa. In the spring of 1943, a combina-

tion of sea power, air blows and land advance from both east and west culminated in the closing of a trap in northern Tunisia on more than a quarter of a million enemy troops.

Already the decision had been made to invade Sicily and then Italy. The huge amphibious assault was a success and a significant battle test, even though many Germans slipped across the straits into Italy. Escaping catastrophe on the beaches at Salerno, the Americans set up their beachhead; British landings were unopposed. Mussolini fell, but the Germans decided to try to hold Italy. The American attempt to advance up the west coast met numerous setbacks: German defenses were stiff, the terrain was rugged and at times Allied manpower was drained to build up forces in England for the projected cross-Channel invasion. Consequently, the war in Italy was hard and slow. Allied airfields on the peninsula became useful in the air war on Germany and Austria, but the advance of ground troops was bitterly contested. As a result, war's end in Italy came only shortly before the collapse of Germany.

Strategic air bombing did not accomplish all the results predicted by its leaders, but its blows were helpful in bringing Germany to defeat. American air forces began to arrive in the United Kingdom in the spring of 1942. Growth was slow, and experience had to be gained. In time the British and the Americans cooperated in a massive around-the-clock bombing of the continent that saw the Royal Air Force concentrating on heavy night-time saturation raids, while the Americans flew by day, gradually building great strength in high-level precision bombing. In time the Allied air forces gained superiority and even command of the air. Post-war analysis indicates that Germany's aviation industry was not destroyed but diversified and that oil, not the aircraft industry, should have been the first target. On the other hand, the Allied air forces had been successful in attaining their main objective, virtual elimination of the German flying personnel.

The air war played an important role in the invasion of France, for tactical as well as strategic air units struck long and hard at the Luftwaffe before the invasion. D-Day in Normandy was long in planning and preparation. To an Englishman, Lieutenant General Sir Frederick Morgan, went the assignment of planning the operation, and to an American, General Dwight D. Eisenhower, went the task of directing the actual invasion and the subsequent Allied campaign in Western Europe.

Success on D-Day, June 6, 1944, owed much to air power which had cleared the skies of enemy planes, naval forces which transported and protected the invading forces and the careful planning, training and build-up of these forces.

After the landings and establishment of strong beachheads, the Allies carried on heavy fighting and then made a breakthrough. Although they did not trap as many of the Germans as they hoped at Falaise, the Allies forced the enemy into general retreat. The next problem of the Allies came to be logistical, as swift moving Allied forces pursued faster moving German troops. An assault on southern France in the middle of August brought new Allied units into the area.

When the Germans stopped retreating at the Siegfried line, General Eisenhower was forced to reappraise his own situation, and his forces made herculean efforts to solve their logistical problems. During a fall deadlock, Eisenhower had to deal with the desires of British General Montgomery or American General Patton each to use his forces in a concerted drive on the heart of Germany. Eisenhower decided, however, to advance more slowly along a broad front.

Meanwhile, the Germans were encountering defeat on the Eastern Front as well and felt themselves gradually squeezed as in a vise. Although on the Western Front the Germans had made a successful stand at Arnhem, the commanding general, Gerd von Rundstedt, realized that Germany could not win, but he still hoped to make the victory a costly one for the Allies. Unfortunately for him, Hitler chose to enter directly into military planning. He sent in additional forces to the Western Front and ordered von Rundstedt to launch an offensive designed to break through the lines, advance toward the sea and strike at the Allies from the rear. The effort failed and in effect cost Hitler a Panzer Brigade.

The Allies also encountered a setback. Failure to clear the approaches to Antwerp killed hope of a quick breakthrough before winter, and Allied military leaders were forced to content themselves with limited objectives. Once again Montgomery sought permission to lead the sole advancing force, and Eisenhower refused in favor of defense and preparations for a move all along the line.

There was a significant exception to the defenses. This was a narrow line of men and equipment guarding the Ardennes forest between the U. S. First and Third Armies. It was in this sector that Hitler determined to make his breakthrough. The German generals were unhappy, but after the unsuccessful attempt on Hitler's life on June 20, 1944, even generals were careful of their words.

In reducing the line of defense in the Ardennes, General Bradley had taken a calculated risk, which in the first stages of the attack it appeared he might have lost. Deliberately using bad weather to reduce air defenses, on December 16, the Germans began what has come to be called the Battle of the Bulge. They surprised the enemy and broke through almost to Bastogne. Suffering heavy casualties, the Allies stood their ground, and gradually reinforcements turned the tide against the Germans. Bastogne held, the weather cleared and the thrust failed. The Germans had inflicted severe losses, surprised the enemy and slowed up Allied action for six weeks, but it was the Germans, and not the Allies, who could not stand the attrition, for they, too, lost heavily in manpower, supplies and equipment.

After eliminating the Ardennes Bulge, Eisenhower planned three massive attacks, from the north to the Saar and Colmar. Gradually, the Allies pushed the enemy to the Rhine and then across. By March, 1945, the Germans clearly could not win, but they kept on fighting. At the same time, the Russians were implacably advancing from the East.

Eisenhower's next move was to order the encirclement of the Ruhr, and the operation was completed by April 1, 1945. Other Allied forces advanced toward the Elbe, and organized resistance ended in this area April 18. As his armies advanced Eisenhower made a decision for which he was later criticized. This was to continue to try to destroy German military power rather than to seize a geographical objective such as Berlin. Further, he felt that the Americans were not strong enough to knife through to Berlin. He determined, therefore, to have his forces advance to meet the Russians and cut Germany in half.

Hitler was one of the last to admit the coming defeat. He made a final effort to disperse his government and, deciding to remain in

Berlin, on April 28 he went to a self-decreed death. There remained the vexatious problem of bringing the war to an end in Europe, persuading the Allies to agree and restoring some order out of the chaos of defeat and anarchy. The victorious forces set up military governments, destroyed the Nazi Party, seized Nazi leaders, and tried to minister to the needs of the defeated populations.

26. Military Planning

London Conference, July 1942

May 6, 1942

MEMORANDUM FOR GENERAL GEORGE MARSHALL:
Chief of Staff

1. I have yours of May sixth regarding the Pacific Theatre versus "Bolero." In regard to the first paragraph I did not issue any directive on May first regarding the increase of combat planes to Australia to a total of 1,000 and the ground forces to a total of 100,000. I did ask if this could properly be done. I understand now that this is inadvisable at the present time and I wholly agree with you and Admiral King.
2. In regard to additional aircraft to the South Pacific Theatre, it is my thought that all we should send there is a sufficient number of heavy and medium bombers and pursuit planes in order to maintain the present objective* there at the maximum.
3. I do not want "Bolero" slowed down.
4. The success of raiding operations seems to be such that a large scale Japanese offensive against Australia or New Zealand can be prevented.

SOURCES: Quoted in Maurice Matloff and Edwin M. Snell, *Strategic Planning for Coalition Warfare, 1941–1942 (United States Army in World War II: The War Department)* (Washington, 1953), p. 220. Reprinted by permission of the Department of the Army.

* The original word "strength" was crossed out and the word "objective" was written by hand, presumably by Roosevelt.

F.D.R.

North Africa

(a) The Commander in Chief, Allied Force, will command all forces assigned to Operation TORCH, under the principle of unity of command.

(b) The Western Naval Task Force will pass to the command of the Commander in Chief, Allied Force, upon crossing the meridian of 40° West Longitude. This command may be exercised either directly by the Commander in Chief or through the Naval Commander, Allied Force. (Prior to that time these forces will remain under the command of the Commander in Chief, United States Atlantic Fleet, who will arrange their movements so that they will meet the schedule of the Commander in Chief, Allied Force.)

(c) Command relations of Subordinate Task Forces are initially set up as given in sub-paragraphs (d), (e), (f), and (g). They are subject to change as found necessary by the Commander in Chief, Allied Force.

(d) The command of those units of the Western Task Force which are embarked in the Western Naval Task Force, will vest in the Commander, Western Naval Task Force, until such time as the Commanding General, Western Task Force, has established his headquarters on shore and states he is ready to assume command.

(e) When the Commanding General, Western Task Force, assumes command on shore, the naval forces designated to give further support to the occupation of FRENCH MOROCCO will pass to his control, acting through the Commander, Western Naval Task Force.

(f) Following the assault operations and when and as released by Commander in Chief, Allied Force, the United States naval

SOURCE: Quoted in George F. Howe, *Northwest Africa: Seizing the Initiative in the West* (*United States Army in World War II: The Mediterranean Theater of Operations*) (Washington, 1957), p. 38. Reprinted by permission of the Department of the Army.

forces assigned thereto will revert to the command of the Commander in Chief, United States Atlantic Fleet.

(g) The United States naval forces assigned for the operation of ports and for naval local and sea frontier defenses—Sea Frontier Forces, Western Task Force, and the Naval Operating Base, Center Task Force—will be under the command of the respective commanding generals of those task forces, under the principle of unity of command.

(h) The Commander in Chief, United States Atlantic Fleet, will exercise command over all forces employed for the cover and ocean escort in the ATLANTIC of follow-up convoys between the UNITED STATES and NORTH AFRICA.

Planning responsibilities were likewise classified as follows:

(a) The Commander in Chief, Allied Force, will designate the tactical and logistic plans to be prepared by the task force commanders.

(b) The Commander in Chief, Atlantic Fleet, will be responsible for planning for the organization of United States Naval Task Forces to be assigned to the Commander in Chief, Allied Force, for the operations of the Atlantic Fleet (less the elements assigned to Commander in Chief, Allied Force) in support of Operation TORCH, and for subsequent covering operations and convoy escorts in support thereof.

(c) The Army will be responsible for planning for the logistic support and requirements of the Army Forces assigned to Operation TORCH.

(d) The Commander in Chief, United States Atlantic Fleet, will be responsible for planning for the logistic support and requirements of the United States Naval Forces assigned to Operation TORCH.

Invasion of Western Europe

The Combined Chiefs of Staff directive to General Eisenhower declared:

SOURCE: Quoted in Forrest C. Pogue, *The Supreme Command* (*United States Army in World War II: The European Theater of Operations*) (Washington, 1954), pp. 53, 55. Reprinted by permission of the Department of the Army.

1. You are hereby designated as Supreme Allied Commander of the forces placed under your orders for operations for the liberation of Europe from the Germans. Your title will be Supreme Commander, Allied Expeditionary Force.

2. *Task.* You will enter the continent of Europe, and, in conjunction with the other United Nations, undertake operations aimed at the heart of Germany and the destruction of her armed forces. The date for entering the Continent is the month of May 1944. After adequate channel ports have been secured, exploitation will be directed to securing an area that will facilitate both ground and air operations against the enemy.

3. Notwithstanding the target date above, you will be prepared at any time to take immediate advantage of favorable circumstances, such as the withdrawal by the enemy on your front, to effect a re-entry into the Continent with such forces as you have available at the time; a general plan for this operation when approved will be furnished for your assistance.

4. *Command.* You are responsible to the Combined Chiefs of Staff and will exercise command generally in accordance with the diagram at Appendix A. Direct communication with the United States and British Chiefs of Staff is authorized in the interest of facilitating your operations and for arranging necessary logistic support.

5. *Logistics.* In the United Kingdom the responsibility for logistics organization, concentration, movement and supply of forces to meet the requirements of your plan will rest with British Service Ministries so far as British Forces are concerned. So far as United States Forces are concerned, this responsibility will rest with the United States War and Navy Departments. You will be responsible for the co-ordination of logistical arrangements on the continent. You will also be responsible for co-ordinating the requirements of British and United States Forces under your command.

6. *Co-ordination of operations of other Forces and Agencies.* In preparation for your assault on enemy occupied Europe, Sea and Air Forces, agencies of sabotage, subversion and propaganda, acting under a variety of authorities, are now in action. You may recommend any variation in these activities which may seem to you desirable.

7. *Relationship to United Nations Forces in other areas.* Responsibility will rest with the Combined Chiefs of Staff for supplying information relating to operations of the forces of the U.S.S.R. for your guidance in timing your operations. It is understood that the Soviet forces will launch an offensive at about the same time as OVERLORD with the object of preventing the German forces from transferring from the Eastern to the Western front. The Allied Commander-in-Chief, Mediterranean Theater, will conduct operations designed to assist your operation, including the launching of an attack against the south of France at about the same time as OVERLORD. The scope and timing of his operations will be decided by the Combined Chiefs of Staff. You will establish contact with him and submit to the Combined Chiefs of Staff your views and recommendations regarding operations from the Mediterranean in support of your attack from the United Kingdom. The Combined Chiefs of Staff will place under your command the forces operating in Southern France as soon as you are in a position to assume such command. You will submit timely recommendations compatible with this regard.

8. *Relationship with Allied Governments—the re-establishment of Civil Governments and Liberated Allied Territories and the administration of Enemy Territories.* Further instructions will be issued to you on these subjects at a later date.

Military Planning at Yalta

TOP SECRET   YALTA, 9 February 1945
REPORT TO THE PRESIDENT AND PRIME MINISTER OF THE AGREED
    SUMMARY OF CONCLUSIONS REACHED BY THE COMBINED CHIEFS
    OF STAFF AT THE "ARGONAUT" CONFERENCE

1. The agreed summary of the conclusions reached at ARGONAUT Conference is submitted herewith:

I. *Over-all Objective*

2. In conjunction with Russia and other Allies, to bring about at the earliest possible date the unconditional surrender of Germany and Japan.

SOURCE: *Foreign Relations* (1955), *Conferences at Malta and Yalta 1945*, pp. 827–831.

II. *Over-all Strategic Concept for the Prosecution of the War*

3. In cooperation with Russia and other Allies, to bring about at the earliest possible date the unconditional surrender of Germany.

4. Simultaneously, in cooperation with other Pacific Powers concerned, to maintain and extend unremitting pressure against Japan with the purpose of continually reducing her military power and attaining positions from which her ultimate surrender can be forced. The effect of any such extension on the over-all objective to be given consideration by the Combined Chiefs of Staff before action is taken.

5. Upon the defeat of Germany, in cooperation with other Pacific Powers and with Russia, to direct the full resources of the United States and Great Britain to bring about at the earliest possible date the unconditional surrender of Japan.

III. *Basic Undertakings in Support of Over-all Strategic Concept*

6. Whatever operations are decided on in support of the over-all strategic concept, the following established undertakings will be a first charge against our resources, subject to review by the Combined Chiefs of Staff in keeping with the changing situation:

   a. Maintain the security and war-making capacity of the Western Hemisphere and the British Isles.
   b. Support the war-making capacity of our forces in all areas.
   c. Maintain vital overseas lines of communication.
   d. Continue the disruption of enemy sea communications.
   e. Continue the offensive against Germany.
   f. Undertake such measures as may be necessary and practicable to aid the war effort of Russia to include coordinating the action of forces.
   g. Undertake such measures as may be necessary and practicable in order to aid the war effort of China as an effective ally and as a base for operations against Japan.
   h. Provide assistance to such of the forces of the liberated areas in Europe as can fulfill an active and effective role in the war against Germany and/or Japan. Within the limits of our available resources to assist other co-belligerents to the extent they are able to employ this assistance against the Enemy Powers in the present war. Having regard to the successful accomplishment of the other basic undertakings, to provide such supplies to the liberated areas as will effectively contribute to the war-making capacity of the United Nations against Germany and/or Japan.

i. Reorient forces from the European Theater to the Pacific and Far East as a matter of highest priority having regard to other agreed and/or inescapable commitments as soon as the German situation allows.

j. Continue operations leading to the earliest practicable invasion of Japan.

IV. *Execution of the Over-all Strategic Concept*

DEFEAT OF GERMANY

The U-Boat War

7. We are concerned with the possibility that German U-boats may again constitute a serious threat to our North Atlantic shipping lanes. It is too early yet to assess the extent to which such an offensive could achieve success, and we propose to review the matter again on 1 April 1945.

8. Meanwhile, we have agreed on the following countermeasures:

a. To build up as much as is practicable the strength of surface hunting groups and anti-U-boat air squadrons.

b. To maintain and, if possible, increase "marginal" bomber effort on assembly yards, concentrating as far as is practicable against Hamburg and Bremen.

c. To maintain "marginal" effort against operating bases, being ready to increase this when bases become crowded beyond the capacity of concrete pens.

d. To increase, by 100% if possible, the air mining effort against U-boats, including the training areas.

e. To mine water beyond range of *d.* above by using surface minelayers and carrier-borne aircraft.

f. To intensify operations against enemy minesweepers.

g. To maintain and intensify operations against the enemy shipping used to supply U-boat bases.

Operations in Northwest Europe

9. In two telegrams, SCAF 180 as amended by SCAF 194, the Supreme Commander, Allied Expeditionary Force, has presented his appreciation and his plan of operations for Northwest Europe. His plan is as follows:

a. To carry out immediately a series of operations north of the Moselle with a view to destroying the enemy and closing the Rhine north of Düsseldorf.

b. To direct our efforts to eliminating other enemy forces west of the Rhine, which still constitute an obstacle or a potential threat to our subsequent Rhine crossing operations.

c. To seize bridgeheads over the Rhine in the North and the South.

d. To deploy east of the Rhine and north of the Ruhr the maximum number of divisions which can be maintained (estimated at some 35 divisions). The initial task of this force, assisted by air action, will be to deny to the enemy the industries of the Ruhr.

e. To deploy east of the Rhine, on the axis Frankfurt-Kassel, such forces, if adequate, as may be available after providing 35 divisions for the North and essential security elsewhere. The task of this force will be to draw enemy forces away from the North by capturing Frankfurt and advancing on Kassel.

10. We have taken note of SCAF 180 as amended by SCAF 194 and of the Supreme Commander's assurance that he will seize the Rhine crossings in the North just as soon as this is a feasible operation and without waiting to close the Rhine throughout its length. Further, that he will advance across the Rhine in the North with maximum strength and complete determination, immediately the situation in the South allows him to collect the necessary forces and do this without incurring unreasonable risks.

Strategy in the Mediterranean

11. We have reviewed our strategy in the Mediterranean in the light of the development of the situation in Europe and of the fact that the enemy is at liberty at any time to make a voluntary withdrawal in Italy. We have agreed that our primary object in the war against Germany should be to build up the maximum possible strength on the Western Front and to seek a decision in that theater.

12. In accordance with this concept we have agreed to withdraw certain forces from the Mediterranean Theater and to place them at the disposal of the Supreme Commander, Allied Expeditionary Force, and to redefine the tasks of the Supreme Allied Commander, Mediterranean.

13. Our proposals are contained in the directive to the Supreme Allied Commander, Mediterranean, attached as Appendix "A."

The War against Japan

Over-All Objective in the War Against Japan

14. We have agreed that the over-all objective in the war against Japan should be expressed as follows:

> To force the unconditional surrender of Japan by:
> a. Lowering Japanese ability and will to resist by establishing sea and air blockades, conducting intensive air bombardment, and destroying Japanese air and naval strength.
> b. Invading and seizing objectives in the industrial heart of Japan.

Operations in the Pacific Area

15. We have taken note of the plans and operations proposed by the United States Chiefs of Staff in C. C. S. 417/11 (Appendix "B").

Operations in Southeast Asia Command

16. We have agreed to the following policy in respect of employment in Southeast Asia Command of United States resources deployed in the India-Burma Theater:

> a. The primary military object of the United States in the China and India-Burma Theaters is the continuance of aid to China on a scale that will permit the fullest utilization of the area and resources of China for operations against the Japanese. United States resources are deployed in India-Burma to provide direct or indirect support for China. These forces and resources participate not only in operating the base and the line of communications for United States and Chinese forces in China, but also constitute a reserve immediately available to China without permanently increasing the requirements for transport of supplies to China.
> b. The United States Chiefs of Staff contemplate no change in their agreement to SACSEA's use of resources of the U. S. India-Burma Theater in Burma when this use does not prevent the fulfillment of their primary object of rendering support to China including protection of the line of communications. Any transfer of forces engaged in approved operations in progress in Burma which is contemplated by the United States Chiefs of Staff and which, in the opinion of the British Chiefs of Staff, would jeopardize those operations, will be subject to discussion by the Combined Chiefs of Staff.

17. We have reviewed the progress of the campaign in Burma and agreed upon the terms of a directive to the Supreme Allied

Commander, Southeast Asia. This directive is attached as Appendix "C."

Planning Dates for the End of the War Against Germany and Japan

18. We feel that it is important to agree and promulgate planning dates for the end of the war against Germany and Japan. These dates are necessary for the purpose of planning production and the allocation of manpower.

We recommend that the planning dates for the end of the war against Germany should be as follows:

    a. Earliest date—1 July 1945.
    b. Date beyond which the war is unlikely to continue—31 December 1945.

We recommend that the planning date for the end of the war against Japan should be set at 18 months after the defeat of Germany.

All the above dates to be adjusted periodically to conform to the course of the war.

27. Combat Conditions

ASSAULT PROBLEMS IN ITALY

The 1949 squabble over unification was intensified by this issue. We must accept the principle of unity of command in peacetime if we are to have it in war—where lack of it may prove disastrous. Otherwise, we will have extra echelons of command existing side by side, as we had in Italy, with the result that never were so few commanded by so many.

Problems of this nature were very much in my mind on that circuitous route across the Mediterranean to Salerno. I suppose that I was making mental preparations for the worst that could

SOURCE: Mark W. Clark, *Calculated Risk* (New York, 1950), pp. 187–188, 190–191. Copyright, 1950 by Mark W. Clark. Reprinted by permission of Harper & Row, Publishers, Inc.

happen; but I recall that I also discussed with my staff such pleasant possibilities as a direct move into Naples Harbor if the Italian surrender cleared our path to a greater extent than we actually anticipated.

It is interesting to recall that as we approached Italian shores we entertained a number of theories that were going to be knocked sky-high when the fighting got under way. One of these, which was particularly held by the British, was that if we struck Italy with sufficient force and secured suitable ports and airfields for big-scale operations, the Germans would soon decide not to give battle but to pull back to north Italy. This theory, which originated in high intelligence sources in London and was reflected throughout the British intelligence in the Mediterranean, was based on the argument that the enemy would be unable to maintain his strength in Italy because of poor transportation facilities through mountainous territory and because of our air superiority. We gave the theory a good try. Allied bombers worked over the enemy communication lines for many weeks and, finally, for months and even years. The Brenner Pass, the tunnels, the bridges, were battered steadily, but the theory was a complete flop. The Germans kept right on increasing their strength in Italy until the very end and were able to battle us for every foot of Italian soil.

On September 8, we sat in Hewitt's cabin and listened to the radio broadcasts of the unconditional surrender of the Italian government. Before sundown that evening our transports and warships were in three lines approaching a designated area off Salerno, where minesweepers moved in to clear a path to the beaches. The sea was smooth, the sky was clear, and at ten minutes to midnight we lay, with engines stopped, only a few miles from the shore. I joined Hewitt on the bridge of the Ancon. I have already said that this naval phase of the assault was out of my hands, but I had not realized how helpless I would feel as everywhere in the darkness around us the officers and men of the Fifth Army started that last dash toward the beaches. There was nothing we could do but wait.

Our landings were on a strip of coast about thirty-six miles long, extending from Maiori, just west of the town of Salerno, southward to Paestum and Agropoli. As the men clambered into landing craft and the small boats maneuvered noisily into position all around us,

I could see flashes of gunfire on the north sector of the assault zone where British warships were laying down a barrage in front of the British X Corps' first wave. On the south sector the American VI Corps was attempting to land quietly without previous bombardment, but there were ominous hints that the enemy was alerted. Flares and the flames of demolition fires could be seen in that area as the 142nd Regimental Combat Team, led by Colonel John D. Forsythe, and the 141st Regimental Combat Team under Colonel Richard J. Werner—both of the 36th Division—felt their landing crafts touch bottom on the shore at 3:30 AM.

Then, to end any doubt about surprise, a loudspeaker voice on the shore roared out in English, "Come on in and give up. You're covered." Flares shot high into the air to illuminate the beaches, and German guns previously sited on the beaches opened up with a roar. The assault forces came on in, but not to give up. There was resistance on every beach, and within a short time the defenders were strengthened by artillery and planes so that our opposition increased steadily as dawn approached. Some boats in the first assault wave were unable to reach their designated beaches and had to shift to other sectors, especially Red Beach, where opposition was lighter; while many of the second-wave boats were badly damaged or had to turn back on their first attempt to get ashore. Men were separated from weapons in the confusion or when their boats sank. Radio communication was difficult in most instances because of loss of equipment and the intense enemy fire.

But, owing to sound basic training and countless instances of personal bravery, the assault forces not only held on but slowly advanced inland. Men squirmed through barbed wire, around mines, and behind enemy machine guns and the tanks that soon made their appearance, working their way inland and knocking out German strongpoints wherever possible as they headed for their assembly point on a railroad that roughly paralleled the beach about two miles away. Singly and in small groups, they reached their first objective by devious means. Private J. C. Jones collected fifty stragglers, guided them off the beach through heavy fire, and destroyed several enemy machine-gun posts. Sergeant Manuel S. Gonzales wriggled on his belly through heavy rifle fire and grenade bursts and, with his own grenades, killed an 88-mm. gun crew. Private James M. Logan killed three Germans who rushed at him, firing rifles, from a wall, shot nearby machine gunners, and turned the weapon on the rest of the gun crew as they fled. Lieutenant Clair F. Carpenter and Corporal Edgar L. Blackburn, manning a 75-mm. self-propelled howitzer, in a defile swept by enemy fire from both flanks, knocked out a machine-gun nest and a tank before they were cut down by a heavy burst of fire. There were countless other acts of heroism.

Under great difficulties, heavy weapons were being landed by dawn. Ducks brought in 105-mm. howitzers of the 133rd Field Artillery Battalion, and the 151st Field Artillery Battalion landed at 6 AM, just in time to beat off a dangerous German tank assault on the beachhead. The veteran 531st Shore Engineers began organizing the communication and supply lines, and bulldozer men, ignoring a steady fire which inflicted many casualties among them, built exit routes for vehicles to move from the beaches through the sand dunes.

In this manner our toehold on Fortress Europa was gained, and no soldiers ever fought more bravely than the men of the 36th Division. I have spoken of their landing in detail both because it was the most difficult, since they were untested troops, and because they were among the first Americans to put foot on Hitler-held Continental Europe; but I do not want to seem to overlook the tremendous job that the rest of the Fifth Army was doing at the same time. The British veterans performed in splendid fashion.

The President's Log en Route to Cairo

Sunday, November 14th. (At sea in "Iowa")
1:00 AM
All ship's clocks were set ahead one hour to conform to Zone Plus Three time.
8:00 AM
Position: Latitude 34°–16′00″ N. Longitude 62°–33′14″ W.
Course—105° (true).
Speed—25 knots.
Distance made good since 8:00 AM, Saturday, 553 miles.
Distance made good since departure, 618 miles.

SOURCE: *Foreign Relations, Conferences at Cairo and Tehran 1943*, pp. 279–280.

Wind from 300°, force 6.
Temperature—70°.
Sea—moderate swell.
Weather—slightly cloudy.

During the afternoon the *Iowa* exercised at air defense drill, simulating the repulse of an air attack from starboard. The President witnessed this exercise from the deck just outside his quarters (first superstructure deck, starboard side). Live ammunition was fired from a number of units of the ship's anti-aircraft battery (5-inch, 40 m. m. and 20 m. m. guns) to demonstrate for the Commander-in-Chief what a veritable curtain of fire a ship of this type can offer as a "greeting" for enemy planes bent on attacking.

While the *Iowa* was exercising at this anti-aircraft drill, and during the lull after one round of the series of firings, a moment of extreme tension was brought on by an unexpected explosion, of an underwater nature, in the vicinity of the ship. This explosion was followed by the terse announcement, "This is not a drill." All hands wondered, had we been attacked? This doubt was soon cleared when the *William D. Porter*, our antisubmarine screen to starboard, reported by visual dispatch that she had accidentally fired a torpedo in our direction. Fortunately the wake of the torpedo had been detected and reported by the *Iowa's* lookouts in time for the *Iowa* to maneuver and to avoid being hit. During this maneuvering, the *Iowa*, within the period of but a very few minutes, built up her speed to 31 knots. The torpedo passed approximately 1,200 yards astern of the *Iowa*, moving at an estimated speed of 46 knots and at an estimated depth of 16 feet. The *William D. Porter* explained the accidental firing as probably caused by moisture from previous rough seas grounding the electrical circuit from the firing pin through the impulse case and igniting the black powder impulse charge. An investigation of this incident was immediately ordered by Admiral King, the Commander in Chief, U. S. Fleet, who was a passenger in the *Iowa* at the time.

Had that torpedo hit the *Iowa* in the right spot with her passenger list of distinguished statesmen, military, naval and aerial strategists and planners, it could have had untold effect on the outcome of the war and the destiny of our country. The *William D. Porter's* ship's company presumably did not know who rode the *Iowa*. During the afternoon Admiral McIntire and Lieutenant Commander Fox inspected the ship's medical department and witnessed several major operations.

DECISION ON D-DAY

A number of other details remained to be ironed out during the days at Portsmouth preceding D-day, but the big question mark always before us was the weather that would prevail during the only period of early June that we could use, the fifth, sixth, and seventh.

All southern England was one vast military camp, crowded with soldiers awaiting final word to go, and piled high with supplies and equipment awaiting transport to the far shore of the Channel. The whole area was cut off from the rest of England. The government had established a deadline, across which no unauthorized person was allowed to go in either direction. Every separate encampment, barrack, vehicle park, and every unit was carefully charted on our master maps. The scheduled movement of each unit had been so worked out that it would reach the embarkation point at the exact time the vessels would be ready to receive it. The southernmost camps where assault troops were assembled were all surrounded by barbed-wire entanglements to prevent any soldier leaving the camp after he had once been briefed as to his part in the attack. The mighty host was tense as a coiled spring, and indeed that is exactly what it was—a great human spring, coiled for the moment when its energy should be released and it would vault the English Channel in the greatest amphibious assault ever attempted.

We met with the Meteorologic Committee twice daily, once at nine-thirty in the evening and once at four in the morning. The committee, comprising both British and American personnel, was headed by a dour but canny Scot, Group Captain J. M. Stagg. At these meetings every bit of evidence was carefully presented, carefully analyzed by the experts, and carefully studied by the assembled commanders. With the approach of the critical period the tension continued to mount as prospects for decent weather became worse and worse.

SOURCE: Dwight D. Eisenhower, *Crusade in Europe* (New York, 1948), pp. 248–250. Copyright 1948 by Doubleday & Company, Inc. Reprinted by permission of the publisher.

The final conference for determining the feasibility of attacking on the tentatively selected day, June 5, was scheduled for 4:00 AM on June 4. However, some of the attacking contingents had already been ordered to sea, because if the entire force was to land on June 5, then some of the important elements stationed in northern parts of the United Kingdom could not wait for final decision on the morning of June 4.

When the commanders assembled on the morning of June 4 the report we received was discouraging. Low clouds, high winds, and formidable wave action were predicted to make landing a most hazardous affair. The meteorologists said that air support would be impossible, naval gunfire would be inefficient, and even the handling of small boats would be rendered difficult. Admiral Ramsay thought that the mechanics of landing could be handled, but agreed with the estimate of the difficulty in adjusting gunfire. His position was mainly neutral. General Montgomery, properly concerned with the great disadvantages of delay, believed that we should go. Tedder disagreed.

Weighing all factors, I decided that the attack would have to be postponed. This decision necessitated the immediate dispatch of orders to the vessels and troops already at sea and created some doubt as to whether they could be ready twenty-four hours later in case the next day should prove favorable for the assault. Actually the maneuver of the ships in the Irish Sea proved most difficult by reason of the storm. That they succeeded in gaining ports, refueling, and readying themselves to resume the movement a day later represented the utmost in seamanship and in brilliant command and staff work.

The conference on the evening of June 4 presented little, if any, added brightness to the picture of the morning, and tension mounted even higher because the inescapable consequences of postponement were almost too bitter to contemplate.

At three-thirty the next morning our little camp was shaking and shuddering under a wind of almost hurricane proportions and the accompanying rain seemed to be traveling in horizontal streaks. The mile-long trip through muddy roads to the naval headquarters was anything but a cheerful one, since it seemed impossible that in such conditions there was any reason for even discussing the situation.

When the conference started the first report given us by Group Captain Stagg and the Meteorologic Staff was that the bad conditions predicted the day before for the coast of France were actually prevailing there and that if we had persisted in the attempt to land on June 5 a major disaster would almost surely have resulted. This they probably told us to inspire more confidence in their next astonishing declaration, which was that by the following morning a period of relatively good weather, heretofore completely unexpected, would ensue, lasting probably thirty-six hours. The long-term prediction was not good but they did give us assurance that this short period of calm weather would intervene between the exhaustion of the storm we were then experiencing and the beginning of the next spell of really bad weather.

The prospect was not bright because of the possibility that we might land the first several waves successfully and then find later build-up impracticable, and so have to leave the isolated original attacking forces easy prey to German counteraction. However, the consequences of the delay justified great risk and I quickly announced the decision to go ahead with the attack on June 6. The time was then 4:15 AM, June 5. No one present disagreed and there was a definite brightening of faces as, without a further word, each went off to his respective post of duty to flash out to his command the messages that would set the whole host in motion.

THE LORRAINE CAMPAIGN

During 4 October the Third Platoon of G Company, 11th Infantry, made an assault to force one of the fort entrances. The platoon was driven back by a counterattack but was saved by the heroic action of 2d Lt. L. S. Dilello, who covered the withdrawal with fire from a BAR until he was killed by a hand grenade. Lieutenant Dilello received a posthumous award of the DSC.

About this time General Patton told General Walker to take Driant, saying that "if it took every man in the XX Corps, [he] could not allow an attack by this army to fail." TUSA Diary, 4 Oct

SOURCE: H. M. Cole, *The Lorraine Campaign* (*United States Army in World War II: The European Theater of Operations*) (Washington, 1950), pp. 272–273. Reprinted by permission of the Department of the Army.

44. Actually, the Third Army commander's subsequent actions as regards Driant all show a more reasonable attitude.

In the late afternoon of 5 October the S–3 of the 2d Battalion, Capt. Ferris N. Church, sent back a message with a graphic report from an infantry captain on conditions at the fort: "The situation is critical a couple more barrages and another counterattack and we are sunk. We have no men, our equipment is shot and we just can't go. The trs in G are done, they are just there whats left of them. Enemy has infiltrated and pinned what is here down. We cannot advance nor can K Co, B Co is in same shape I'm in. We cannot delay any longer on replacement. We may be able to hold till dark but if anything happens this afternoon I can make no predictions. The enemy arty is butchering these trs until we have nothing left to hold with. We cannot get out to get our wounded and there is a hell of a lot of dead and missing. There is only one answer the way things stand. First either to withdraw and saturate it with hvy bombers or reinforce with a hell of a strong force. This strong force might hold here but eventually they'll get it by arty too. They have all of these places zeroed in by arty. The forts have 5–6 feet walls inside and 15 foot roofs of reinforced concrete. All our charges have been useless against this stuff. The few leaders are trying to keep what is left intact and that's all they can do. The trs are just not sufficiently trained and what is more they have no training in even basic Inf. Everything is committed and we cannot follow attack plan. This is just a suggestion but if we want this dammed fort lets get the stuff required to take it and then go. Right now you haven't got it. Gerrie, Capt., Inf." TF Warnock Jnl, 5 Oct 44.

AIR RAID ON BERLIN

From a broadcast by Ed Murrow of the Columbia Broadcasting System:

> The flak looked like a cigarette lighter in a dark room—one that won't light. Sparks but no flame. The sparks crackling just above the level of the cloud tops. . . .
> Dead ahead there was a whole chain of red flares looking like

SOURCE: Leo Cherne, *The Rest of Your Life* (Doubleday, Garden City, N.Y., 1944), p. 25. Reprinted by permission of the publisher.

stop lights. . . . Again we could see those little bubbles of colored lead. . . . The clouds were gone, and the sticks of incendiaries from the preceding wave made the place look like a badly laid out city with the street lights on. The small incendiaries were going down like a fistful of white rice thrown on a piece of black velvet. The cookies—the 4,000-pound high explosives—were bursting below like great sunflowers gone mad.

I looked down on the white fires; the white fires had turned red. They were beginning to merge and spread, just like butter does on a hot plate. But this time all those patches of white on black had turned yellow and started to flow together. . . .

I looked to the port beam at the target area. There was a red, sullen, obscene glare. The fires seemed to have found each other— and we were heading home. . . .

Berlin was a kind of orchestrated hell, a terrible symphony of light and flame.

28. Military Leadership: George S. Patton, Jr.

BRADLEY ON PATTON

The evening before this Gafsa attack George had assembled his II Corps' staff for a final briefing.

"Gentlemen," he said, looking about the dimly lighted room, "tomorrow we attack. If we are not victorious, let no one come back alive." With that, George excused himself and retired alone to his room to pray.

These contradictions in Patton's character continued to bewilder his staff. For while he was profane, he was also reverent. And while he strutted imperiously as a commander, he knelt humbly before his God. And while that last appeal for victory even at the price of death was looked upon as a hammy gesture by his corps staff, it helped to make it more clearly apparent to them that to Patton war was a holy crusade.

I still could not accustom myself, however, to the vulgarity with which Patton skinned offenders for relatively minor infractions in

SOURCE: Omar N. Bradley, A Soldier's Story (New York, 1951), pp. 52, 160–161, 355–358. Copyright 1951 by Holt, Rinehart and Winston, Inc. Reprinted by permission of the publisher.

discipline. Patton believed that profanity was the most convincing medium of communication with his troops. But while some chuckled delightedly over the famed expletives he employed with startling originality, the majority, it seemed to me, were more often shocked and offended. At times I felt that Patton, however successful he was as a corps commander, had not yet learned to command himself.

The techniques of command vary, of course, with the personality of the commander. While some men prefer to lead by suggestion and example and other methods, Patton chose to drive his subordinates by bombast and by threats. Those mannerisms achieved spectacular results. But they were not calculated to win affection among his officers or men.

On August 10 George drove up to call on me at the corps CP. He had stopped on the road en route to visit the patients at a nearby corps evacuation hospital. Few commanders spent more time touring the wards than George did, for he found in the bandaged wounds of those soldiers the recognizable badge of courage he respected most. These were men he could understand. He joked with them, talked to them, shook their hands, and pinned on their Purple Hearts.

As George drove into the CP I walked out to meet him. He jumped down from the high running board of his recon car.

"Sorry to be late, Bradley," he said, "I stopped off at a hospital on the way up. There were a couple of malingerers there. I slapped one of them to make him mad and put some fight back in him."

He spoke of it casually, without remorse and without any evidence of wrongdoing. Indeed I would probably have forgotten the incident had it not been brought to my attention two days later.

That was when Kean came to my trailer with the corps surgeon in tow. He handed me a typewritten sheet.

"Here's a report you should see, General. It came in to the surgeon this morning from the CO of the 93rd Evac."

I read it and turned to the surgeon. "Has anyone else seen this?"

"No, sir," he answered, "no one but me."

I handed the report back to Kean. "Seal it in an envelope," I told him, "and mark it to be opened only by you or me. Then lock it up in my safe."

The paper contained an eyewitness report of what afterward

came to be known as the "slapping incident." It had been sub-mitted through channels by the CO of the hospital Patton had visited on his way to corps.

According to the commander, George had strolled unannounced into the receiving tent of the 93rd Evac. There he walked from litter to litter, talking with the wounded and congratulating them on the performance of their divisions.

At length he came to a patient without splints or dressings. George asked what was wrong. The man answered that he was running a high fever. Patton dismissed him without a word.

Another patient was seated nearby, shaking with convulsions.

"And what's happened to you?" Patton asked.

"It's my nerves, sir," the man replied, his eyes filled with tears.

"What did you say?" Patton stiffened.

"It's my nerves," the patient sobbed, "I can't stand the shelling any more."

George raised his voice. "Your nerves, hell," he shouted, "you're just a goddamned coward."

The soldier cried and George slapped him. "Shut up," he said, "I won't have these brave men here who've been shot see a yellow bastard crying."

George struck the man again. His helmet liner fell off and rolled across the dirt floor.

Patton called to the receiving officer, "Don't you admit this yellow bastard. There's nothing the matter with him. I won't have the hospitals cluttered up with sonsabitches who haven't the guts to fight."

Then turning to the patient, he said, "You're going back to the front lines—you may get shot and killed, but you're going back to fight. If you don't, I'll stand you up against a wall and have a firing squad kill you on purpose."

Patton's uproar had alerted the hospital. By that evening an exaggerated version of the tale had started its travels around the island. Within a week it was common gossip.

Eisenhower was told of the slapping, though not through me. The story reached newsmen accredited to Patton's Seventh Army and soon crossed the Mediterranean to the press camp at AFHQ. But though many of these newsmen were critical of Patton, they voluntarily declined to file it.

Reprehensible though Patton's conduct had been, Eisenhower questioned whether it justified his relieving one of the finest ground gainers in the U. S. Army. Instead he reprimanded George and ordered him to apologize not only to the patients and hospital personnel but also to the troops of his Seventh Army.

Inevitably, however, the story leaked to the United States where it touched off a nation-wide dispute that almost cost Patton his career. Although it would have been easy for Eisenhower to dump Patton now that the heat was on, he chose to stand by him.

Patton had crossed the Channel to France on July 6 with the vanguard of Third Army headquarters. He traveled under tight security wraps, for had the enemy learned of his prospective employment on the heels of the breakout, the hoax we had cultivated on the Pas de Calais would have been given away. We assigned George a bivouac in the Cotentin where he was to await commitment under 12th Army Group on August 1—a week after First Army's breakout.

My own feelings on George were mixed. He had not been my choice for Army commander and I was still wary of the grace with which he would accept our reversal in roles. For George was six years my senior and had been my Army commander when I fought II Corps in the Sicilian campaign. I was apprehensive in having George join my command, for I feared that too much of my time would probably be spent in curbing his impetuous habits. But at the same time I knew that with Patton there would be no need for my whipping Third Army to keep it on the move. We had only to keep him pointed in the direction we wanted to go.

George soon caused me to repent these uncharitable reservations, for he not only bore me no ill will but he trooped for 12th Army Group with unbounded loyalty and eagerness. Shortly after the war an officer from Third Army recalled the rancor with which Patton had frequently excoriated his senior commanders. "And yet in all those outbursts," he said, "I never heard the General speak an unkind word of you."

Before many more months had passed, the new Patton had totally obliterated my unwarranted apprehensions; we formed as amiable and contented a team as existed in the senior command. No longer the martinet that had sometimes strutted in Sicily,

George had now become a judicious, reasonable, and likable commander.

Several months later when George outlined a prospective scheme of maneuver, I showed him several faults in it. Instead of replying huffily as he might have a year before, George merely crinkled his eyes and chuckled. "You're right, Brad," he said, "goddammit, you're always right."

The reformation, however, was not totally complete, for George was still an impetuous man and even in Europe this impetuous nature continued to make trouble. The first misstep occurred after only 12 days on the beachhead while Third Army was biding its time impatiently in the Cotentin.

Once the COBRA plan was completed, I briefed Patton on it since he was to join the operation once it got under way. On July 18, two days before we were to brief the First Army newsmen, Dickson came to me red-faced with anger.

"We've heard from our correspondents, General," he said, "that Patton has briefed the press at Third Army on COBRA."

"I'll be damned," I said and reached for the phone. But George was not in.

Patton called back that evening with an apology and an explanation. Yes, he had briefed his *staff* on First Army's plan for the breakout but the press was not cut in. His PRO had leaked the plan to the newsmen.

"I'll can him," he promised, "you can bet your life I'll can him— just as soon as we find another." I hung up. George was too contrite for me to argue further. Eventually he did relieve the PRO but for other reasons.

When news of the attempted assassination of Hitler reached Patton in the Cotentin, he bounded down to our CP at Colombières.

"For God's sake, Brad," George pleaded, "you've got to get me into this fight before the war is over, I'm in the doghouse now and I'm apt to die there unless I pull something spectacular to get me out."

I've often wondered how much this nothing-to-lose attitude prodded Patton in his spectacular race across the face of France. For certainly no other commander could have matched him in reckless haste and boldness. Someday a definitive biography of Patton will go into the issue more exhaustively than I. Until then I shall go on believing that the private whose face he slapped in a Sicilian hospital ward did more to win the war in Europe than any other private in the army.

Only 34 days after he had been committed in the Battle for France, George joined me one day in a plea to Ike that he might retain his allotment of tonnage and thus push on to the German frontier.

"If you don't cut us back we can make it on what we're getting," he said. "I'll stake my reputation on it."

"Careful, George," Ike quipped, "that reputation of yours hasn't been worth very much."

Patton hitched up his belt and smiled. "It's pretty good now," he said.

And if one could judge by the headlines, we agreed that perhaps it was.

EISENHOWER ON PATTON

I notified General Marshall of my desire to have General Patton command the Casablanca expedition and within a short time George reported to me in London, where he was thoroughly briefed on his portion of the plan. Hardly had he returned to Washington before I received a message stating that he had become embroiled in such a distressing argument with the Navy Department that serious thought was being given to his relief from command. Feeling certain that the difficulty, whatever its nature, was nothing more than the result of a bit of George's flair for the dramatic, I protested at once, suggesting that if his personality was causing any difficulty in conferences the issue could be met by sending him out with his troops and allowing some staff member to represent him in the completion of planning details. In any event the matter was passed over.

I well knew that Patton delighted to startle his hearers with fantastic statements; many men who believed they knew him well

SOURCE: Eisenhower, *Crusade in Europe*, pp. 82, 175–176, 179–181.

never penetrated past the shell of showmanship in which he constantly and carefully clothed himself. But he was essentially a shrewd battle leader who invariably gained the devotion of his subordinates. From early life his one ambition was to be a successful battlefield commander. Because of this he was an inveterate reader of military history and his heroes were the great captains of past ages.

All the mannerisms and idiosyncrasies he developed were of his own deliberate adoption. One of his poses, for example, was that of the most hard-boiled individual in the Army. Actually he was so soft-hearted, particularly where a personal friend was concerned, that it was possibly his greatest fault. Later in the war he once vehemently demanded that I discharge eighty of his officers because, as he said, of inefficiency and timidity bordering on cowardice. He was so exercised and so persistent that I agreed, contingent upon his sending me a report in writing. Apparently astonished by my acquiescence, he began postponing from week to week, on one excuse or another, the submission of his list. Finally he confessed, rather sheepishly, that he had reconsidered and wanted to discharge no one.

Patton in the meantime pushed vigorously forward to the center of the island, while with his extreme left flank he threw mobile columns around the western perimeter of the island, entering Palermo within twelve days after the initial landing. His rapidity of movement quickly reduced the enemy ports to the single one of Messina; it broke the morale of the huge Italian garrison and placed Patton's forces in position to begin the attack from the westward to break the deadlock on the eastern flank.

Patton was a shrewd student of warfare who always clearly appreciated the value of speed in the conduct of operations. Speed of movement often enables troops to minimize any advantage the enemy may temporarily gain but, more important, speed makes possible the full exploitation of every favorable opportunity and prevents the enemy from readjusting his forces to meet successive attacks. Thus through speed and determination each successive advantage is more easily and economically gained than the previous one. Continuation of the process finally results in demoralization of the enemy. Thereupon speed must be redoubled—relentless and speedy pursuit is the most profitable action in war.

It was during this campaign that the unfortunate "slapping incident" involving General Patton took place. Patton, on a visit to base hospitals to see the wounded, encountered, in quick succession, two men who had no apparent physical hurts. Of the first one he met, Patton inquired why he was a patient in the hospital. To this the man replied, "General, I guess it's my nerves." Patton flew into a rage. He had, himself, been under a terrific strain for a period of many days. Moreover, he sincerely believed that there was no such thing as true "battle fatigue" or "battle neurosis." He always maintained that any man who began to show signs of breaking under battle conditions could by shock be restored to a sense of responsibility and to adequate performance of duty. At the moment, also, Patton was in a highly emotional state because of the sights he had seen and the suffering he had sensed among the wounded of the hospital. He broke out into a torrent of abuse against the soldier. His tirade drew protests from doctors and nurses, but so violent was his outbreak that they hesitated to intervene.

Within a matter of moments he met a second soldier under somewhat similar circumstances. This time his emotions were so uncontrollable that he swung a hand at the soldier's head. He struck the man's helmet, which rolled along the ground, and by this time doctors and nurses, overcoming their natural timidity in the presence of the commanding general, intervened between Patton and the soldier.

Both enlisted men were, of course, badly upset. One of them was seriously ill. Doctors later testified that he had a temperature of 102. Patton soon gained sufficient control of himself to continue his inspection and left the hospital. But throughout his visit he continued to talk in a loud voice about the cowardice of people who claimed they were suffering from psychoneuroses and exclaimed that they should not be allowed in the same hospital with the brave wounded men.

The story spread throughout the hospital and among neighboring units with lightning speed. I soon received an unofficial report from the surgeon commanding the hospital and only a few hours thereafter was visited by a group of newspaper correspondents who had been to the hospital to secure the details. Their report substantially corroborated the one I had already received from the doctor. The question became, what to do? In forward areas it is frequently necessary, as every battle veteran knows, to use stern measures to insure prompt performance of duty by every man of the organization. In a platoon or in a battalion, if there is any sign of hesitation or shirking on the part of any individual, it must be quickly and sternly repressed. Soldiers will not follow any battle leader with confidence unless they know that he will require full performance of duty from every member of the team. When bullets are flying and every man's safety and welfare depend upon every other man in the team doing his job, men will not accept a weakling as their leader. Patton's offense, had it been committed on the actual front, within an assaulting platoon, would not have been an offense. It would merely have been an incident of battle—no one would have even noted it, except with the passing thought that here was a leader who would not tolerate shirking.

But because of the time and place of his action Patton's offense was a serious one, more so because of his rank and standing. Thus to assault and abuse an enlisted man in a hospital was nothing less than brutal, except as it was explained by the highly emotional state in which Patton himself then existed. His emotional tenseness and his impulsiveness were the very qualities that made him, in open situations, such a remarkable leader of an army. In pursuit and exploitation there is need for a commander who sees nothing but the necessity of getting ahead; the more he drives his men the more he will save their lives. He must be indifferent to fatigue and ruthless in demanding the last atom of physical energy.

All this I well understood, and could explain the matter to myself in spite of my indignation at the act. I felt that Patton should be saved for service in the great battles still facing us in Europe, yet I had to devise ways and means to minimize the harm that would certainly come from his impulsive action and to assure myself that it would not be repeated. I was then working intensively on plans for the invasion of Italy, and could not go immediately to Sicily. In these circumstances I sent to Sicily three different individuals in whose judgment, tact, and integrity I placed great confidence. One of these I sent to see General Patton. Another went to visit the hospital in which the trouble occurred. Still a third was sent to visit the divisions of Patton's army to determine for himself the extent to which the story had spread among the troops and to determine their reaction. I not only wanted independent reports from several sources, but I wanted to accomplish the whole investigation as rapidly as possible.

As a result I determined to keep Patton. I first wrote him a sharp letter of reprimand in which I informed him that repetition of such an offense would be cause for his instant relief. I informed him, also, that his retention as a commander in my theater would be contingent upon his offering an apology to the two men whom he had insulted. I demanded also that he apologize to all the personnel of the hospital present at the time of the incident. Finally, I required that he appear before the officers and representative groups of enlisted men of each of his divisions to assure them that he had given way to impulse and respected their positions as fighting soldiers of a democratic nation.

Patton instantly complied and I kept in touch with results again through a series of observers and inspectors.

PATTON ON PATTON

November 11

I decided to attack Casablanca this day with the 3d Division and one tank battalion. It took some nerve, as both Truscott and Harmon seemed in a bad way, but I felt we should maintain the initiative. Then Admiral Hall came ashore to arrange for naval gunfire and air support and brought fine news. Truscott has taken the airfield at Port Lyautey and there are forty-two P–40's on it. Harmon is marching on Casablanca.

Anderson wanted to attack at dawn, but I made it 7:30, as I wanted no mistakes in the dark. At 4:30 this morning, a French officer came to say that the forces at Rabat had ceased firing, and all the Staff wanted to call off the attack. However, I said it must go on. I remembered 1918, when we stopped too soon. I sent the French officer to Casablanca to tell Admiral Michelier, in command at Casablanca, that if he did not want to be destroyed, he had better quit at once, as I was going to attack—I did not say

SOURCE: George S. Patton, Jr., *War As I Knew It* (Boston, 1947), pp. 9–10, 64, 184–185, 381–382. Reprinted by permission of Houghton Mifflin Company.

when. I then sent word to Admiral Hewitt that if at the last minute the French quit, I would radio "cease firing." That was at 5:30. At 6:40 the enemy quit. It was a near thing, for the bombers were over their targets and the battleships were in position to fire. I ordered Anderson to move into the town, and if anyone stopped him, to attack. No one stopped him, but the hours from 7:30 to 11 were the longest in my life so far.

At 2 o'clock, Admiral Michelier and General Noguès came to treat for terms. I opened the conference by congratulating the French on their gallantry and closed it with champagne and toasts. I also gave them a guard of honor—no use kicking a man when he's down.

Noguès and I are calling on the Sultan in a day or two.

HEADQUARTERS SEVENTH ARMY
U.S. ARMY

August 22, 1943

Soldiers of the Seventh Army:

Born at sea, baptized in blood, and crowned with victory, in the course of thirty-eight days of incessant battle and unceasing labor, you have added a glorious chapter to the history of war.

Pitted against the best the Germans and Italians could offer, you have been unfailingly successful. The rapidity of your dash, which culminated in the capture of Palermo, was equalled by the dogged tenacity with which you stormed Troina and captured Messina.

Every man in the Army deserves equal credit. The enduring valor of the Infantry and the impetuous ferocity of the tanks were matched by the tireless clamor of our destroying guns.

The Engineers performed prodigies in the construction and maintenance of impossible roads over impassable country. The Services of Maintenance and Supply performed a miracle. The Signal Corps laid over 10,000 miles of wire, and the Medical Department evacuated and cared for our sick and wounded.

On all occasions the Navy has given generous and gallant support. Throughout the operation, our Air has kept the sky clear and tirelessly supported the operation of the ground troops.

As a result of this combined effort, you have killed or captured 113,350 enemy troops. You have destroyed 265 of his tanks, 2324 vehicles, and 1162 large guns, and, in addition, have collected a mass of military booty running into hundreds of tons.

But your victory has a significance above and beyond its physical aspect—you have destroyed the prestige of the enemy.

The President of the United States, the Secretary of War, the Chief of Staff, General Eisenhower, General Alexander, General Montgomery, have all congratulated you.

Your fame shall never die.

> G. S. PATTON, JR.,
> Lieut. General, U.S. Army,
> Commanding.

The weather was so bad that I directed all Army chaplains to pray for dry weather. I also published a prayer with a Christmas greeting on the back and sent it to all members of the Command. The prayer was for dry weather for battle.[1]

1. On or about the fourteenth of December, 1944, General Patton called Chaplain O'Neill, Third Army Chaplain, and myself into his office in Third Headquarters at Nancy. The conversation went something like this:

General Patton: "Chaplain, I want you to publish a prayer for good weather. I'm tired of these soldiers having to fight mud and floods as well as Germans. See if we can't get God to work on our side."

Chaplain O'Neill: "Sir, it's going to take a pretty thick rug for that kind of praying."

General Patton: "I don't care if it takes the flying carpet. I want the praying done."

Chaplain O'Neill: "Yes, sir. May I say, General, that it usually isn't a customary thing among men of my profession to pray for clear weather to kill fellow men."

General Patton: "Chaplain, are you teaching me theology or are you the Chaplain of the Third Army? I want a prayer."

Chaplain O'Neill: "Yes, sir."

Outside, the Chaplain said, "Whew, that's a tough one! What do you think he wants?"

It was perfectly clear to me. The General wanted a prayer—he wanted one right now—and he wanted it published to the Command.

The Army Engineer was called in, and we finally decided that our field topographical company could print the prayer on a small-sized card, making enough copies for distribution to the army.

It being near Christmas, we also decided to ask General Patton to include a Christmas greeting to the troops on the same card with the prayer. The

During the attack on Troina, I drove to the Headquarters of General Bradley, who was conducting the attack, accompanied by General Lucas. Just before we got there, I saw a field hospital in a valley and stopped to inspect it. There were some three hundred and fifty badly wounded men in the hospital, all of whom were

---

General agreed, wrote a short greeting, and the card was made up, published, and distributed to the troops on the twenty-second of December.

Actually, the prayer was offered in order to bring clear weather for the planned Third Army break-through to the Rhine in the Saarguemines area, then scheduled for December 21.

The Bulge put a crimp in these plans. As it happened, the Third Army had moved north to attack the south flank of the Bulge when the prayer was actually issued.

PRAYER

Almighty and most merciful Father, we humbly beseech Thee, of Thy great goodness, to restrain these immoderate rains with which we have had to contend. Grant us fair weather for Battle. Graciously hearken to us as soldiers who call upon Thee that, armed with Thy power, we may advance from victory to victory, and crush the oppression and wickedness of our enemies, and establish Thy justice among men and nations. Amen.

REVERSE SIDE

To each officer and soldier in the Third United States Army, I wish a Merry Christmas. I have full confidence in your courage, devotion to duty, and skill in battle. We march in our might to complete victory. May God's blessing rest upon each of you on this Christmas Day.

G. S. PATTON, JR.
Lieutenant General
Commanding, Third United States Army

Whether it was the help of the Divine guidance asked for in the prayer or just the normal course of human events, we never knew; at any rate, on the twenty-third, the day after the prayer was issued, the weather cleared and remained perfect for about six days. Enough to allow the Allies to break the backbone of the Von Rundstedt offensive and turn a temporary setback into a crushing defeat for the enemy.

We had moved our advanced Headquarters to Luxembourg at this time to be closer to the battle area. The bulk of the Army Staff, including the Chaplain, was still in Nancy. General Patton again called me to his office. He wore a smile from ear to ear. He said, "God damn! look at the weather. That O'Neill sure did some potent praying. Get him up here. I want to pin a medal on him."

The Chaplain came up next day. The weather was still clear when we walked into General Patton's office. The General rose, came from behind

very heroic under their sufferings, and all of whom were interested in the success of the operation. Just as I was leaving the hospital, I saw a soldier sitting on a box near the dressing station. I stopped and said to him, "What is the matter with you, boy?" He said, "Nothing; I just can't take it." I asked what he meant. He said, "I just can't take being shot at." I said, "You mean that you are malingering here?" He burst into tears and I immediately saw that he was an hysterical case. I, therefore, slapped him across the face with my glove and told him to get up, join his unit, and make a man of himself, which he did. Actually, at the time he was absent without leave.

I am convinced that my action in this case was entirely correct, and that, had other officers had the courage to do likewise, the shameful use of "battle fatigue" as an excuse for cowardice would have been infinitely reduced.

29. Military Leaders Disagree

Eisenhower and Berlin

From Eisenhower to Marshall

30 March

Frankly the charge that I have changed plans has no possible basis in fact. The principal effort north of the Ruhr was always adhered to with the object of isolating that valuable area. Now that I can foresee the time that my forces can be concentrated in the Kassel area I am still adhering to my old plan of launching from

SOURCE: Eisenhower, *Crusade in Europe*, pp. 399–401.

---

his desk with hand outstretched and said, "Chaplain, you're the most popular man in this Headquarters. You sure stand in good with the Lord and soldiers." The General then pinned a Bronze Star Medal on Chaplain O'Neill.

Everyone offered congratulations and thanks and we got back to the business of killing Germans—with clear weather for battle P.D.H.[arkins]

there one main attack calculated to accomplish, in conjunction with the Russians, the destruction of the enemy armed forces. My plan will get the ports and all the other things on the north coast more speedily and decisively than will the dispersion now urged upon me by Wilson's message to you.

After sending this preliminary message we drew up, for General Marshall's information, a complete digest of our plan and dispatched it by following radio:

This is in reply to your radio.

The same protests except as to "procedure" contained in that telegram were communicated to me by the Prime Minister over telephone last night.

I am completely in the dark as to what the protests concerning "procedure" involve. I have been instructed to deal directly with the Russians concerning military co-ordination. There is no change in basic strategy. The British Chiefs of Staff last summer protested against my determination to open up the Frankfurt route because they said it would be futile and would draw strength away from a northern attack. I have always insisted that the northern attack would be the principal effort in that phase of our operations that involved the isolation of the Ruhr, but from the very beginning, extending back before D-day, my plan, explained to my staff and senior officers, has been to link up the primary and secondary efforts in the Kassel area and then make one great thrust to the eastward.

Even cursory examination of the decisive direction for this thrust, after the link-up in the Kassel area is complete, shows that the principal effort should under existing circumstances be toward the Leipzig region, where is concentrated the greater part of the remaining German industrial capacity, and to which area the German ministries are believed to be moving. My plan does not draw Montgomery's British and Canadian forces to the southward. You will note that his right flank will push forward along the general line Hanover–Wittenberge. Merely following the principle that Field Marshal Brooke has always emphasized, I am determined to concentrate on one major thrust and all that my plan does is to place the U. S. Ninth Army back under Bradley for that phase of operations involving the advance of the center from Kassel to the Leipzig region, unless, of course, the Russian forces should be met on this side of that area. Thereafter, that position will be consolidated while the plan clearly shows that Ninth Army may again have to move up to assist the British and Canadian armies in clearing the whole coast line to the westward of Lübeck.

After strength for this operation has been provided, it is considered that we can launch a movement to the southeastward to prevent Nazi occupation of a mountain citadel.

I have thoroughly considered the naval aspects of this situation and clearly recognize the advantages of gaining the northern coast line at an early date. It is for this reason that I have made that objective the next one to be achieved after the primary thrust has placed us in a decisive position. The opening of Bremen, Hamburg, and Kiel involves operations against the Frisian Islands and Heligoland and extensive mine sweeping. All this and operations into Denmark and Norway form part of a later phase.

May I point out that Berlin itself is no longer a particularly important objective. Its usefulness to the German has been largely destroyed and even his government is preparing to move to another area. What is now important is to gather up our forces for a single drive and this will more quickly bring about the fall of Berlin, the relief of Norway, and the acquisition of the shipping and the Swedish ports than will the scattering around of our effort.

As another point I should like to point out that the so-called "good ground" in northern Germany is not really good at this time of year. That region is not only badly cut up with waterways, but in it the ground during this part of the year is very wet and not so favorable for rapid movement as is the higher plateau over which I am preparing to launch the main effort.

To sum up:

> I propose, at the earliest possible moment, in conjunction with the Soviets to divide and destroy the German forces by launching my main attack from the Kassel area straight eastward toward the heart of what remains of the German industrial power until that thrust has attained the general area of Leipzig and including that city, unless the Russian advance meets us west of that point. The second main feature of the battle is to bring Montgomery's forces along on the left and as quickly as the above has been accomplished to turn Ninth Army to the left to assist him in cleaning out the whole area from Kiel and Lübeck westward.
>
> After the requirements of these two moves have been met, I will thrust columns southeastward in an attempt to join up with the Russians in the Danube Valley and prevent the establishment of a Nazi fortress in southern Germany.
>
> Naturally, my plans are flexible and I must retain freedom of ac-

tion to meet changing situations. Maximum flexibility will result from a concentration of maximum force in the center.

An interesting sidelight on the foregoing telegram is that it was originally drafted, in my headquarters, by one of my British assistants.

Churchill and Berlin

CHURCHILL TO ROOSEVELT

April 1, 1945

Having dealt with and I trust disposed of these misunderstandings between the truest friends and comrades that ever fought side by side as Allies, I venture to put to you a few considerations upon the merits of the changes in our original plans now desired by General Eisenhower. . . . I say quite frankly that Berlin remains of high strategic importance. Nothing will exert a psychological effect of despair upon all German forces of resistance equal to that of the fall of Berlin. It will be the supreme signal of defeat to the German people. On the other hand, if left to itself to maintain a siege by the Russians among its ruins and as long as the German flag flies there, it will animate the resistance of all Germans under arms.

There is moreover another aspect which it is proper for you and me to consider. The Russian armies will no doubt overrun all Austria and enter Vienna. If they also take Berlin, will not their impression that they have been the overwhelming contributor to our common victory be unduly imprinted in their minds, and may this not lead them into a mood which will raise grave and formidable difficulties in the future? I therefore consider that from a political standpoint we should march as far east into Germany as possible and that should Berlin be in our grasp we should certainly take it. This also appears sound on military grounds.

SOURCE: Forrest C. Pogue, *The Supreme Command* (*United States Army in World War II: The European Theater of Operations*) (Washington, 1954), pp. 442–443. Reprinted by permission of the Department of the Army.

30. German Reactions

Fuehrer Headquarters
3 November 1943

Top Secret

The Fuehrer

HITLER DIRECTIVE No. 51

For the last two and one-half years the bitter and costly struggle against Bolshevism has made the utmost demands upon the bulk of our military resources and energies. This commitment was in keeping with the seriousness of the danger, and the over-all situation. The situation has since changed. The threat from the East remains, but an even greater danger looms in the West: the Anglo-American landing! In the East, the vastness of the space will, as a last resort, permit a loss of territory even on a major scale, without suffering a mortal blow to Germany's chance for survival.

Not so in the West! If the enemy here succeeds in penetrating our defenses on a wide front, consequences of staggering proportions will follow within a short time. All signs point to an offensive against the Western Front of Europe no later than spring, and perhaps earlier.

For that reason, I can no longer justify the further weakening of the West in favor of other theaters of war. I have therefore decided to strengthen the defenses in the West, particularly at places from which we shall launch our long-range war against England. For those are the very points at which the enemy must and will attack; there—unless all indications are misleading—will be fought the decisive invasion battle.

Holding attacks and diversions on other fronts are to be ex-

SOURCE: Reprinted in Gordon A. Harrison, *Cross-Channel Attack* (*United States Army in World War II: The European Theater of Operations*) (Washington, 1951), pp. 464–467. Reprinted by permission of the Department of the Army.

pected. Not even the possibility of a large-scale offensive against Denmark may be excluded. It would pose greater nautical problems and could be less effectively supported from the air, but would nevertheless produce the greatest political and strategic impact if it were to succeed.

During the opening phase of the battle, the entire striking power of the enemy will of necessity be directed against our forces manning the coast. Only an all-out effort in the construction of fortifications, an unsurpassed effort that will enlist all available manpower and physical resources of Germany and the occupied areas, will be able to strengthen our defenses along the coasts within the short time that still appears to be left to us.

Stationary weapons (heavy AT guns, immobile tanks to be dug-in, coast artillery, shore-defense guns, mines, etc.) arriving in Denmark and the occupied West within the near future will be heavily concentrated in points of main defensive effort at the most vulnerable coastal sectors. At the same time, we must take the calculated risk that for the present we may be unable to improve our defenses in less threatened sectors.

Should the enemy nevertheless force a landing by concentrating his armed might, he must be hit by the full fury of our counterattack. For this mission ample and speedy reinforcements of men and materiel, as well as intensive training must transform available larger units into first-rate, fully mobile general reserves suitable for offensive operations. The counterattack of these units will prevent the enlargement of the beachhead, and throw the enemy back into the sea.

In addition, well-planned emergency measures, prepared down to the last detail, must enable us instantly to throw against the invader every fit man and machine from coastal sectors not under attack and from the home front.

The anticipated strong attacks by air and sea must be relentlessly countered by Air Force and Navy with all their available resources. I therefore order the following:

A) Army:

1. The Chief of the Army General Staff and the Inspector General of Panzer Troops will submit to me as soon as possible a schedule covering arms, tanks, assault guns, motor vehicles, and

ammunition to be allocated to the Western Front and Denmark within the next three months. That schedule will conform to the new situation. The following considerations will be basic:

a) Sufficient mobility for all panzer and panzer grenadier divisions in the West, and equipment of each of those units by December 1943 with 93 Mark IV tanks or assault guns, as well as large numbers of antitank weapons.

Accelerated reorganization of the 20 Luftwaffe Field Divisions into an effective mobile reserve force by the end of 1943. This reorganization is to include the issue of assault guns.

Accelerated issue of all authorized weapons to the SS Panzer Grenadier Division Hitler Jugend, the 21st Panzer Division, and the infantry and reserve divisions stationed in Jutland.

b) Additional shipments of Mark IV tanks, assault guns, and heavy AT guns to the reserve panzer divisions stationed in the West and in Denmark, as well as to the Assault Gun Training Battalion in Denmark.

c) In November and December, monthly allotments of 100 heavy AT guns models 40 and 43 (half of these to be mobile) in addition to those required for newly activated units in the West and in Denmark.

d) Allotment of large numbers of weapons (including about 1,000 machine guns) for augmenting the armament of those static divisions that are committed for coastal defense in the West and in Denmark, and for standardizing the equipment of elements that are to be withdrawn from sectors not under attack.

e) Ample supply of close-combat AT weapons to units in vulnerable sectors.

f) Improvement of artillery and AT defenses in units stationed in Denmark, as well as those committed for coastal protection in the occupied West. Strengthening of GHQ artillery.

2. The units and elements stationed in the West or in Denmark, as well as panzer, assault gun, and AT units to be activated in the West, must not be transferred to other fronts without my permission. The Chief of the Army General Staff, or the Inspector General of Panzer Troops will submit to me a report through the Armed Forces Operations Staff as soon as the issue of equipment to the panzer and assault gun battalions, as well as to the AT battalions and companies, has been completed.

3. Beyond similar measures taken in the past, the Commander in Chief West will establish timetables for, and conduct maneuvers and command post exercises on, the procedure for bringing up units from sectors not under attack. These units will be made capable of performing offensive missions, however limited. In that connection I demand that sectors not threatened by the enemy be ruthlessly stripped of all forces except small guard detachments. For sectors from which reserves are withdrawn, security and guard detachments must be set aside from security and alarm units. Labor forces drawn largely from the native population must likewise be organized in those sectors, in order to keep open whatever roads might be destroyed by the enemy air force.

4. The Commander of German Troops in Denmark will take measures in the area under his control in compliance with paragraph 3 above.

5. Pursuant to separate orders, the Chief of Army Equipment and Commander of the Replacement Army will form Kampfgruppen in regimental strength, security battalions, and engineer construction battalions from training cadres, trainees, schools, and instruction and convalescent units in the Zone of the Interior. These troops must be ready for shipment on 48 hours' notice.

Furthermore, other available personnel are to be organized into battalions of replacements and equipped with the available weapons, so that the anticipated heavy losses can quickly be replaced.

B) Luftwaffe:

The offensive and defensive effectiveness of Luftwaffe units in the West and in Denmark will be increased to meet the changed situation. To that end, preparations will be made for the release of units suited for commitment in the anti-invasion effort, that is, all flying units and mobile Flak artillery that can be spared from the air defenses of the home front, and from schools and training units in the Zone of the Interior. All those units are to be earmarked for the West and possibly Denmark.

The Luftwaffe ground organization in southern Norway, Denmark, northwestern Germany, and the West will be expanded and supplied in a way that will—by the most far-reaching decentralization of own forces—deny targets to the enemy bombers, and split the enemy's offensive effort in case of large-scale operations. Particularly important in that connection will be our fighter forces. Possibilities for their commitment must be increased by the establishment of numerous advance landing fields. Special emphasis is to be placed on good camouflage. I expect also that the Luftwaffe will unstintingly furnish all available forces, by stripping them from less threatened areas.

C) Navy:

The navy will prepare the strongest possible forces suitable for attacking the enemy landing fleets. Coastal defense installations in the process of construction will be completed with the utmost speed. The emplacing of additional coastal batteries and the possibility of laying further flanking mine fields should be investigated.

All school, training, and other shore-based personnel fit for ground combat must be prepared for commitment so that, without undue delay, they can at least be employed as security forces within the zone of the enemy landing operations.

While preparing the reinforcement of the defenses in the West, the Navy must keep in mind that it might be called upon to repulse simultaneous enemy landings in Norway and Denmark. In that connection, I attach particular importance to the assembly of numerous U-boats in the northern area. A temporary weakening of U-boat forces in the Atlantic must be risked.

D) SS:

The Reichsfuehrer-SS will determine what Waffen-SS and police forces he can release for combat, security, and guard duty. He is to prepare to organize effective combat and security forces from training, replacement, and convalescent units, as well as schools and other home-front establishments.

E) The commanders in chief of the services, the Reichsfuehrer-SS, the Chief of the Army General Staff, the Commander in Chief West, the Chief of Army Equipment and Commander of the Replacement Army, the Inspector General of Panzer Troops, as well as the Commander of German Troops in Denmark will report to me by 15 November all measures taken or planned.

I expect that all agencies will make a supreme effort toward utilizing every moment of the remaining time in preparing for the decisive battle in the West.

All authorities will guard against wasting time and energy in useless jurisdictional squabbles, and will direct all their efforts toward strengthening our defensive and offensive power.

Adolf Hitler

ROMMEL ON INVASION

H.Q. 5 July 1944

To C.-IN-C. WEST.
HERR GENERALFELDMARSCHALL VON KLUGE.

I send you enclosed my comments on military events in Normandy to date.

The rebuke which you levelled at me at the beginning of your visit, in the presence of my Chief of Staff and Ia, to the effect that I, too, "will now have to get accustomed to carrying out orders," has deeply wounded me. I request you to notify me what grounds you have for making such an accusation.

ROMMEL
Generalfeldmarschall

In the document enclosed with this letter, which Rommel had already forwarded to Hitler, he stated once again, in all clarity, his criticism of the conduct of the war in Normandy.

COMMANDER-IN-CHIEF
ARMY GROUP B.   *MEMORANDUM*   *H.Q. 3 July 1944*

The reasons why it has been impossible to maintain a lasting hold on the Normandy coast, the Cherbourg peninsula and the fortress of Cherbourg, are set out below:

(1) The garrison forces stationed in Normandy were too weak and in some cases badly over-age (e.g. 709th Division, where the average age was 36); their equipment was inadequate for modern requirements, ammunition stocks were too small, constructional work on fortifications was in arrears and the supply situation was utterly inadequate.

(2) Repeated requests for reinforcements made by Army Group B before the invasion—above all, at the end of May,

SOURCE: Erwin Rommel, *The Rommel Papers*, ed. B. H. Liddell Hart (London, 1953), pp. 481–485. Reprinted by permission of Harcourt Brace Jovanovich, Inc.

when the threat to Normandy became apparent—were refused. Most important of these was a request for the 12th
S.S. Panzer Division *Hitler Jugend* to be moved into the
Lessay-Coutances area to enable it to launch an immediate
and overwhelming counter-attack on an enemy landing on
either the west or east coast of the Cotentin. To bring the
12th S.S. Panzer Division up from its station south of the
Seine, in the expected conditions of enemy air superiority,
would have required at least two days and would have been
bound to involve them in heavy losses. Colonel-General
Jodl was aware of this fact, for shortly before the enemy
invasion he again had me asked through General Buhle,
how long the 12th S.S. Panzer Division would require to
get into action in Normandy. However, my persistent demands for the dispatch of this division were turned down
and all I received was a promise that in the event of an
enemy attack it would be put under my command immediately.

(3) My suggestion to position the Panzer Lehr Division where
it could intervene rapidly in a coastal battle in either Normandy or Brittany was also not fulfilled, due to fears of a
possible enemy airborne landing in the neighborhood of
Paris.

(4) The Army Group requested that strong anti-aircraft forces
should be deployed by the end of May, above all, at those
points where the enemy has already been making heavy
and unhindered air attacks against our battery positions
and fortifications. On the advice of G.O.C. 3rd A.A. Corps,
I proposed that the entire A.A. Corps should be stationed
as a formation between the Orne estuary and Montebourg
[*18 miles S.E. of Cherbourg*], as this area was showing
signs of being particularly threatened by the enemy activity. The request was not complied with and the A.A.
Corps was instead deployed in a mobile role, with one of
its four regiments on either side of the Somme and one
weak regiment between the Orne and the Vire. This division of the A.A. Corps' strength—so prejudicial to the defence of Normandy—was justified on the grounds of short-
age of petrol. Thus two regiments remained in the vicinity

of the V2 launching points to provide protection for them when fire was opened.

(5) Since it was to be expected that the forward movement of reinforcements would present great difficulty after the attack had opened, I suggested that the Normandy defences should be strengthened by moving 7th Nebelwerfer Brigade into the area south of Carentan. This request was also not approved, and the brigade was not put under my command until after the landing. Consequently, it did not go into action during the first days of the invasion.

(6) To deny the enemy good landing conditions I pressed repeatedly for the Bay of the Seine to be mined in good time by the navy and air force, using the latest type of mines. This bay, with its shallow waters, is particularly suited for mining. This request also was not acted upon. Mine-laying did not start until after the enemy landing had taken place and then under conditions of extreme difficulty and mainly from the air.

(7) Orders were given by the Quartermaster-General for stocks of ammunition in Normandy to be cut during May, as part of the scheme for withdrawing ammunition from C.-in-C. West's command in order to build up reserve stocks in Base and Army Ammunition Depots. This would have made holdings of ammunition even smaller than they already were. The Army Group, however, on the initiative of General Marcks, succeeded in resisting this measure.

(8) Despite the existence of the railway network and sea routes, supply conditions, especially in Normandy, were already becoming difficult even before the invasion, due to the heavy bombing of railway installations.

(9) After the enemy had succeeded in gaining his foothold on the Continent, it was the intention of Army Group B when its reinforcements had arrived, first to wipe out the bridgehead north of Carentan, thus eliminating all danger to the Cotentin peninsula and the fortress of Cherbourg, and not until then to launch an attack on the enemy between the Orne and the Vire. The O.K.W., however, did not agree and gave orders for our main weight to be shifted to the eastern flank at the Orne estuary.

(10) The advance elements of 12th S.S. Panzer Division Hitler Jugend, did not arrive in the area north-west of Caen until 09.30 hours on the 7th June, after a 75-mile approach march, during which they sustained substantial losses from low-flying aircraft. There being then neither the time nor the space for a formation operation, its attack could not be driven home.

Panzer Lehr Division had 110 miles to cover, and its leading elements did not arrive at the battle front west of Caen until 13.00 hours on the 7th June. They, too, were hindered in their advance by low-flying aircraft, and the wheeled units became separated from the tracked. As a result, their attack could no longer be put in; they were, in fact, hard put to it to maintain their position against the enemy, who had by that time grown strong. An unfortunate result of this was that the division failed to establish contact with, and provide support for, the units of 352nd Infantry Division which were still fighting at Bayeux.

The leading elements of 2nd Panzer Division, which had to be brought up from its station on either side of the Somme (160 miles as the crow flies), arrived on the 13th June. A further seven days were needed before it could go into action as a division.

3rd Parachute Division required six days for its approach march from Brittany to its battle area north-east of St. Lô (135 miles as the crow flies), during which time it was under constant threat from the air. By the time it arrived, the attack it was due to launch on Bayeux was no longer possible, as strong enemy forces had already taken possession of the Forest of Cerisy.

77th Division required six days before it could intervene with substantial forces in the fighting in the north of the Cotentin peninsula.

All the reserves that came up arrived far too late to smash the enemy landing by counter-attacks. By the time they arrived the enemy had disembarked considerably stronger forces and himself gone over to the attack under cover of powerful air and artillery support.

(11) Support by our air force was not forthcoming on the scale originally foreseen. The enemy had command of the air

over the battle-ground up to a point some 60 miles behind the front. In sorties of immense strength he smashed the defence installations in the coastal zones and effectively opposed the approach march of our reserves and the supply of our troops, principally by damage to the railway system.

(12) Naval activity was also not on the scale that had originally been promised. (Only 6 U-boats, for example, instead of 40.) Due to adverse weather conditions no outpost ship watch was kept on the Bay of the Seine on the night of the 5th June. U-boat activity against the landing fleet was on a relatively small scale. As a result of the enemy air attack on le Havre on the 12th June, the navy lost a large part of its craft suitable for use against the landing fleet.

The mining of the Bay of the Seine, which was undertaken immediately after the invasion, has also shown no noticeable success to date. Landings are still taking place on the very largest scale and the daily bombardment by naval guns, "on a scale hitherto unknown" (Report by 2nd S.S. Panzer Corps), is causing serious difficulties for our front.

(13) The Army Group has had no part in the machinery of supply. It has no Quartermaster staff of its own and had at first no authority to give instructions to the Quartermaster at Headquarters West.

(14) Channels of command were unsatisfactory. At the start of the invasion, the Army Group had no control over the mobile formations of Panzer Group West (see above), nor over the Nebelwerfer Brigade. On the "direction" of the A.A. Corps, etc., I have already given my views in a report. Only unified, close-knit command of all services, after the pattern of Montgomery and Eisenhower, will vouchsafe final victory.

ROMMEL
Generalfeldmarschall

Hardly had von Kluge inspected the front in Normandy, when he changed his views completely. He also acknowledged the justice of the words which Rommel had written to the Fuehrer's H.Q. at the end of June: "The enemy's command of the air restricts all movement in terms of both space and time, and renders calculation of time impossible. For armoured or motorised troops in divisional strength upwards, it limits the possibilities of command and manœuvre to night or bad weather operations, which cannot as a rule develop into anything more than operations with limited objective. Daylight action is, however, still possible—given sufficient A.A. defence—for a small armoured combat group."

31. War Crimes

TOP SECRET
DRAFT AGREEMENT ON TREATMENT OF GERMANY IN THE INITIAL CONTROL PERIOD

Department of State Memorandum

4. War criminals and those who have participated in planning or carrying out Nazi enterprises involving or resulting in atrocities or war crimes shall be arrested, with a view to their ultimate disposal. Nazi leaders and influential Nazi supporters and any other persons dangerous to the occupation or its objectives shall be arrested and interned.

TOP SECRET
PROSECUTION OF WAR CRIMINALS

Following preliminary discussion with British authorities in London in April, Judge Rosenman, acting as personal representative of President Truman, presented to the British, French and Soviet representatives at San Francisco early in May a draft of a proposed agreement between the four governments containing this government's suggested plan for the punishment of war criminals. This draft was based on an earlier report submitted to President Roosevelt by the Secretaries of State and War and the Attorney General.

SOURCE: *Foreign Relations, Berlin Conference, (The Potsdam Conference)*, pp. 574–577.

NATURE OF PROPOSALS

In brief, the proposed agreement contemplated:

(a) That in conformity with the Moscow Declaration (Roosevelt, Churchill and Stalin) of November 1, 1943, European Axis war criminals, against whom there is proof of personal participation in specific atrocities, be returned to the former occupied countries where their crimes were committed for prosecution and punishment by the authorities of such countries;

(b) That the major war criminals in Europe, whose crimes have no particular geographical localization, and organizations, official or unofficial, charged with crimes or complicity therein, be tried before one or more international military tribunals, such tribunals to be composed of a member (and alternate) each designated by the United States, France, Great Britain and U. S. R. respectively;

(c) That each of the four governments designate a representative who, acting as a group, shall prepare charges and conduct the prosecutions contemplated by (b) above; and

(d) That all members of the United Nations be invited to adhere to the agreement.

SUBSEQUENT DEVELOPMENTS

On May 2 President Truman issued a press statement regarding the appointment of Mr. Justice Jackson as "Chief of Counsel for the United States in preparing and prosecuting the charges of atrocities and war crimes against such of the leaders of the European Axis powers, and their principal agents and accessories, as the United States may agree with any of the United Nations to bring to trial before an international military tribunal." The British and French governments have each recently announced the appointment of similar representatives. On June 7 [6], Mr. Justice Jackson submitted a report to the President summarizing developments since his designation as Chief of Counsel and outlining the basic features of the plan of prosecution.

On June 26, at the invitation of the British Government, Mr. Justice Jackson and representatives of Great Britain, France and U. S. R. began conferences in London with a view to formulating a final agreement. Prior to that date the three interested governments were furnished for purposes of discussion at the conferences, with a draft agreement prepared by Mr. Justice Jackson revising, but not in any substantial way, the draft agreement submitted at San Francisco.

ATTITUDE OF OTHER GOVERNMENTS

It is understood that the British and French governments are in general agreement with the proposals advanced by this Government. On June 14 a representative of the Soviet Embassy called on Mr. Justice Jackson and left with him an *Aide-Mémoire* raising certain questions regarding this Government's proposal. Mr. Justice Jackson indicates that, with few exceptions, they related to matters of inconsequential detail which would cause no difficulty whatever and that it was probable that the remaining questions raised could be ironed out at the London conference.

WAR CRIMES COMMISSION

Sixteen countries, including the United States, Great Britain and France, are represented on the United Nations War Crimes Commission. The U. S. S. R. is not represented on the Commission, and it has been the subject of a number of attacks by the Soviet press.

The terms of reference of the Commission are found in notes addressed in 1942 by the British Government to various other governments suggesting the establishment of the Commission, in which reference was made to the Lord Chancellor's announcement in the House of Lords on October 7, 1942, that "The Commission will investigate war crimes committed against nationals of the United Nations recording the testimony available, and the Commission will report from time to time to the Governments of those nations cases in which such crimes appear to have been committed, naming and identifying wherever possible the persons responsible."[1] The Commission is also charged with making recommendations of a "politicolegal" nature to the governments.

Upon the basis of the cases presented to it, and also on its own initiative, the Commission prepares lists of war criminals, which it is authorized to communicate directly to the Theater Commanders. The latter have been authorized by the Combined Chiefs

1. See the statement by Viscount Simon in *Parliamentary Debates: House of Lords Official Report*, 5th series, vol. 124, col. 582.

of Staff to take the persons on the lists into custody without requirement of further proof.

Since the Commission has no judicial or prosecuting functions, there would seem to be no conflict of jurisdiction between it and the proposed military tribunals to adjudicate cases against major war criminals or the joint prosecutors of such cases. It is understood to be the Department's view that the Commission should be kept in existence, for the time being at least, as it serves a useful purpose as a clearing house for information on war criminals. Moreover its continued existence probably serves to make the small nations represented on it feel that, even though they may not have a direct part in the prosecution of major criminals under the plan discussed above, they nevertheless are participating in the over-all plan and determination of all of the United Nations to prosecute and punish all war criminals.

WASHINGTON, June 29, 1945.

32. Hidden Treasure

Gold

General Patton's army had overrun and discovered Nazi treasure, hidden away in the lower levels of a deep salt mine. A group of us descended the shaft, almost a half mile under the surface of the earth.

At the bottom were huge piles of German paper currency, apparently heaped up there in a last frantic effort to evacuate some of it before the arrival of the Americans. In one of the tunnels was an enormous number of paintings and other pieces of art. Some of these were wrapped in paper and burlap, others were merely stacked together like cordwood.

In another tunnel we saw a hoard of gold, tentatively estimated by our experts to be worth about $250,000,000, most of it in gold bars. These were in sacks, two 25-pound bars to each sack. There was also a great amount of minted gold from the different coun-

SOURCE: Eisenhower, *Crusade in Europe*, pp. 407–408.

tries of Europe and even a few millions of gold coins from the United States.

Crammed into suitcases and trunks and other containers was a great amount of gold and silver plate and ornament obviously looted from private dwellings throughout Europe. All the articles had been flattened by hammer blows, obviously to save storage space, and then merely thrown into the receptacle, apparently pending an opportunity to melt them down into gold or silver bars.

Attention had been originally drawn to the particular tunnel in which all this gold was stored by the existence of a newly built brick wall in the center of which was a steel safe door of the most modern type. The safe door was so formidable that heavy explosive charges would certainly have been necessary for its demolition. However, to an American soldier who inspected it the surrounding brick wall did not look particularly strong, and he tested out his theory with a mere half stick of TNT. With this he blew an enormous hole completely through the obstruction and the hoard was exposed to view. We speculated as to why the Germans had not attempted to provide a concealed hiding place for the treasure in the labyrinth of tunnels instead of choosing to attempt its protection by a wall that could easily have been demolished by a pickax. The elaborate steel door made no sense to us at all, but an American soldier who accompanied me remarked, "It's just like the Germans to lock the stable door but to tear out all its sides." Patton's story of the incident that led to the exploration of the mine was in itself intriguing.

It is probable, of course, that sooner or later the mine would have been carefully searched by the captors. But according to Patton, except for the instincts of human decency on the part of two Americans, we might not have discovered it until much of it had been more securely hidden away. The story was this:

In the little neighboring town the advancing Americans had established a curfew law. Any civilian in the streets after dark was instantly picked up for questioning. One evening a roving patrol in a jeep saw a German woman hurrying along the street after curfew and stopped to speak to her. She protested that she was rushing off to get a midwife for her neighbor, who was about to have a child. The American soldiers decided to check on the story, being quite ready to help if it should prove to be correct. They took the German woman into their jeep, picked up the midwife, and returned to the accouchement, which was all as described by the German woman. The soldiers, still helpful, remained long enough to return the German woman and her midwife friend to their homes. As they were going along the street they passed the mouth of one of the salt mines of that region and one of the women remarked, "That's the mine in which the gold is buried."

This remark excited the curiosity of the soldiers and they questioned the women sufficiently to learn that some weeks earlier great loads of material had been brought from the east to be put into the mine. The soldiers reported the story to their superiors, who in turn sought out some of the German officials of the mining corporation and the whole treasure fell into our hands.

Drawings for Jet Engines

We spent an hour at the BMW factory, while Lieutenant Robinson discussed arrangements for the assembling of a number of their latest jet engines for shipment to the United States for tests. The manager had been my guide during the trip I made through the factory in 1938. While we were talking, a man came up to Lieutenant Robinson, a little white and shaky, to tell him that before the invading troops arrived, he had been given the drawings for one of the jet engines with orders to destroy them. (The BMW officers had said some days ago that their drawings had been destroyed.) However, he had disobeyed orders and buried the drawings in some land belonging to a friend of his. Would we like to have them? He would show us where they were. The location was about a two-and-a-half-hour bicycle ride away.

After the discussion with the BMW officers was over and arrangements for building the jet engines completed, we tied his bicycle on the front of our jeep and drove to the property where the drawings were buried. We had to walk the last hundred yards or so through a pine woods with bits of radar-deceiving tinsel scattered in with the pine needles on the ground. Our guide finally

SOURCE: Charles A. Lindbergh, *The Wartime Journals of Charles A. Lindbergh* (New York, 1970), pp. 958–959. Reprinted by permission of Harcourt Brace Jovanovich, Inc.

stopped beneath a large pine tree and began feeling about on the ground and lining up marks which he probably made a note of at the time of burial.

I studied the ground carefully where he started digging, but could see no unusual marks of any kind. The earth had obviously been replaced with the utmost care, tramped down, needles scattered over the top, and the surplus carried away. Soon, the spade struck the top of a metal box. It turned out to be about the size of a file box and was hermetically sealed by welding. There was another box buried a few feet away; also a long cylinder which contained the larger drawings. We loaded all three into our jeep; then stopped to have tea with the owner of the property. He had been in New York in 1927, he told me, at the time I returned from the flight to Paris.

DOCUMENTS

LONDON, March 20, 1945

OBJECTIVES FOR THE COMBINED TEAMS OF THE BRITISH FOR-
EIGN OFFICE AND THE U.S. DEPARTMENT OF STATE IN
SEARCHING GERMAN ARCHIVES

The Foreign Office and the Department of State have found that their interests in locating and microfilming German archives are so similar that it has been decided to have their teams work together in closest cooperation, members of each team to consider themselves as working jointly for the interests of the two Governments. These teams are under the general agency of the CIOS, and will cooperate with other CIOS representatives working on targets of mutual interest. CIOS leaders may not, however, divert our team members for use in investigating CIOS targets other than those for which these teams are specifically sent out or targets of opportunity arising therefrom. (See CIOS minutes 11th Meeting, 31 January 1945, par. 4, page 6 as corrected in minutes of the 12th Meeting, 14 February, par. 1, page 3.) With this reservation, team members will bear in mind their responsibility to proceed in harmony with CIOS directives, and, of course, to comply with all applicable military regulations in their zone of operations.

SOURCE: *Foreign Relations* (1945), III: 1102–1103.

It may be assumed that the Foreign Office and the Department of State have a general interest in the whole range of information regarding German financial, economic, political and military affairs both as to domestic conditions and activities abroad. Obviously with the limited personnel available, we must restrict the field of our own study of German archives. Numerous other agencies of our two Governments will be making studies of German records for their own purposes and their reports will be available to the Foreign Office and Department of State. Our teams might well confine their efforts to a study of such major Government and Nazi Party records as deal with German international relations in the fields of diplomacy, politics and broad economic policies.

The finding of evidence on war crimes and Nazi investments and flight of capital abroad, as well as any study of propaganda methods, cultural activities, means of maintaining control in Germany, tracing of enemy agents abroad, fifth column activities, etc. will be the primary responsibility of other agencies, but the combined teams should always be on the alert for information which may be of value in these fields as well as in their own spheres of special interest. Such finds should be reported immediately to the team leaders who will notify the appropriate authorities. In like manner we may expect to receive from other investigators notifications of items of interest to us. For this reason it is important to maintain friendly contact with other teams working in fields similar to ours.

Documentation within even the limits proposed above is, of course, vast and will require months of work in examining and microfilming if the German Archives, or any substantial part of them, can be located and preserved for exploitation. With this in mind, it is important that the interests of the two offices be determined so that records which may be of immediate value will be given first attention by the combined teams.

E. R. PERKINS
R. C. THOMSON

33. Allied Plans for Germany

MEMORANDUM BY PRESIDENT ROOSEVELT TO THE SECRETARY
OF WAR

WASHINGTON, August 26, 1944

This so-called "Handbook"[1] is pretty bad. I should like to know how it came to be written and who approved it down the line. If it has not been sent out as approved, all copies should be withdrawn and held until you get a chance to go over it.

It gives me the impression that Germany is to be restored just as much as The Netherlands or Belgium, and the people of Germany brought back as quickly as possible to their pre-war estate.

It is of the utmost importance that every person in Germany should realize that this time Germany is a defeated nation. I do not want them to starve to death but, as an example, if they need food to keep body and soul together beyond what they have, they should be fed three times a day with soup from Army soup kitchens. That will keep them perfectly healthy and they will remember that experience all their lives. The fact that they are a defeated nation, collectively and individually, must be so impressed upon them that they will hesitate to start any new war.

SOURCE: *Foreign Relations* (1944), I: 544.

1. *Handbook of Military Government in Germany*, 1 September 1944, issued "By Command of General Eisenhower" by W. B. Smith, Lieutenant General, Chief of Staff, Supreme Headquarters, Allied Expeditionary Force, mimeographed (Hickerson files, Lot 55D374, Box 5339).

H. Freeman Matthews on the Morgenthau Plan

MEMORANDUM BY THE DEPUTY DIRECTOR OF THE OFFICE
OF EUROPEAN AFFAIRS

TOP SECRET   (WASHINGTON,) September 20, 1944

The Secretary had a meeting in his office this morning attended by Secretary Morgenthau and Secretary Stimson. The Secretary of the Treasury gave an account of what took place at Quebec while he was present. Mr. McCloy, Assistant Secretary of War, Mr. White of the Treasury, and I were also present.

Secretary Morgenthau said that the question of the economic treatment of Germany came up at dinner on Wednesday night, September 13th, and Prime Minister Churchill was violently opposed to the policy eventually set forth in the President's memorandum to the Secretary of State. He quoted Mr. Churchill as inquiring with annoyance whether he had been brought over to Quebec to discuss such a scheme as that and as stating that it would mean "England would be chained to a dead body" (Germany). Secretary Morgenthau turned to Secretary Stimson and said: "He was even more angry than you Harry." The discussion broke up apparently with the suggestion that Mr. Morgenthau (and apparently Mr. White) should discuss the question with Lord Cherwell, which they apparently did on the basis of the Treasury's memorandum. Having convinced Lord Cherwell, the latter discussed the question again with the Prime Minister. The proposal apparently appealed to the Prime Minister on the basis that Great Britain would thus acquire a lot of Germany's iron and steel markets and eliminate a dangerous competitor. In any event, he came around completely and proved to be an advocate of the Treasury policy. Mr. Morgenthau said that several attempts were made to write up the understanding, none of which pleased Mr. Churchill. At Mr. Morgenthau's suggestion, the Prime Minister thereupon called in his secretary and dictated his understanding of what had been agreed. The result is the document quoted in the

SOURCE: *Foreign Relations, The Conferences at Malta and Yalta 1945*, pp. 134–135.

President's memorandum to the Secretary of State, dated September 15th. Mr. Morgenthau insisted that this was entirely the Prime Minister's drafting.

In reply to a question from Secretary Stimson, Mr. Morgenthau denied that there was any connection between the Prime Minister's acceptance of the German policy embodied in the memorandum and his eager desire to obtain a commitment on Lend-Lease in Phase 2. Mr. Morgenthau admitted, however, that the latter was clearly the Prime Minister's principal objective (in the non military field) at Quebec and that his interest in the Far Eastern campaign was to a great extent motivated by Lend-Lease.

The next day Mr. Eden arrived and, said Mr. Morgenthau, was very much upset at the decision taken on the economic treatment of Germany. He had quite a heated discussion with the Prime Minister and the latter instructed Mr. Eden not to take it up in the War Cabinet until he (Churchill) returned; that he was bent on pushing it through. Mr. Morgenthau seemed surprised at Mr. Eden's opposition as he had gained the opposite impression in his conversation with the Foreign Secretary in London a short time ago.

Mr. Morgenthau said that there was no discussion whatsoever in his presence of the partition of Germany or of German territorial amputations.

On Lend-Lease Mr. Morgenthau said that he found the President was prepared to accept the Prime Minister's thesis without question, but he (Mr. Morgenthau) had insisted that a committee be set up to work it out. Neither Mr. Morgenthau nor Mr. White seemed to feel that the committee would be any too effective in the long run in obtaining British cooperation in the field of commercial policy and other economic questions, but they felt that at least it gave us a foot in the door. In answer to my specific question, Mr. Morgenthau said that the President at no time raised any question as to what policy the British should pursue in return for our Lend-Lease assistance.

The Secretary expressed his shocked feelings at the way such vital matters were settled without any consultation with our Government experts or regard for what has gone before.

H. FREEMAN MATTHEWS

Cordell Hull on the Morgenthau Plan

My conversation with the President on October 1 had obviated the need to take any action on his memorandum. This latter showed me, however, the line of thought he had been pursuing. In his mind the future of Britain was linked inversely with the future of Germany. Britain needed to get back her export trade after the war, but he felt that she could not do so if Germany were permitted to develop an extensive export trade in competition. Therefore he embraced Morgenthau's plan. But he forgot, despite Churchill's initialing of the agreement, that the British Government was the last to desire the conversion of Germany into a pastoral country, because Britain's livelihood would be impaired if Europe's economy collapsed because of a wrecked Germany.

The President's memorandum also showed plainly that he had not understood the meaning of what he had agreed to at Quebec. At about this time Secretary Stimson had a talk with the President, from which Stimson drew the same conclusion. He informed me that he had thereupon read to the President several sentences from the President's memorandum of September 15, concluding with the phrase "looking forward to converting Germany into a country primarily agricultural and pastoral in its character."

Stimson informed me that the President was frankly staggered at hearing these sentences and said that he had no idea how he could have initialed the memorandum, and that he had evidently done so without much thought.

In any event, the President, after my conversation with him, ceased to embrace Morgenthau's ideas on Germany. Three weeks after my memorandum of September 29 he sent me a reply dated October 20 which he began by saying: "I think it is all very well for us to make all kinds of preparations for the treatment of Germany, but there are some matters in regard to such treatment that lead me to believe that speed on these matters is not an essential at the present moment. It may be in a week, or it may be in a month, or it

SOURCE: Cordell Hull, *The Memoirs of Cordell Hull* (New York, 1948), II: 1621. Copyright 1948 by Cordell Hull. Reprinted with permission of the Macmillan Company.

may be several months hence. I dislike making detailed plans for a country which we do not yet occupy."

Plans for Surrender

THE AMBASSADOR IN THE UNITED KINGDOM WINANT TO
THE SECRETARY OF STATE

LONDON, January 6, 1945
[Received January 12]

SIR: With reference to telegram No. 188 of January 5, 9 PM, Comea 143, which reported the establishment of an Allied Consultation Committee in the European Advisory Commission to consult with representatives of certain European United Nations Governments, I have the honor to transmit copies of a Summary of the Instrument of Unconditional Surrender of Germany which has been prepared in the Commission for the purpose of serving as a basis for discussion in the meetings of the new Committee.

Respectfully yours,

For the Ambassador:
E. ALLAN LIGHTNER, JR.
Secretary, U. S. Delegation,
European Advisory Commission

[Enclosure]

SUMMARY OF INSTRUMENT OF UNCONDITIONAL SURRENDER
OF GERMANY

LONDON, 7 December, 1944

The Instrument of Unconditional Surrender of Germany, as recommended by the European Advisory Commission to the Three Governments, is a relatively short document of a predominantly military character.

It is designed to be signed on the Allied side by representatives of the Supreme Commands of the United Kingdom, the United States and the Soviet Union, and on the German side by representatives of the German Government and of the German High Command.

SOURCE: *Foreign Relations* (1945), III: 168–169, 229.

The Instrument consists essentially of three parts:

The first is the preamble which includes an unqualified acknowl-edgement on the part of Germany of the complete defeat of the German armed forces on land, at sea and in the air, and an announcement by her of her unconditional surrender. The Repre-sentatives of the Supreme Commands of the United Kingdom, the United States of America and the Soviet Union, acting by author-ity of their respective Governments and in the interests of the United Nations, thereupon announce the terms of surrender.

The second part comprises a series of articles which provide:

(i) for the cessation of hostilities by Germany in all theatres of war against the forces of the United Nations;

(ii) for the complete disarmament and disposal of the armed forces of Germany or armed forces under German control;

(iii) for the standstill of all such forces in their positions at the time of surrender, pending instructions from the Allied Rep-resentatives;

(iv) for the evacuation by the said forces of all territories outside the frontiers of Germany as they existed on 31st December, 1937, according to instructions to be given by the Allied Rep-resentatives;

(v) for the holding by the German authorities at the disposal of the Allied Representatives, intact and in good condition, of all war material, naval vessels, merchant shipping, aircraft, transportation and communications facilities and equipment, military, naval and air installations, and factories designed to produce the foregoing or otherwise to further the conduct of war;

(vi) for the release of United Nations' prisoners of war and of United Nations' and other nationals who are under restraint for political reasons, and for their protection and maintenance prior to their repatriation;

(vii) for the stationing of forces and civil agencies in any or all parts of Germany by the Allied Representatives as they may determine.

The third part is a General Article setting forth the supreme authority of the Three Powers with respect to Germany, including the power completely to disarm and to demilitarise Germany and to take such other steps as the Three Powers may deem requisite for future peace and security. The General Article further states that the Allied Representatives will present additional political,

administrative, economic, financial, military and other requirements arising from the surrender of Germany, and will issue
Proclamations, Orders, etc., for the purpose of laying down such
additional requirements and of giving effect to the other provisions
of the Instrument of Surrender. The German authorities will carry
out unconditionally the requirements of the Allied Representatives, and fully comply with such Proclamations, Orders, etc.

THE UNITED STATES POLITICAL ADVISER FOR GERMANY MURPHY TO THE DIRECTOR OF THE OFFICE OF EUROPEAN AFFAIRS MATTHEWS

LONDON, April 16, 1945

DEAR DOC: Just a word about the current trend. Apparently
there is on the part of some of our officers no particular eagerness
to occupy Berlin first. It is not at all impossible that our forces may
linger along the Elbe "consolidating" their position. This will be
true in the event there is substantial German resistance. One
theory seems to be that what is left of Berlin may be tenaciously
defended house by house and brick by brick. I have suggested the
modest opinion that there should be a certain political advantage
in the capture of Berlin even though the military advantage may be
insignificant.

Plans for Surrender: The Allies

PRESIDENT TRUMAN TO THE BRITISH PRIME MINISTER CHURCHILL

WASHINGTON, 26 April 1945

Referring to your Number 13 it appears to me, particularly in
view of the fact that the Armies now in the Soviet zone are American, that any agreement entered into regarding withdrawal to the
designated post hostility zones of occupation in Germany and
Austria should be tripartite.

I therefore suggest for your consideration that you address the
following message to Marshal Stalin and to me:

SOURCE: *Foreign Relations* (1945), III: 244–245.

"1. The Anglo-American armies will soon make contact in Germany with Soviet forces, and the approaching end of German resistance makes it necessary that the United States, Great Britain, and the Soviet Union decide upon an orderly procedure for the occupation by their forces of the zones which they will occupy in Germany and in Austria.

2. Our immediate task is the final defeat of the German Army. During this period the boundaries between the forces of the three Allies must be decided by Commanders in the field, and will be governed by operational considerations and requirements. It is inevitable that our armies will in this phase find themselves in occupation of territory outside the boundaries of the ultimate occupational zones.

3. When the fighting is finished, the next task is for the Allied Control Commissions to be set up in Berlin and Vienna, and for the forces of the Allies to be redisposed and to take over their respective occupational zones. The demarcation of the zones in Germany has already been decided upon and it is necessary that we shall without delay reach an agreement on the zones to be occupied in Austria at the forthcoming meeting proposed by you in Vienna.

4. It appears now that no signed instrument of surrender will be forthcoming. In this event governments should decide to set up at once the Allied Control Commissions, and to entrust to them the task of making detailed arrangements for the withdrawal of the forces to their agreed occupational zones.

5. In order to meet the requirements of the situation referred to in paragraph 2 above, namely the emergency and temporary arrangements for the tactical zones, instructions have been sent to General Eisenhower. These are as follows:

(a) To avoid confusion between the two armies and to prevent either of them from expanding into areas already occupied by the other, both sides should halt as and where they meet, subject to such adjustments to the rear or to the flanks as are required, in the opinion of the local commanders on either side, to deal with any remaining opposition.

(b) As to adjustments of forces after cessation of hostilities in an area, your troops should be disposed in accordance with military requirements regardless of zonal boundaries. You will, in so far as permitted by the urgency of the situation, obtain the approval of the Combined Chiefs of Staff prior to any major adjustment in contrast to local adjustments for operational and administrative reasons.

6. It is requested that you will issue similar instructions to your commanders in the field."

Upon the receipt of the above message from you, I will at once inform Marshal Stalin than I am in full agreement therewith.[1]

THE AMBASSADOR IN FRANCE CAFFERY TO THE SECRETARY OF STATE

PARIS, May 5, 1945—midnight
[Received May 5—8:47 PM]

From Murphy for Matthews. Representatives of Admiral Dönitz and General Busch are now at SHAEF discussing surrender of balance of German forces in the north including Norway. By agreement with the Soviet High Command Russian officers (General Suslaparoff) are participating and the Allied position is unconditional surrender to the Russians as well as the Anglo-American side. These conversations may go on thru the night and while there is no assurance the Germans will sign, as they apparently hoped to negotiate a surrender to SHAEF without the Russians, it is believed that after telegraphic consultation with Dönitz they will sign probably tomorrow.

Kesselring also has requested permission to send plenipotentiaries and has been informed they will be received on condition that they prepared to surrender unconditionally to the Russians and to ourselves. Otherwise local surrenders will be effected to the individual unit commanders. [Murphy.]

CAFFERY

SOURCE: *Foreign Relations* (1945), III: 777–780.

1. In his telegram 18, April 27, to President Truman, Prime Minister Churchill stated that he had addressed to Marshal Stalin the message quoted above. Churchill added the following comment: "I think Stalin is pleased at our having informed him in such quick unity of our spontaneous view of the Himmler-Bernadotte contacts. Even if there is a short delay or setback, all our forces will be in a much more favourable position. I thank you so much for promoting the easy way in which we are handling this three-cornered business." (Department of Defense Files)

THE AMBASSADOR IN FRANCE CAFFERY TO THE SECRETARY
OF STATE

PARIS, May 6, 1945—11 PM
[Received May 6—7:30 PM]

For Matthews from Murphy. Field Marshal Jodl arrived at SHAEF this afternoon from 21st Army Group Headquarters. He is understood to possess full powers for the surrender of German forces. SHAEF officers are inclined to be optimistic of a successful outcome and the first impression they have is that the Germans have decided upon unconditional surrender and that their primary concern is to save as many of their forces as possible from falling into Russian hands. The surrender will embrace the entire area north and south and I believe it will be signed Sunday night or Monday morning. [Murphy.]

CAFFERY

MEMORANDUM OF TELEPHONE CONVERSATION, BY THE
ACTING SECRETARY OF STATE

WASHINGTON, May 7, 1945—1:45 PM

Admiral Leahy telephoned me and said that the situation on the announcement of V-E Day was terribly confused and he wanted me to know the background of the latest information. He stated that we have an agreement with Stalin and Churchill to make the announcement at 9 o'clock tomorrow morning but Churchill today raised the devil because he said he had to make the announcement right away and wanted to make it at noon today. Admiral Leahy said the President declined to do it then and said that he had arranged with Stalin and Churchill to announce it at 9 o'clock and he could not violate his agreement without the assent of Stalin. Admiral Leahy said they had been trying to get in touch with Stalin but so far have had nothing from him except the vague thought that he doesn't know the terms and can't make an announcement as yet. Admiral Leahy said he had heard later through BBC that Churchill was going to make the announcement at 3 o'clock. He said that he also had heard that de Gaulle is going to announce it at 2 o'clock. He stated that nobody has any control over de Gaulle and that this action was typical of him. I agreed with

Admiral Leahy and remarked that de Gaulle was acting just like a naughty boy. Admiral Leahy said he spoke to the President about 20 minutes ago and thought it was definite for 9 o'clock tomorrow morning. He said that the only way the thing would be stopped would be for Stalin to ask us not to announce it yet. Admiral Leahy also said that he had been in touch with Eisenhower who said he had made no announcement and has kept it as secret as it could be kept. He said he would not make any announcement until it was released here. I said I understood it had leaked through AP. Admiral Leahy said the Germans are talking freely in plain language about it so everyone knows it. I said at any rate the only people who would be displeased about the whole thing would be the newspapermen.

MARSHAL STALIN TO PRESIDENT TRUMAN[1]

Moscow, May 7, 1945

I am in receipt of your message of May 7,[2] about announcing Germany's surrender. The Supreme Command of the Red Army is not sure that the order of the German High Command on unconditional surrender will be executed by the German armies on the Eastern Front. We fear, therefore, that if the Government of the U. S. S. R. announces today the surrender of Germany we may find ourselves in an awkward position and mislead the Soviet public. It should be borne in mind that the German resistance on the Eastern Front is not slackening but, judging by the intercepted radio messages, a considerable grouping of German troops have explicitly declared their intention to continue the resistance and to disobey Dönitz's surrender order.

For this reason the Command of the Soviet troops would like to wait until the German surrender takes effect and to postpone the Government's announcement of the surrender till May 9, 7 PM Moscow time.[3]

1. Reprinted from Stalin's Correspondence, vol. ii, p. 230.
2. Telegram 260, in which President Truman indicated that he would announce Germany's surrender on May 8, at 9 AM Washington time, if this was agreeable to Marshal Stalin.
3. On May 8, at 8:15 AM Washington time, President Truman made the formal announcement that Germany had surrendered on all fronts. Later that day he handed the following message to Soviet Ambassador Gromyko:

THE CHARGÉ IN THE SOVIET UNION KENNAN TO THE
SECRETARY OF STATE

Moscow, May 7, 1945—2 PM
[Received 3:15 PM]

I wish to invite attention to my several telegrams pointing out the markedly casual and inconspicuous treatment which the Soviet press has given to the surrenders of German forces in Italy and in the Western Theater and the general crumbling of German resistance there. News of these events has been made available to the Soviet public only in minor back page items in the daily press, has been accompanied by no editorial comment of any sort and has not been singled out in any way for the attention of the readers.

It is not possible to be sure of the motives dictating this extreme reserve in releasing news of victories which one might have thought would be highly gratifying to both the Soviet Government and public. The most likely explanation, in my opinion, is that the Soviet leaders, while not daring to withhold the news entirely are not happy over the fact that the big local surrenders have been exclusively to our forces and not to theirs; that they do not wish it to be suggested that the forces of the Western nations are less feared and hated that [than?] the Soviet forces among the peoples of central Europe and that they choose not to draw the attention of their public to the full extent of German disintegration until they are able to announce complete surrender and cessation of resistance on all fronts, including their own, and to attribute this primarily to the heroic efforts of the Red Army.[4]

"Please inform Marshal Stalin that his message to me was received in the White House at 1 o'clock this morning. However, by the time the message reached me, preparations had proceeded to such an extent that it was not possible to give consideration to a postponement of my announcement of the German surrender."

4. In telegram 1492, May 8, noon, from Moscow, Mr. Kennan commented further on the failure of the Soviet Government to announce the signature of the act of surrender and observed: "The official justification for this state of affairs would doubtless be that there was still resistance here and there against Soviet forces in Eastern Europe but I think the true explanation lies deeper. For Russia, peace, like everything else, can come only by ukase and the end of hostilities must be determined not by the true course of events

Sent Department as 1487, repeated to Paris for Reber and Murphy as 101.

KENNAN

THE AMBASSADOR IN FRANCE CAFFERY TO THE SECRETARY OF STATE

PARIS, May 7, 1945—10 PM
[Received May 7—6:33 PM]

From Murphy for Matthews. General Eisenhower has informed Combined Chiefs of Staff that the mission entrusted to his Allied Command has now been completed.[5] [Murphy.]

CAFFERY

The Surrender

The text of the Act of Military Surrender signed by General Jodl follows:

1. We the undersigned, acting by authority of the German High Command, hereby surrender unconditionally to the Supreme Commander, Allied Expeditionary Force and simultaneously to the Soviet High Command all forces on land, sea, and in the air who are at this date under German control.

2. The German High Command will at once issue orders to all German military, naval and air authorities and to all forces under German control to cease active operations at 2301 hours Central European time on 8 May and to remain in the positions occupied

SOURCE: Pogue, *The Supreme Command*, pp. 488–489.

---

but by decision of the Kremlin. Among the lesser injuries for which the Germans may have to answer to Russia, when the smoke has cleared away, perhaps not the least may be their willfulness in capitulating at a time and place which the Kremlin has not selected."

Telegram 1519, May 9, noon, from Moscow, reported that the unconditional surrender of Germany was made known in Moscow via radio broadcast at 2 AM, May 9.

5. On May 7, 1945, at Rheims, France, the German High Command surrendered unconditionally to the Supreme Commander, Allied Expeditionary Force and to the Soviet High Command. The ratification of the unconditional surrender of all German Armed Forces to the Supreme Allied Commands took place in Berlin on May 8, 1945.

at that time. No ship, vessel, or aircraft is to be scuttled, or any damage done to their hull, machinery or equipment.

3. The German High Command will at once issue to the appropriate commanders, and ensure the carrying out of any further orders issued by the Supreme Commander, Allied Expeditionary Force and by the Soviet High Command.

4. This act of military surrender is without prejudice to, and will be superseded by any general instrument of surrender imposed by, or on behalf of the United Nations and applicable to GERMANY and the German armed forces as a whole.

5. In the event of the German High Command or any of the forces under their control failing to act in accordance with this Act of Surrender, the Supreme Commander, Allied Expeditionary Force and the Soviet High Command will take such punitive or other action as they deem appropriate.

Signed at Rheims at 0241 on the 7th day of May, 1945.

On behalf of the German High Command.

JODL

IN THE PRESENCE OF
On behalf of the Supreme Commander,
Allied Expeditionary Force

W. B. SMITH

On behalf of the Soviet High Command

SUSLOPAROFF

F. SEVEZ

Major General, French Army

(Witness)

General Jodl also signed the following statement:

It is agreed by the German emissaries undersigned that the following German officers will arrive at a place and time designated by the Supreme Commander, Allied Expeditionary Force, and the Soviet High Command prepared with plenary powers, to execute a formal ratification on behalf of the German High Command of this act of Unconditional Surrender of the German armed forces.

Chief of the High Command

Commander-in-Chief of the Army

Commander-in-Chief of the Navy

Commander-in-Chief of the Air Forces

After the Surrender

MEMORANDUM OF TELEPHONE CONVERSATION BY THE
DIRECTOR OF THE OFFICE OF EUROPEAN
AFFAIRS MATTHEWS

WASHINGTON, May, 12, 1945

Mr. McCloy telephoned me this morning and said that he was both much embarrassed and much annoyed to find on his return from San Francisco that the instrument of surrender which had been signed both at Rheims and at Berlin was a brand new document and not the one so carefully and painstakingly negotiated over a period of eight months in the European Advisory Commission. He said it was simply incredible to him that this document, which had the formal approval of the four governments and the Joint Chiefs of Staff, had been simply forgotten and ignored. He read me a telegram from General Eisenhower which indicated that instead of consulting the G–5 people at SHAEF, they had put the matter in the hands of G–3 and G–1 and people like General Spaatz who knew none of the background. Mr. McCloy said he still could not understand how General Bedell Smith could have overlooked the document because he was familiar with it, nor did he understand why Bob Murphy had not been consulted. Mr. McCloy said that in any event he wished to apologize for this serious oversight and promised to send a telegram to General Eisenhower to make sure that no other documents are signed or proclamations issued which may run counter to the governmental agreements negotiated in the European Advisory Commission. He also said that he thought we should examine carefully to see whether we should still force a German signature of the agreed surrender document or whether the proposed proclamation to be issued by the four governments based on those terms may be adequate for the purpose and for the setting up of the control machinery. I told him that Winant was negotiating in the EAC on the latter basis and that he would look into it carefully as soon as the completed text has been agreed upon.

SOURCE: *Foreign Relations* (1945), III: 289–290, 294–297, 544–545, 549–554.

THE UNITED STATES POLITICAL ADVISER FOR GERMANY
MURPHY TO THE DIRECTOR OF THE OFFICE OF
EUROPEAN AFFAIRS MATTHEWS

PARIS, May 14, 1945

DEAR DOC: The story of the negotiation with the German High Command of the short surrender document reported in my 2517, May 10, 7 PM, and my 2493, May 9, 9 PM, is amusing.

In considering this matter, the fact that the conversations were closely held by a few officers at different headquarters (SHAEF at Rheims and the 21st Army Group which then had its headquarters at Luneburg) should be remembered because the physical aspects had a good deal to do with it.

I think it is fair to say that SHAEF had made up its mind to restrict these conversations to the military and to exclude Foreign Office or State Department participation.

As you know, our main office of necessity is at Versailles where the US Group CC are housed, but I maintain an office also at SHAEF Forward, Rheims. Jake Beam stays there regularly and I go to Rheims about three or four times a week. Jake was not told anything about the initial stages of the negotiations. I was at Rheims on May 5, and Smith told me that he was expecting the arrival sometime that evening of Admiral von Friedeburg who was coming down from Headquarters 21st Army Group. I waited until the arrival of the party and after a conversation with them which I did not attend as I was not invited, Smith informed me that the Germans had no authority to sign anything, and that as the German ciphers had been left at 21st Army Group Headquarters, probably prolonged communications via 21st Army Group to Admiral Doenitz' headquarters at Flensburg would be necessary. I returned to Versailles that evening and had no further advice from Headquarters regarding the progress of the negotiations until a telephone call at 2 AM May 7 saying that Colonel General Jodl had arrived and that a signature of the surrender document would be made within minutes. This advice came from Secretary of the General Staff. I assumed that the reference to the surrender document referred to the EAC text. I was amazed therefore to discover only very much later in the day that a new text had been provided, but I was still ignorant of the source. I immediately returned to Rheims to discover that a group consisting of military officers only were proceeding forthwith to Berlin for the signature of a similar document. Upon inquiry I discovered that it was the opinion of several officers who had worked on this matter both British and American (G–3 SHAEF, Generals Bull and Whiteley) that as there was no Combined Chiefs of Staff directive concerning the use of the text, elaborated in the EAC and approved by the Governments, that SHAEF was not required to use that text which it was believed was only applicable in case a recognizable German Government existed at the time of signature.

I have driven home to all of the top SHAEF officers on both the American and British sides the point that the Russians saw to it that their delegation to Berlin had with it a representative of the Foreign Office (Vyshinski).

I enclose a copy in paraphrase of a telegram sent by Bedell Smith to the War Department on May 10 offering an explanation of the procedure followed by SHAEF in this matter and having reference to the Department's 1950 of May 9 addressed to me the contents of which were conveyed to General Eisenhower and General Smith. As you will probably understand, General Eisenhower entrusted to General Smith the entire responsibility for procedure in negotiating the surrender document.

Yours ever,

BOB

LIEUTENANT GENERAL WALTER BEDELL SMITH TO MAJOR GENERAL JOHN E. HULL[1]

Paris, 10 May 1945

A query from the State Department as to why the instrument of unconditional surrender as negotiated in the EAC was not used has just been shown to me by Ambassador Murphy. I must say that we are all shocked to realize that the hours of work and worry spent

---

1. Maj. Gen. John E. Hull, Assistant Chief of Staff, Operations Division, War Department General Staff. In a letter to General Smith, dated May 11, General Hull wrote in part as follows:

"The EAC document being on a governmental basis, would not, as such, be referred to the Combined Chiefs of Staff for review. This coupled with

here in preparing an instrument of surrender were completely unnecessary in view of the existence of a document which our three governments had agreed upon.

As a matter of fact a directive from the Combined Chiefs of Staff on the subject of the surrender terms negotiated in the EAC had never been received by us. Through Mr. Winant we did receive an informal copy and when negotiations began Ambassador Winant reminded me of this by telephone, and stated that a revised document had just been prepared. I suggested that he take immediate steps to invite the attention of Washington to the fact that we had never received a directive from the Combined Chiefs of Staff so that we might receive instructions on it through Combined Chiefs of Staff channels if indeed there was an approved surrender form. We proceeded with the short surrender document which was drafted here since we heard nothing further and in view of the urgent circumstances.

I find on checking back that we did receive a JCS paper on the subject of the surrender terms negotiated in the EAC which would have given us a guide to the existence of a set of agreed surrender terms. Although this was unfortunately overlooked, I do not think that any harm has been done as our own draft and the accompanying instructions cover practically everything covered in the EAC text. We did a great deal of worrying about Russia which we might have avoided had we been a little bit more alert however, and there has been a lot of unnecessary work done. The State Department is being informed by Murphy that any requirement of the EAC draft

---

the fact that no request was made on the CCS to forward the document to SHAEF for guidance, I think, explains why SHAEF did not receive a directive from the CCS. I believe this lack of a request was due, in part, to the absence of an approved EAC document that included the French. In January, the State Department requested the JCS views as to amending the Instrument of Surrender and other EAC documents to include the French. To this request the JCS on 24 January replied they had no objection. JCS papers on this (JCS 1226 series) were forwarded to CG. ETOUSA on 31 January. Nothing further on the matter of including the French was brought to the attention of the JCS but Mr. Winant in a cable to the State Department on 9 May 1945 said that an instrument including the French had not at that time been approved by the four governments." (Political Advisor for Germany Files)

not covered by our own papers can be made the subject of additional instructions to the German High Command.

Why the Russians did not raise this question is a mystery to me since matters in Berlin were obviously being handled by Vyshinski who must have been thoroughly conversant with the whole affair. As Murphy remembered all the circumstances, if we had brought him into the picture we would not have missed this bet.

REPORT ON THE WORK OF THE EUROPEAN ADVISORY COMMISSION

SECTION I: ORGANISATION AND PROCEDURE OF THE COMMISSION

The European Advisory Commission was established by the Governments of the United Kingdom, the United States of America and the Union of Soviet Socialist Republics pursuant to an agreement concluded on 1st November, 1943, at the Moscow Conference of Foreign Ministers. The Conference decided that the Commission would be composed of representatives of the three Powers, assisted where necessary by civilian and military advisers; that it would have its seat in London, where a joint Secretariat would be established; and that the Presidency would be held in rotation by the representatives of the three Powers.

The principal terms of reference of the Commission were defined as follows:

(1) "The Commission will study and make recommendations to the three Governments upon European questions connected with the termination of hostilities which the three Governments may consider appropriate to refer to it. . . ."

(2) "As one of the Commission's first task the three Governments desire that it shall, as soon as possible, make detailed recommendations to them upon the terms of surrender to be imposed upon each of the European States with which any of the three Powers are at war, and upon the machinery required to ensure the fulfilment of those terms. . . ." In its study of these matters, the Commission was directed to take into account relevant information furnished by the three Governments, as well as the experience already gained in the imposition and enforcement of unconditional surrender upon Italy.

(3) "Representatives of the Governments of other United Nations will, at the discretion of the Commission, be invited to take

part in meetings of the Commission when matters especially affecting their interests are under discussion."

SECTION II: AGREEMENTS SIGNED BY THE COMMISSION
SURRENDER, OCCUPATION AND CONTROL OF GERMANY

(1) Unconditional Surrender of Germany

At the first formal meeting the Commission agreed that its initial task should be that of drawing up the terms of surrender of Germany and devising machinery for their enforcement. Each of the Delegations (United Kingdom, United States and Union of Soviet Socialist Republics) accordingly prepared draft proposals on this subject. The United Kingdom Delegation proposed a "Draft German Armistice" (15th January, 1944) based on the principle of unconditional surrender and designed to confer on the Allied Powers far-reaching political and military authority. In presenting this draft, which comprised 70 articles, the United Kingdom Delegation emphasized the view that whatever form of surrender was ultimately imposed upon Germany in the light of the conditions prevailing at the time, a relatively long armistice document would in the initial stages of discussion be the most convenient way of ensuring thorough consideration of all the issues involved. The United States Delegation circulated two documents. The first of these (25th January 1944), in the form of a memorandum rather than a draft instrument ready for signature, comprised 27 provisions to be imposed on Germany, while the second, a "Draft Instrument and Acknowledgment of Unconditional Surrender" (6th March, 1944), contained thirteen general articles under which the Allies assumed supreme military and political authority over Germany. The United States Delegation proposed that this instrument be accompanied by proclamations and orders setting forth in greater detail the more specific requirements which Germany would be obliged to carry out. The Delegation of the Union of Soviet Socialist Republics circulated (18th February, 1944) "Draft Terms of Surrender" in 20 articles. This document was primarily military in character designed to effect the cessation of hostilities, the disarmament of the German forces, the surrender of military material and the occupation of Germany. The final article, however, provided that the Allies would present additional political, economic and military requirements connected with the surrender of Germany which would undertake to carry them out unconditionally.

The Commission discussed these proposals at considerable length in a series of formal and informal meetings and as a result unanimously resolved to draft a surrender instrument which would be relatively brief and predominantly military in character, while reserving to the Allied Governments complete freedom to impose subsequently such additional terms as might be deemed necessary. It was understood that many of the detailed political and economic provisions which had appeared in the initial United Kingdom proposal and which were not to be included in an instrument of a relatively brief character, could be incorporated in agreed form in a general order or other document of a similar nature. (See below, "Agreement on Additional Requirements.")

With the assistance of a committee of experts, which considered the military terms in all the draft documents on the unconditional surrender of Germany, the Commission analysed, compared and coordinated the relevant provisions of the proposals before it, and as a result formulated, article by article, a single tentative draft of the surrender instrument. This document, after undergoing successive revisions and modifications at the hands of a committee of experts, a drafting committee, and the Commission itself, emerged later as the approved text of the "Unconditional Surrender of Germany," signed by the Representatives of the United Kingdom, the United States of America and the Union of Soviet Socialist Republics on 25th July, 1944. The accompanying Report by the Commission explained that the Surrender Instrument was predominantly military, comprising an unqualified acknowledgment of the complete defeat of Germany, a short series of military articles providing for the cessation of hostilities and for disarmament, and a general article setting forth the supreme authority of the Allies and binding Germany to carry out unconditionally such further requirements as the Allies might impose. The Report also contained an interpretation of Article 2 (b) of the Instrument and informed the Governments of the action which the Commission contemplated taking in the matter of consultation with other Allied Governments. [E.A.C. (44) 7th Meeting].

By an Agreement signed on 1st May, 1945, by the Representatives of the United Kingdom, the United States of America, the Union of Soviet Socialist Republics and the Provisional Government of the French Republic, the "Unconditional Surrender of Germany" was amended to allow for full participation of the Provisional Government of the French Republic in the imposition of surrender terms upon Germany. [E.A.C. (45) 1st Meeting.]

(2) *Declaration regarding the Defeat of Germany and the Assumption of Supreme Authority with respect to Germany*

While the "Unconditional Surrender of Germany" was prepared on the assumption that it would be signed on the one hand by the Allied Representatives and on the other by representatives of the German Government and German High Command, the Commission recognized in its initial discussions that the complete defeat of the German armed forces might result in there being at the close of hostilities no Central Government in Germany capable of signing a general surrender or giving effect to the requirements of the Allies. As military operations developed, the possibility of such a situation arising became more probable and the Commission accordingly undertook to recast the "Unconditional Surrender of Germany" in the form of a Declaration to be issued, without German signature, by the Governments of the United Kingdom, the United States of America, the Union of Soviet Socialist Republics and the Provisional Government of the French Republic. On the basis of the "Unconditional Surrender of Germany," a United Kingdom proposal circulated on 30th March, 1945, and amendments to the latter proposed by the other Delegations, the Commission drafted and on 12th May, 1945, signed the "Declaration regarding the Defeat of Germany and the Assumption of Supreme Authority with respect to Germany." [E.A.C. (45) 3rd Meeting.]

Following a number of local military surrenders, brief unconditional surrender terms were signed by the German military authorities provisionally at Rheims on 7th May and finally at Berlin on 8th May, 1945. The Declaration was approved by the four Governments by 21st May, 1945. The Commission agreed on 4th June to recommend to the four Governments that the four Commanders-in-Chief meet in Berlin for the purpose of signing and publishing the Declaration. In accordance with this recommendation, the Declaration was signed and issued at Berlin on 5th June.

(3) *Zones of Occupation in Germany and the Administration of Greater Berlin*

From March to September, 1944, the Commission considered the problem of zones of military occupation in Germany and the administration of Greater Berlin. The Commission had before it basic proposals on this subject presented by the United Kingdom Delegation on 15th January, 1944, by the Union of Soviet Socialist Republics Delegation on 18th February, 1944, and by the United States Delegation on 12th June, 1944, as well as various revised proposals circulated at informal meetings. The first stage in reaching a complete agreement was the signature by the Representatives of the United Kingdom, the United States of America and the Union of Soviet Socialist Republics on 12th September, 1944, of a Protocol which defined the boundaries of three zones of occupation in Germany within her frontiers as they were on 31st December, 1937, delimited three sectors of occupation in the Berlin area, and provided for the establishment of an Inter-Allied Governing Authority for Berlin. The Protocol also provided that the Eastern zone in Germany and the North Eastern sector of Berlin would be occupied by armed forces of the Union of Soviet Socialist Republics, but did not allocate the other zones or the sectors in Berlin as between the United Kingdom and United States forces. [E.A.C. (44) 9th Meeting.] A further Agreement signed in the Commission on 14th November, 1944, made certain alterations in the boundaries between the North Western and South Western zones, assigned the North Western zone in Germany, as well as the North Western part of Berlin, to the United Kingdom, and assigned the South Western zone, as well as the Southern part of Berlin to the United States. [E.A.C. (44) 12th Meeting.] The Crimea Conference decided that a French zone in Germany should be formed from the United Kingdom and the United States zones and referred the matter to the European Advisory Commission for implementation. An Agreement signed in the Commission on 26th July, 1945, defined the boundaries of the French zone, fixed the new limits of the United Kingdom and United States zones, and provided for French participation in the administration of Greater Berlin. On account of the physical conditions prevailing in the area, the Commission did not attempt in this Agreement to fix the boundaries of a French sector of occupation in Berlin, but recommended that the limits of this sector, which would have to be formed from the United Kingdom and United States sectors on account of the greater destruction in the Soviet area, be determined by the Control Council in Berlin. [E.A.C. (45) 7th Meeting.] On the date this Agreement was signed, an exchange of letters took place between the Governments of the United Kingdom and the United States of America and the Provisional Government of the French Republic regarding a possible future adjustment between the French zone and the United States and United Kingdom zones of occupation. The United States and French Representatives also exchanged letters relating to the use by the French authorities of certain records located at Karlsruhe and to the free passage to be accorded United States forces across and above the French zone.

(4) Control Machinery in Germany

Between February and November, 1944, the Commission considered the subject of Allied Machinery required for effective control of Germany. At this stage the three Governments were not yet prepared to formulate in detail the content of their policy towards Germany, but the Commission considered it essential to agree in advance on machinery through which the Allies could carry out in Germany whatever policies the Governments might finally lay down. On the basis of a number of proposals circulated by the United Kingdom, United States and Union of Soviet Socialist Republics Delegations, the Commission undertook to work out an agreement on control machinery which could be put into operation whether or not a German central authority existed at the time of surrender. The Agreement on Control Machinery signed on 14th November, 1944, provided for a tripartite Control Council and subsidiary agencies through which the Allies would exercise supreme authority in the period during which Germany would be carrying out the basic requirements of unconditional surrender. The purpose of these agencies comprised the control and disarmament of Germany, including the most urgent tasks of economic disarmament, the abolition of the Nazi regime, and the preparation of conditions for the establishment in Germany of organs based on democratic principles. [E.A.C. (44) 11th Meeting.]

An additional Agreement signed by the Representatives of the

United Kingdom, the United States of America, the Union of Soviet Socialist Republics and the Provisional Government of the French Republic on 1st May, 1945, provided for participation of the Provisional Government of the French Republic in the control machinery on an equal basis. [E.A.C. (45) 2nd Meeting.]

(5) *Certain Additional Requirements to be Imposed on Germany*

From the beginning of the discussions of German surrender, it was realized that effective control over Germany would eventually require an agreement supplementing the predominantly military clauses of the Surrender Instrument by providing for joint action of the Allies in the political and economic spheres. The Commission agreed in March, 1944, that certain broad political and economic requirements should be imposed upon Germany at the time of, or shortly after, the surrender, and the way for such action was prepared by Article 13(b) of the Declaration issued on 5th June, 1945. After preliminary discussions in late 1944 and early 1945, the Commission during May and June, 1945, worked out a long document embodying some of the more urgent of these requirements. The "Agreement on Certain Additional Requirements to be Imposed on Germany" was signed in the Commission on 25th July, 1945, and submitted to the four Governments with the recommendation that it be transmitted, after approval by the four Governments, to the Allied Representatives in Berlin for their guidance. The Agreement covered a wide range of matters of common concern to the four Powers, including the abolition of Nazi and militaristic organizations, surrender of war criminals, and joint control over German foreign relations, production, trade, finance, transportation and movement of persons. The accompanying Report contained a number of interpretations and explanations of certain articles in the text of the Agreement. [E.A.C. (45) 6th Meeting.] When signing the Report the United Kingdom Representative made an oral statement regarding paragraph 3(d).

IV

War against Japan

34. Introduction

Having immobilized the U. S. Pacific Fleet by the surprise attack on Pearl Harbor, the Japanese moved quickly toward their military objectives. In their advance they took the American possessions, Guam and Wake, and by the middle of February had seized Singapore.

Once the war started, it was realized that the Philippines would be a target. One of the mysteries of the war is why the forces around Manila, even though warned, were so helpless before the first Japanese air attacks. Within two weeks the Japanese had eliminated enemy air power and effective naval operations and had made successful amphibious landings on Luzon. General MacArthur determined to make his stand on the peninsula of Bataan. The defense was heroic, heartbreaking and futile. On Washington's orders a submarine took General MacArthur to Australia to fight another day, and General Jonathan M. Wainright was left to conduct the defense and go with his forces into captivity when surrender became inevitable. Although the Philippines were lost, the Allies agreed that they must be retaken, for political as much as military reasons, and they established an advance base at Port Arthur in Australia as a start toward recovery.

There were tremendous obstacles in the way of the war in the Pacific and Far East. In the first place, the British and Americans had already agreed that defeat of Germany was the prime objective. Support to the Pacific war at first, therefore, would be minimal and for defensive action. However, Admiral King was a strong supporter of the Pacific war, and from Australia General MacArthur sent urgent appeals for more men and supplies. Even if these could be provided, distances made logistics difficult. It was twice as far from San Francisco to Brisbane as it was from New York to Liverpool.

Given the task of planning operations in the Pacific, the U. S. Joint Chiefs of Staff assigned the huge Pacific Ocean Area to Admiral Chester W. Nimitz and a deputy, Vice Admiral R. A. Ghormley. During 1942, however, the only offensive action the American forces could take was to engage in a few nuisance raids.

Encouraged by their successes, the Japanese planned to extend their conquests. The Battle of the Coral Sea, the first large naval engagement in which surface vessels did not fire at each other, was tactically a Japanese victory, but it dissuaded the Japanese from their plan to capture Port Moresby in New Guinea. Even more important was the Battle of Midway in June 1942, which showed that if used properly air power could defeat a superior naval force. The battle stopped the enemy's forward thrust and may be considered a turning point in the war.

Dropping their plans for further expansion, the Japanese started to strengthen some of their newly won holdings. One such move was to begin construction of an airfield on Guadalcanal in the Solomons, to be part of a ring of defenses around Rabaul, a stronghold on New Britain. Knowledge of the move on Guadalcanal prompted the Allied forces to start a limited offensive, the beginning of amphibious assault in the Pacific. The struggle for Guadalcanal was hard-fought, and it was not until January, 1943, that the Japanese lost possession of the island. Meanwhile other Allied and Japanese forces became locked in combat in Papua, in New Guinea. It was another case of evenly matched forces engaged on a narrow front, a struggle which the Allies won early in 1943.

During 1943 the strategy of the war against Japan began to come into focus. Instead of fighting along one route toward Japan, the Allies would move along two. General MacArthur was a vigorous supporter of the approach primarily along large land masses such as New Guinea and the Philippines. The Navy would play a supporting role. While he did not gain the publicity accorded MacArthur, Admiral Nimitz was an able supporter of the other approach. This was through the central Pacific. It was argued that by judicious island-hopping and by-passing of Japanese forces, advance would be faster, less costly and surer.

The result was a combination of the two approaches. MacArthur began the slow march along the northern coast of New Guinea on the way to the Philippines. Under his command also the invasion of New Georgia and Bougainville in the Solomons formed part of the effort to isolate Rabaul.

Nimitz's operations in the Central Pacific started with attacks on the Gilberts after making the Hawaiian Islands the training ground for the Pacific advance. Of two islands attacked in the Gilberts,

Tarawa proved to be the more difficult to take, and the invaders learned hard lessons of amphibious assault. This experience helps explain the smoother operations which followed in the assault on the Marshalls which followed early in 1944. Nimitz decided to skip four Japanese-held atolls and attack one, Kwajalein. The attack was so successful that Nimitz ordered the seizure of another atoll, Eniwetok, which was in American hands by the end of February. Not long afterwards, forces under MacArthur seized two islands in the Admiralties, which later provided excellent bases for support of both lines of advance.

In 1944, the dual approach continued as MacArthur's forces advanced on Hollandia, and Nimitz's forces invaded the Marianas. The attack on Hollandia was perhaps more important in the war of attrition than it was strategically, but it was a significant part of the move along great land masses. Continuing, MacArthur's forces attacked Japanese positions on Wakde and Biak, islands off the coast of New Guinea. Although the way was difficult, the Allied forces gradually reached their objectives.

In March, 1944, the Joint Chiefs of Staff decided on the invasion of the Marianas. There was the matter of regaining Guam, and also the islands were needed for bases from which the new long-range bombers, the B-29s, could operate against Japan. The action on Saipan in the middle of June, 1944, was bitterly contested, and victory was not won until July 9. During the course of the campaign U.S. carrier forces inflicted a sharp defeat on the Japanese Navy and Air Force in the Battle of the Philippine Sea, sometimes called the Marianas Turkey Shoot. Although the island of Tinian fell easily, Japanese forces put up a stiffer struggle on Guam before losing.

Some of the hardest fighting in the Pacific took place on Peleliu in the Palaus. Admiral Halsey had wanted to by-pass the Palaus, but Admiral Nimitz accepted the view that their conquest was necessary for the campaign planned for the Philippines.

After New Guinea, General MacArthur needed only one more island before advancing on the Philippines. This was Morotai, attacked September 15, 1944. Poor landing conditions hurt the invader more than did the enemy, and the island turned out to be a disappointment since good airfields could not readily be constructed on it.

Americans returned to the Philippines on the island of Leyte, midway in the archipelago. The assault was a large and highly complicated operation, making use of experience gained in months of fighting. The accompanying naval Battle for Leyte Gulf was of great significance in that this victory gave the Allies control of the Pacific Ocean. The hard-fought conquest of Leyte doomed Japanese control of Luzon and the rest of the Philippines although the Japanese by no means laid down their arms. Suicide tactics appearing on a large scale hampered but did not stop the invasion of Luzon in January, 1945. Some twenty thousand Japanese held out for a month in Manila, and it took until June 30 for the major portions of Luzon to come under Allied control.

In the Pacific, the next point of attack was Iwo Jima in the Bonins about half-way between the Marianas and Japan. This was an island that could not be by-passed, and in February skilled opponents met on this rough little spot in the Pacific. Fighting from concealed positions, the Japanese put up a stubborn defense; they were seldom visible and retired with their wounded and dead into caves and tunnels. Major resistance ended by the middle of March, although fighting continued for some time thereafter.

The next objective was Okinawa, much larger and nearer Japan. The Japanese could be expected to make every effort to hold this defensive position. The assault on Okinawa was the largest amphibious operation of the Pacific war and engaged some 183,000 troops. Suicidal tactics featured Japanese attempts to prevent the landings, as several hundred Kamikaze planes at a time headed for the island. The depths of Japanese desperation can be seen in the fact that the 69,000 ton *Yamato*, the world's largest battleship, left Japan to shell American beachheads on Okinawa without enough fuel for the return trip. American planes sank it on the way.

Landing on the narrow middle of Okinawa, the invaders cut the island in two and gradually isolated and defeated the Japanese forces, the bulk of which were in the southern part of the island. Conquest of Okinawa was an important part of the war of attrition against Japan. It would also provide bases of operation should invasion of Japan become necessary.

Important in the war of attrition also, if not in the strategic approach to Japan, were operations in the China-Burma-India theater. At one time it was hoped that China might become the base for air attacks on Japan, but with the arrival of B-29s it appeared that the Marianas were preferable. The theater was a frustrating experience for men like General Joseph W. Stilwell, who had to deal with Chinese leaders, but at least many Japanese troops were prevented from fighting elsewhere.

While the Allies were advancing across the Pacific and into the Philippines, the mainland of Japan was coming under increasing air attacks. These were of two sorts, B-29 raids and carrier air attacks. The first B-29 raids from Saipan hit Japan on November 24, 1944. For the next three months, the raids concentrated on high-level precision attacks on aircraft industries. In January, 1945, the XXI Bomber Command received a new and more aggressive commander, General Curtis E. Lemay, who early in February introduced fire bombs against leading cities of Japan. These raids began in earnest in March. The raid on Tokyo on March 8 was the most devastating air attack the world had seen. A million persons were rendered homeless, 83,793 were killed and 40,918 injured. The purpose of such attacks was to force surrender without invasion. As such raids continued, carrier aircraft joined to make air attack a night-and-day affair. Meanwhile, American submarines were making a graveyard of the seas around Japan.

The final attempt to reach surrender without invasion came in the form of the atom bomb. The Potsdam Proclamation failed to induce the Japanese to surrender, and on August 6, 1945, an atom bomb dropped on Hiroshima, giving a terrible example of the devastating power of the new weapon. The single bomb killed between 70,000 and 80,000 people. Two days later Soviet Russia entered the war against Japan, and one day after that a second atom bomb fell on Nagasaki, causing 35,000 dead and 60,000 injured.

Some Japanese leaders had been attempting to work toward peace, but their efforts failed. The principal intermediary, Soviet Russia, was not interested, the Japanese Government was not clearly enough identified with some of the peace feelers, the United States did not make it sufficiently understood that the emperor would not be removed and Japanese leaders were reluctant to admit publicly that the war was being lost. These were a few of the factors that complicated and perhaps delayed the ending of the war. After the atom bombs and Soviet Russia's declaration of war, the Japanese Emperor entered the picture and supported a proposal for peace which finally brought World War II to an end in the Pacific.

35. Military and Diplomatic Documents

a. *Military Directives*

March 30, 1942

DIRECTIVE TO THE SUPREME COMMANDER IN THE SOUTHWEST PACIFIC AREA

BY AGREEMENT AMONG THE GOVERNMENTS OF AUSTRALIA, NEW ZEALAND, UNITED KINGDOM, AND THE UNITED STATES.

1. The SOUTHWEST PACIFIC AREA has been constituted as defined in Annex One. Definitions of other areas of the PACIFIC Theater are as shown therein.

2. You are designated as the Supreme Commander of the SOUTHWEST PACIFIC Area, and of all armed forces which the governments concerned have assigned, or may assign to this area.

3. As Supreme Commander you are not eligible to command directly any national force.

4. In consonance with the basic strategic policy of the governments concerned your operations will be designed to accomplish the following:

a. Hold the key military regions of Australia as bases for future offensive action against Japan, and in order to check the Japanese conquest of the SOUTHWEST PACIFIC AREA.

b. Check the enemy advance toward Australia and its essential lines of communication by the destruction of enemy combatant, troop, and supply ships, aircraft, and bases in Eastern Malaysia and the New Guinea-Bismarck-Solomon Islands Region.

SOURCE: Reprinted in Louis Morton, *Strategy and Command: The First Two Years* (Washington, 1962), pp. 614–615. Reprinted by permission of the Department of the Army.

c. Exert economic pressure on the enemy by destroying vessels transporting raw materials from the recently conquered territories to Japan.

d. Maintain our position in the Philippine Islands.

e. Protect land, sea, and air communications within the SOUTHWEST PACIFIC Area, and its close approaches.

f. Route shipping in the SOUTHWEST PACIFIC Area.

g. Support the operations of friendly forces in the PACIFIC OCEAN Area and in the INDIAN Theater.

h. Prepare to take the offensive.

5. You will not be responsible for the internal administration of the respective forces under your command, but you are authorized to direct and coordinate the creation and development of administrative facilities and the broad allocation of war materials.

6. You are authorized to control the issue of all communiques concerning the forces under your command.

7. When task forces of your command operate outside the SOUTHWEST PACIFIC Area, coordination with forces assigned to the areas in which operating will be effected by the Joint Chiefs of Staff, or the Combined Chiefs of Staff, as appropriate.

8. Commanders of all armed forces within your Area will be immediately informed by their respective governments that, from a date to be notified, all orders and instructions issued by you in conformity with this directive will be considered by such commanders as emanating from their respective governments.

9. Your staff will include officers assigned by the respective governments concerned, based upon requests made directly to the national commanders of the various forces in your Area.

10. The governments concerned will exercise direction of operations in the SOUTHWEST PACIFIC Area as follows:

a. The Combined Chiefs of Staff will exercise general jurisdiction over grand strategic policy and over such related factors as are necessary for proper implementation, including the allocation of forces and war materials.

b. The Joint U.S. Chiefs of Staff will exercise jurisdiction over all matters pertaining to operational strategy. The Chief of Staff, U.S. Army will act as the Executive Agency for the Joint U.S. Chiefs of Staff. All instructions to you will be issued by or through him.

XIV Corps' Field Order No. 1,
16 January 1943

HQ XIV CORPS,
APO #709
1200 16 Jan 43

1. a. See current Summary.

b. See Operations Overlay.

2. This Corps, from present positions, will attack to the west at a time and on a date to be announced later, seize the high ground in the vicinity of (68.0–201.8)–(67–200)–(65–198) to the south thereof, and be prepared to continue the attack to the northwest. See Operations Overlay.

3. a. 2d Marine Division (less 2d and 8th Marine Regiments), one (1) Infantry regiment American Division attached, will attack to the west and seize that part of the Corps objective within its zone of action. It will maintain connection and contact with the 25th Infantry Division during the attack, will cover its left (south) flank, and will assist the 25th Infantry Division by fire in taking the high ground in the vicinity of (66.0–198.5). It will protect the shore line from the MATANIKAU RIVER (excl) to the objective (incl) against any attempted enemy landing.

b. 25th Infantry Division will attack to the west and seize that part of the Corps objective within its zone of action. It will envelop or turn the enemy's right (south) flank and will protect the left (south) flank of the Corps.

c. The Perimeter Defense (less one (1) Infantry regiment American Division), with 2d and 8th Marine Regiments attached, will intensify patrolling to insure protection of airfields and rear installations of the Corps. It will extend beach protection to insure against possible enemy landings as far west as the MATANIKAU RIVER (incl). One (1) Infantry regiment will be kept immediately available for use by the Corps Commander in support of the

Source: Reprinted in John Miller, Jr., Guadalcanal: The First Offensive (United States Army in World War II: The War in the Pacific) (Washington, 1949), pp. 362–363. Reprinted by permission of the Department of the Army.

attack or in defense of rear areas; it will be committed to action only on orders of the Corps Commander. A second regiment of Infantry will be so utilized that it can be assembled in two and one half (2½) hours for use by the Corps Commander.

d. 147th Infantry—will prepare to cover KOLI POINT AIR-FIELD with two (2) rifle companies reinforced. The remainder of the 147th Infantry at KOLI POINT will await orders there in Corps reserve and will be committed to action only on orders of the Corps Commander.

e. Artillery.

(1) Americal Division Artillery, with 10th Marines (less two (2) battalions) (75–mm Pack How), Battery A 1st Marine Amphibious Corps (155–mm How), and Battery F 244th Coast Artillery (155–mm Gun) attached, will support the attack of the 2d Marine Division. It will be prepared to reinforce the fires in the zone of action of the 25th Infantry Division with two (2) battalions of light artillery and one (1) battalion of medium artillery.

(2) Two (2) battalions 10th Marines (75–mm How) will remain on Perimeter Defense.

(3) 25th Infantry Division Artillery will be prepared to reinforce the fires in the zone of action of the 2nd Marine Division with two (2) battalions of light-artillery and one (1) battalion of medium artillery.

(4) A fifteen (15) minute artillery, sea, and air preparation will precede the attack. Thereafter, artillery, without instructions from other headquarters, will promptly take under fire targets of opportunity.

f. 2d Marine Air Wing will support the attack and will engage targets of opportunity as indicated by organic air surveillance and this headquarters, paying particular attention to enemy artillery and concentrations of enemy troops. Requests for air-ground support missions will be transmitted to the AC of S, G–3, this headquarters.

g. Naval gunfire support, utilizing such naval vessels as are available, will be coordinated by the Corps Artillery Officer. This support will include an initial preparation of (15) minutes, commencing at H-15, in the areas (67.8–201.8)–(67.5–201.0) (66.8–

200.2) and (67.8–201.8)–(66.2–200.0), followed by missions on targets of opportunity as far west as Visale Mission as indicated by air surveillance, shore surveillance, and this headquarters.

> h.   (1) An artillery, sea, and air preparation of fifteen (15) minutes will precede the attack. Thereafter, these units will fire on targets of opportunity.
>
>   (2) Isolated points of enemy resistance will be contained and by-passed; they will be reduced later. Maximum use will be made of artillery and air support in effecting reductions.
>
>   (3) All Infantry units will keep their supporting artillery and the AC of S, G–3, this headquarters, advised of their locations at all times in order that targets of opportunity may be fired upon promptly. . . .

b. Differing Military Views

MAKIN FOR NAURU

Nauru was an uplifted circular atoll with no lagoon, no protection except on the lee side, a narrow beach and inshore of that a cliff about 100 ft. high. It lay about 380 [nautical] miles west of Tarawa toward Truk. The operation called for would have divided our fleet into two parts, out of supporting distance of each other, each one engaged in conducting a difficult amphibious operation. The Japanese Fleet at Truk was about equal to our own in strength, and, except for our submarines, we had no means of knowing what it was doing. I protested against this situation, but got no change. The more we studied the problem of how to capture Nauru, the less we liked it. Finally, Gen. Holland Smith wrote a letter recommending we not take Nauru. Admiral Turner and I both added our endorsements concurring, and I handed it to Admiral Nimitz at his morning conference, at which Admiral King and Admiral C. M. Cooke were present (about 25 Sept). Admiral King read the letter and then asked me what I proposed to take instead of Nauru. I replied "Makin," and said that Makin was in

SOURCE: Reprinted in Morton, *Strategy and Command*, p. 523.

the direction we were going and would be of much more value to us than Nauru, that Nauru had been of value to the Japanese, but it would not be after we took the Gilberts. After some discussion Admiral King agreed to the change, and recommended it to the JCS. (Ltr, Spruance to Hoover, 17 Jul 59.)

KWAJALEIN FOR WOTJE AND MALOELAP

I argued as strongly as I could with Admiral Nimitz against Kwajalein, proposing instead Wotje and Maloelap. My argument was based . . . on the insecurity of our line of communications in to Kwajalein after the withdrawal of the Pacific Fleet. . . . With the air pipe line through Eniwetok open back to Japan and with the activity which had been shown by Japanese air in the Marshalls in their attacks on our fleet forces during the Gilberts operation, I felt that our support shipping moving into Kwajalein would have a tough time of it. In my arguments I was supported by Admiral Turner and General Holland Smith, but I was overruled by Admiral Nimitz. (Ltr, Spruance to Isely, 3 Jul 49.)

IWO JIMA AND OKINAWA FOR FORMOSA

When Admirals King and Nimitz visited Saipan about 12 July 1944—shortly after the end of organized resistance—Admiral King asked me for my ideas on my next operation. At this time the Philippines campaign had not yet been definitely decided upon, but I expected to be relieved by Admiral Halsey after the completion of the Marianas operation, which still involved the capture of Guam and Tinian. My reply to Admiral King was that I would like to take Okinawa.

Before I arrived back in Pearl Harbor in the *Indianapolis* about 4

SOURCE: Reprinted in Philip A. Crowl and Edmund G. Love, *Seizure of the Gilberts and Marshalls* (*United States Army in World War II: The War in the Pacific*) (Washington, 1955), pp. 168–169. Reprinted by permission of the Department of the Army.

SOURCE: Reprinted in Charles S. Nichols, Jr. and Henry I. Shaw, Jr., *Okinawa: Victory in the Pacific* (Marine Corps Monographs, 15) (Washington, 1955), pp. 16–17.

September 1944, I gave considerable thought to the question of the next operation for the Fifth Fleet. I came to the conclusion that Okinawa was the proper objective, but that Iwo Jima would have to be captured first. On reporting to Admiral Nimitz, he informed me that my next operation would be Amoy and Formosa. I then recommended that we take first Iwo Jima and then Okinawa instead, but was told that the decision had already been made for Formosa, and that, as soon as I was ready, I should fly to California for about two weeks' leave.

Shortly before I was due to return to Pearl Harbor, I received orders to delay and to attend the CominChCinCPac conference in San Francisco about 28 September. It was at this conference that Admiral Nimitz recommended to Admiral King the substitution of Iwo Jima and Okinawa for Amoy and Formosa. This change was necessary because General Buckner had said he did not have enough service troops for an objective as large as Formosa, but he could handle Okinawa. The Marines had said they could take Iwo Jima. The paper submitting Admiral Nimitz' recommendations for the change was, I believe, prepared by his War Plans Officer, Captain Forrest Sherman. It was the clear and logical presentation needed to overcome Admiral King's strong belief in the value of Formosa.[1]

c. MacArthur Speaks

It is my opinion that purely military considerations demand the reoccupation of the Philippines in order to cut the enemy's communications to the south and to secure a base for our further advance. Even if this were not the case and unless military factors demanded another line of action it would in my opinion be necessary to reoccupy the Philippines.

The Philippines is American Territory where our unsupported forces were destroyed by the enemy. Practically all of the 17,000,-

SOURCES: Reprinted in Cannon, *Leyte*, p. 4; Albert C. Wedemeyer, *Wedemeyer Reports!* (New York, 1958), pp. 240–241. Reprinted by permission of the author.

1. Adm R. A. Spruance Ltr to CMC, 28Sept54.

000 Filipinos remain loyal to the United States and are undergoing the greatest privation and suffering because we have not been able to support or succor them. We have a great national obligation to discharge.

Moreover, if the United States should deliberately bypass the Philippines, leaving our prisoners, nationals, and loyal Filipinos in enemy hands without an effort to retrieve them at earliest moment, we would incur the gravest psychological reaction. We would admit the truth of Japanese propaganda to the effect that we had abandoned the Filipinos and would not shed American blood to redeem them; we would undoubtedly incur the open hostility of that people; we would probably suffer such loss of prestige among all the peoples of the Far East that it would adversely affect the United States for many years. . . .

From a broad strategic standpoint I am convinced that the best course of offensive action in the Pacific is a movement from Australia through New Guinea to Mindanao. This movement can be supported by land based aircraft which is utterly essential and will immediately cut the enemy lines from Japan to his conquered territory to the southward. By contrast a movement through the mandated islands will be a series of amphibious attacks with the support of carrier based aircraft against objectives defended by naval units and ground troops supported by land based aviation. Midway stands as an example of the hazards of such operations. Moreover, no vital strategic objective is reached until the series of amphibious frontal attacks succeeds in reaching Mindanao. The factors upon which the old ORANGE plan was based have been greatly altered by the hostile conquests of Malaya and the Netherlands East Indies and by the availability of Australia as a base.

d. Combined Chiefs of Staff Report to Truman and Churchill

TOP SECRET   BABELSBERG, July 24, 1945
Enclosure to C.C.S. 900/3

REPORT TO THE PRESIDENT AND PRIME MINISTER OF THE AGREED
  SUMMARY OF CONCLUSIONS REACHED BY THE COMBINED CHIEFS
  OF STAFF AT THE "TERMINAL" CONFERENCE

1. The agreed summary of conclusions reached at the TERMINAL Conference is submitted herewith.

I. OVER-ALL OBJECTIVE

2. In conjunction with other Allies to bring about at the earliest possible date the unconditional surrender of Japan.

II. OVER-ALL STRATEGIC CONCEPT FOR THE PROSECUTION OF THE WAR

3. In cooperation with other Allies to bring about at the earliest possible date the defeat of Japan by: lowering Japanese ability and will to resist by establishing sea and air blockades, conducting intensive air bombardment, and destroying Japanese air and naval strength; invading and seizing objectives in the Japanese home islands as the main effort; conducting such operations against objectives in other than the Japanese home islands as will contribute to the main effort; establishing absolute military control of Japan; and liberating Japanese-occupied territory if required.

4. In cooperation with other Allies to establish and maintain, as necessary, military control of Germany and Austria.

III. BASIC UNDERTAKINGS AND POLICIES FOR THE PROSECUTION OF THE WAR

5. The following basic undertakings are considered fundamental to the prosecution of the war:—

a. Maintain the security and war-making capacity of the Western Hemisphere and the British Commonwealth as necessary for the fulfillment of the strategic concept.

b. Support the war-making capacity of our forces in all areas, with first priority given to those forces in or designated for employment in combat areas in the war against Japan.

c. Maintain vital overseas lines of communication.

6. In order to attain the over-all objective, first priority in the provision of forces and resources of the United States and Great Britain, including reorientation from the European Theater to the

SOURCE: *Foreign Relations, The Conference of Berlin (The Potsdam Conference)* II: 1462–1464, 1468–1469.

Pacific and Far East, will be given to meeting requirements of task necessary to the execution of the over-all strategic concept and to the basic undertakings fundamental to the prosecution of the war.

The invasion of Japan and operations directly connected therewith are the supreme operations in the war against Japan; forces and resources will be allocated on the required scale to assure that invasion can be accomplished at the earliest practicable date. No other operations will be undertaken which hazard the success of, or delay these main operations.

7. The following additional tasks will be undertaken in order to assist in the execution of the over-all strategic concept:—

a. Encourage Russian entry into the war against Japan. Provide such aid to her war-making capacity as may be necessary and practicable in connection therewith.

b. Undertake such measures as may be necessary and practicable in order to aid the war effort of China as an effective ally against Japan.

c. Provide assistance to such of the forces of liberated areas as can fulfill an active and effective role in the present war in accordance with the over-all strategic concept. Within the limits of our available resources assist co-belligerents to the extent they are able to employ this assistance in the present war. Having regard to the successful accomplishment of basic undertakings, to provide such supplies to the liberated areas as will effectively contribute to the capacity of the United Nations to prosecute the war against Japan.

d. In cooperation with other Allies conduct operations, if required, to liberate enemy-occupied areas.

IV. THE WAR AGAINST JAPAN

Strategic Direction of the War

8. We have discussed the strategic direction of the war against Japan and have agreed as follows:—

a. The control of operational strategy in the Pacific Theater will remain in the hands of the United States Chiefs of Staff.

b. The United States Chiefs of Staff will provide the British Chiefs of Staff with full and timely information as to their future plans and intentions.

c. The United States Chiefs of Staff will consult the British Chiefs of Staff on matters of general strategy on the understanding that in the event of disagreement the final decision on the action to be taken lie with the United States Chiefs of Staff.

d. In the event the British Chiefs of Staff should decide that they cannot commit British troops in support of a decision made by the United States Chiefs of Staff as indicated in c. above, the British Chiefs of Staff will give to the United States Chiefs of Staff such advance notice of their decision as will permit them to make timely rearrangements.

e. In the event the U. S. S. R. enters the war against Japan, the strategy to be pursued should be discussed between the parties concerned.

Operations in the Pacific

9. We have taken note of the plans and operations proposed by the United States Chiefs of Staff in Appendix "A."

10. We have considered the scope and nature of British participation in operations in the Pacific area. Our conclusions are as follows:

a. The British Pacific Fleet will participate as at present planned.

b. A British very long range bomber force of 10 squadrons, increasing to 20 squadrons when more airfields become available, will participate. There is little prospect that airfield space for more than 10 squadrons of this force will become available before 1 December 1945 at the earliest.

c. We have agreed in principle that a Commonwealth land force and, if possible, a small tactical air force, should take part in the final phase of the war against Japan, subject to the satisfactory resolution of operational and other problems. In addition, some units of the British East Indies Fleet may also take part.

11. In connection with paragraph 10 c. above, we have agreed that the appropriate British commanders and staff should visit Admiral Nimitz and General MacArthur and draw up with them a plan for submission to the Combined Chiefs of Staff.

PLANS AND OPERATIONS IN THE PACIFIC

1. In conformity with the over-all objective to bring about the unconditional surrender of Japan at the earliest possible date, the United States Chiefs of Staff have adopted the following concept of operations for the main effort in the Pacific:

a. From bases in Okinawa, Iwo Jima, Marianas, and the Philippines to intensify the blockade and air bombardment of Japan in order to create a situation favorable to:

b. An assault on Kyushu for the purpose of further reducing Japanese capabilities by containing and destroying major enemy forces and further intensifying the blockade and air bombardment in order to establish a tactical condition favorable to:

c. The decisive invasion of Honshu.

2. We have curtailed our projected expansion in the Ryukyus by deferring indefinitely the seizure of Miyako Jima and Kikai Jima. Using the resources originally provided for Miyako and Kikai, we have accelerated the development of Okinawa. By doing this, a greater weight of effort will more promptly be brought to bear against Japan and the risk of becoming involved in operations which might delay the seizure of Kyushu is avoided.

3. In furtherance of the accomplishment of the over-all objectives, we have directed:

a. The invasion of Kyushu.

b. The continuation of operations for securing and maintaining control of sea communications to and in the western Pacific as are required for the accomplishment of the over-all objective.

c. The defeat of the remaining Japanese in the Philippines by such operations as can be executed without prejudice to the over-all objective.

d. The seizure of Balikpapan. (This operation is now approaching successful completion.)

e. The continuance of strategic air operations to support the accomplishment of the over-all objective.

4. Planning and preparation for the campaign in Japan subsequent to the invasion of Kyushu are continuing on the basis of

meeting the target date for the invasion of Honshu. This planning is premised on the belief that defeat of the enemy's armed forces in the Japanese homeland is a prerequisite to unconditional surrender, and that such a defeat will establish the optimum prospect of capitulation by Japanese forces outside the main Japanese islands. We recognize the possibility also that our success in the main islands may not obviate the necessity of defeating Japanese forces elsewhere; decision as to steps to be taken in this eventuality must await further developments.

5. We are keeping under continuing review the possibility of capitalizing at small cost upon Japanese military deterioration and withdrawals in the China Theater, without delaying the supreme operations.

6. We have directed the preparation of plans for the following:

a. Keeping open a sea route to Russian Pacific ports.

b. Operations to effect an entry into Japan proper for occupational purposes in order to take immediate advantage of favorable circumstances such as a sudden enemy collapse or surrender.

e. Japanese Military Plans

GENERAL OUTLINE OF POLICY OF FUTURE WAR GUIDANCE, ADOPTED BY LIAISON CONFERENCE, 7 MARCH 1942, AND REPORT OF PRIME MINISTER AND CHIEFS OF STAFF TO EMPEROR
13 MARCH 1942

1. In order to bring BRITAIN to submission and to demoralize the UNITED STATES, positive measures shall be taken by seizing opportunities to expand our acquired war gains, and by building a political and military structure capable of withstanding a protracted war.

2. By holding the occupied areas and major communication lines, and by expediting the development and utilization of key

SOURCE: Reprinted in Morton, *Strategy and Command*, pp. 611–613.

resources for national defense; efforts shall be made to establish a self-sufficient structure, and to increase the nation's war potential.

3. More positive and definite measures of war guidance shall be adopted by taking the following situations into consideration: Our national power, the progress of operations, the German-Soviet war situation, the relations between the UNITED STATES and the SOVIET UNION, and the trend in CHUNGKING.

4. Our policy toward the SOVIET UNION shall be based on the "Plan for Expediting the Termination of the War against the UNITED STATES, BRITAIN, the NETHERLANDS, and CHIANG Kai-shek," adopted on 5 Nov 41; and the "Measures to be Immediately Effected in Line with the Development of the Situation," adopted on 10 Jan 42. However, under the present circumstances, no efforts shall be made to mediate a peace between GERMANY and the SOVIET UNION.

5. Our policy toward CHUNGKING shall be based on the "Matters Concerning Measures to be taken toward CHUNG-KING, in Line with the Development of the Situation," adopted on 24 Dec 41.

6. Cooperation with GERMANY and ITALY shall be based on the "Plan for Expediting the Termination of the War against the UNITED STATES, BRITAIN, the NETHERLANDS and CHIANG Kai-shek," adopted on 15 Nov 41.

Report to the Throne

We humbly report to Your Majesty on behalf of the Imperial General Headquarters and the Government.

At this point, when our initial operations are about to come to a favorable end by dint of the august virtue of Your Majesty, the Imperial General Headquarters and the Government have, after a careful appraisal, since the latter part of February, of our acquired war gains and their effect, the changes in the world situation, and the present war potentialities of our Empire, agreed on the "General Outline on Future War Guidance." We will now give our explanations.

1. Regarding the general outline on war guidance to be effected hereafter in the war against the UNITED STATES and BRITAIN:

Various measures must be planned and executed in anticipation of a protracted war. It will not only be most difficult to defeat the UNITED STATES and BRITAIN in a short period, but, the war cannot be brought to an end through compromise.

It is essential to further expand the political and military advantages achieved through glorious victories since the opening of hostilities, by utilizing the present war situations to establish a political and strategic structure capable of withstanding a protracted war. We must take every possible step, within the limits of our national power, to force the UNITED STATES and BRITAIN to remain on the defensive. Any definite measure of vital significance to be effected in this connection will be given thorough study, and will be presented to Your Majesty for approval each time.

2. Regarding the need for building national power and fighting power for the successful prosecution of a protracted war.

We deem it highly essential to constantly maintain resilience in our national defense, and build up the nation's war potential so that we will be capable of taking the steps necessary to cope with the progress of situation.

If a nation should lose its resilience in national defense while prosecuting a war, and become unable to rally from an enemy blow, the result would be short of her desired goal, no matter what victory she might achieve in the process. This is amply proved in the precious lessons learned from the annals of war.

Consequently, in our Empire's war guidance policy, we have especially emphasized that, while taking steps to bring the enemy to submission, we must fully build up the nation's war potential to cope with a protracted war.

3. Regarding the adoption of a new and more positive measure of war guidance.

We have made it clear that the question of whether to adopt new and more positive measures for war guidance for the attainment of the objective of the Greater East Asia War should be decided after careful study, not only of the war gains acquired so far, but other factors of extensive and profound significance; such as, the enemy's national power and ours, especially the increase in the fighting power on both sides; the progress of our operations, our relations with the SOVIET UNION and CHINA, the German-Soviet war, and various other factors.

By "more positive measures of war guidance" we mean such measures as the invasion of INDIA and AUSTRALIA.

4. Regarding the measures to be immediately taken toward the SOVIET UNION.

We have made it clear that the measures to be taken toward the SOVIET UNION will be based on the established policy which was adopted earlier at a liaison conference. The essentials of that policy are as follows:

a. Utmost efforts shall be made to prevent the expansion of hostilities.

b. JAPAN shall endeavor to the utmost to prevent war with the SOVIET UNION while operations are being conducted in the Southern Area.

c. While maintaining peace between JAPAN and the SOVIET UNION, efforts shall be made to prevent the UNITED STATES and BRITAIN from strengthening their cooperation with the SOVIET UNION, and to alienate the latter from the former, if possible. However, this does not imply that our military preparations against the SOVIET UNION will be neglected, and it is our belief that all possible operations preparations should be made to achieve a quick and decisive victory in case of war.

With regard to the peace between GERMANY and the SOVIET UNION, not only does a compromise seem utterly hopeless, under the present circumstances, but we fear that our mediatory efforts at this point would be detrimental to Japanese-German relations, and would also mean risking a complication in Japanese-Soviet relations. Consequently, we have made it clear that we have no intention of taking any positive steps toward mediation.

5. Regarding the measures to be immediately taken toward Chungking:

We have made it clear that measures toward Chungking will be based on the policy which was adopted at the earlier conference that, "taking advantage of the restlessness in the Chungking Regime which was caused by our application of strong pressure on a vulnerable spot of theirs, our measures toward Chungking shall be shifted, at a proper time, from intelligence activities to activities to bring the regime to submission. The time and method therefore shall be decided at a liaison conference."

Meanwhile, the campaign in BURMA is progressing faster than

originally expected, and RANGOON is already in our hands. We believe that our progress in BURMA is already having serious effects on the Chungking Regime, but since we greatly fear that any attempt to bring the Chungking Regime to submission, at too early a stage, would produce an adverse result, our intention is to postpone it to a date that will be decided later.

6. Regarding measures to be taken toward GERMANY and ITALY.

Since we keenly realized that strengthening cooperation with GERMANY and ITALY will become increasingly necessary to achieve our war aims, we have decided that we must adhere closely to the established policy regarding cooperation with GERMANY and ITALY.

We hereby respectfully report to Your Majesty.

> 13 Mar 42
> Prime Minister TOJO Hideki
> Chief of the Naval General Staff NAGANO Osami
> Chief of the Army General Staff SUGIYAMA Gen

Imperial Headquarters Plan, March 1942

1. To aim at subjugating England first and then undermining America's will to fight. For this purpose, to endeavor to exploit the fruits of our initial victories and erect an impregnable defense, politically as well as militarily, to cope with a protracted war, devising further offensive strategies at an opportune momemt.

2. To establish a self-supporting system and augment the nation's strength to prosecute the war by consolidating the occupied regions, securing the lines of communication, and exploiting the important resources required for our defense.

3. Detailed strategies for the conduct of the offensive to be worked out in due time in accordance with the progress of operations, development of the Russo-German war, the trend of relations between the Soviet Union and the United States, and the attitude of the Chungking regime.

Source: Quoted in Toshikazu Kase, *Journey to the "Missouri,"* (New Haven, 1950), pp. 104–105. Reprinted by permission of Yale University Press.

4. As regards the Soviet Union, to continue the policy of preserving tranquillity in the north, endeavoring at the same time to prevent the strengthening of the ties between the Soviet Union on the one hand and Great Britain and the United States on the other.

5. To try through military pressure and political maneuvers to bring about the defection of the Chungking regime.

6. Policy toward Germany and Italy was decided upon prior to the outbreak of the war. This policy to remain unaltered, namely, that the three powers will cooperate in bringing about the speedy downfall of England and will, parallel with this, endeavor to undermine the morale of the United States.

f. Combat Conditions: Philippines

LIFE ON CORREGIDOR

Under the deepening shadow of death life on Corregidor took on a faster, more intense tempo. The smallest and most simple pleasures became sought after and treasured as they became increasingly rare and dangerous—an uninterrupted cigarette, a cold shower, a stolen biscuit, a good night's sleep in the open air.

There was a heightened feeling that life was to be lived from day to day, without illusions of an ultimate victory. Many sought forgetfulness in gambling. There was no other way to spend the accumulated pay that bulged in their pockets and they rattled the dice or played endless bridge, rummy and poker.

Jam sessions attracted great crowds which gathered in the dark and hummed softly or tapped feet to the nostalgic swing of the organ, a haunting guitar, or a low moaning trombone. Sometimes a nurse and her boy friend of the evening would melt into a dance. . . . The eyes of the onlookers would grow soft and thoughtful, while other couples would steal out into the perilous night. . . .

Still others sought the consolations of religion and the symbols

SOURCE: Quoted in Louis Morton, *The Fall of the Philippines* (*United States Army in World War II: The War in the Pacific*) (Washington, 1953), pp. 542–543. Reprinted by permission of the Department of the Army.

of another world, a better world of sweet and eternal peace. The Catholics gathered at dawn in the officers mess of Malinto Tunnel where one of the tables was converted into a simple altar, and kneeling on the bare cement under the high white washed vault they listened devoutly and a little desperately to the same hushed phrases that had been whispered in the Catacombs.[1]

To my terror [he wrote] it began to move toward us. There was a high rocky hill to my right and another to my left. Neither afforded any shelter whatsoever. We began to run hoping to get around the side of the hill. The barrage walked after us at about a pace equal to our own. We rounded the hill and saw in front of us the ruins of the Ordnance warehouses blown up by bombs in December. The ground was heap after heap of concrete chunks and exploded 75 shells and casings. Suddenly the barrage behind us lifted and came down about 400 yds in front of us slightly to our left. We ran to the right. The curtain of fire lifted again and came down on our right moving towards us. Terror and desperation seized us. We were panting, sweating, and scared. It seemed as if the Jap artillery was playing cat and mouse with us. . . .

We ran down the old trolley tracks with barrages or concentrations behind and on both sides of us. Suddenly again up ahead shells began to land. . . . We reached a drainage ditch and threw ourselves in it. Dead leaves had cloaked its depth so that we sank down about 3 feet. It was hot, dirty, and almost smothering. But we were so exhausted by terror and by running that we could only lie there panting and perspiring.[2]

PRISONERS OF WAR
REPORT BY M. MICHEL VERLINDEN,
FORMERLY BELGIAN CONSUL AT MANILA

Conditions in Santo Tomas

The conditions in Santo Tomas should at the first glance be the same for everybody but this is not the case. The most fortunate are those who have friends outside in the Spanish, neutrals, or Filipino

1. Maude R. Williams, The Last Days of Corregidor, Supp., pp. 3–5. This typescript diary is in two parts. A copy is on file in OCMH.
2. Gulick, Memoirs of Btry C, 91st CA (ps), pp. 137–39.

communities. Then come those who have some funds and are able to secure food, etc., from outside contacts and the real unfortunate are those who were stranded in Manila without friends or those residing in the Philippines, whose funds are now exhausted. Most of the people in Santo Tomas have lost from 10 to 50 pounds, [and] the lack of proper diet and their inactivity have rendered them very weak. The morale being different for every individual, the effects of the lack of proper diet and the hardships of being confined react differently on everyone. It is contended that, in general, the women take it better than the men.

When I left Manila, I was urged by many American friends and others to do everything I can to try to convince the American Authorities to do the utmost to evacuate them from the Philippine Islands and I am sure that the majority, if not all, would be willing to leave the country even if they would have to abandon all hopes of recovering their properties.

This will give an idea of the seriousness of the situation there and I am afraid that the conditions during the rainy season have made the situation worse.

It is true that there are some classes for children, conferences, games, entertainment, etc., for the Internees, but this is only done to pass the time away and for nothing else. Living in a room together with 20 or 60 other people makes life very uncomfortable, poor sanitary conditions and poor washing facilities for laundry, etc., also make life very uncomfortable.

TREATMENT OF AMERICAN AND FILIPINO PRISONERS

After the surrender of Bataan the American and Filipino Soldiers were taken to camps near Tarlac and knowledge came from several sources that they were exhausted and that for 36 hours the Japanese did not give them any food whatsoever and they were left without shelter. American nurses and then Filipino nurses offered their services to help those which were sick. These proposals were refused by the Japanese. Some Filipino doctors offered their service but this was also refused. After a few days, I understand that those prisoners in Tarlac received regular meals consisting of fish and

SOURCE: *Foreign Relations* (1942), I: 852–854.

rice, and tea. An American nurse which had seen some of these soldiers told me that they are in pitiful conditions and that she feared that quite a few would not survive unless something was done for them. I have no knowledge that up to the time of my departure that American soldiers and/or officers had been sent away from the Philippines.

THE AMBASSADOR IN THE UNITED KINGDOM WINANT
TO THE SECRETARY OF STATE

LONDON, November 18, 1942—5 PM
[Received 9:46 PM]

The following information regarding prisoners at Fort Santiago and conditions there has been received from Gaston Willoquet.

Approximately 86 persons were arrested by the Japanese upon their entry into Manila and detained at first in Villamor Hall of the University of the Philippines. . . .

The prisoners were incarcerated in wooden cages or cells built in the interior courtyard of Fort Santiago; there were 16 of these cages in all of varying sizes. His cell was about 12 feet by 14 feet, and about 13 ft. high at the far end and in the door there were openings about 4 feet square fitted with wooden slats with interstices between. Toilet facilities consisted of a bucket sunk in the floor at one corner of the cell and a tap of running water in another corner. Empty sacks were the only bedding. During the day the cells were dark, but during the night they were lighted by a small electric light in the ceiling.

Food consisted of a plate of boiled rice three times a day, with very occasionally a little vegetables. The prisoners were not allowed to communicate with anyone outside, nor to receive food from outside. No books, pens or paper were allowed them, and for the first 3 weeks they were not allowed to bathe, to receive clean clothing, or even to wash their own clothes. For the first 3 weeks they were allowed no exercise but thereafter they were allowed 5 minutes exercise in the prison yard where they were permitted to bathe every 2 or 3 days.

The cells were very crowded. Willoquet states that on one occasion the Japanese crowded 26 Filipinos into a cell about 5 feet by 13 feet. No sleep was permitted from 7 AM to 7 PM and conversation was prohibited, although a certain amount of conversation was nevertheless carried on not only with inmates of the same cell but also with inmates of neighboring cells.

With the exception of Vespa, who was apparently terribly beaten, and some of the Filipinos, there was no physical brutality against the prisoners at Fort Santiago, nor were the white prisoners subjected to interrogation while there. Practically all, however, had been interrogated prior to their imprisonment. About the middle of April the members of the Chinese consular staff were seen being led out in bonds and they are believed to have been shot.

Willoquet attributes the imprisonment of the Free French to denunciation by the Vichy French, German, Italian and Spanish Consuls at Manila.

WINANT

g. Combat Conditions

GUADALCANAL

The feelings of the men who suffered the bombardments are expressed by the historian of the 67th Fighter Squadron:

> Almost daily, and almost always at the same time—noon, "Tojo Time"—the bombers came. There would be 18 to 24 of them, high in the sun and in their perfect V-of-V's formation. They would be accompanied by 20 or more Zeroes, cavorting in batches of 3, nearby. Their bombing was accurate, and they would stay in formation and make their bombing run even as they knew the deadly fire from the Grummans would hit any minute.
>
> There was a routine of noises at Tojo Time. First the red and white flag (a captured Japanese rising sun) would go up at the pagoda. That meant scramble. Every airplane that would fly would start up immediately and all would rush for the runway, dodging bomb craters. Often through the swirling dust the ground crews would see a wing drop. That meant another plane had taxied [into] a dud hole or a small crater, indistinct in the tall grass. The first planes to the runway took off first, and two at a time, whether . . . Grummans, dive-bombers or P-400s.
>
> The formations would join later in the air. The P-400s and dive-bombers would fly away to work over the Jap territory. The Grummans would climb for altitude, test-firing their guns on the

SOURCE: Quoted in Miller, *Guadalcanal*, p. 109.

way. The whining of engines at high r.p.m., the chatter of machine guns, and settling dust.

On the ground the men would put in a few more minutes' work, watching the pagoda all the while. Then the black flag would go up. It was amazing how fast the tired and hungry men could sprint. . . . In a moment the field would be deserted.

Then the high, sing-song whine of the bombers would intrude as a new sound, separate from the noise of the climbing Grummans. Only a few moments now. The sing-song would grow louder. Then: swish, swish, swish. And the men would pull the chin straps of their helmets tighter and tense their muscles and press harder against the earth in their foxholes. And pray.

Then: WHAM! (the first one hit) WHAM! (closer) WHAM! (walking right up to your foxhole) . . . WHAAA MM! (Oh Christ!) WHAM! (Thank God, they missed us!) WHAM! (the bombs were walking away) WHAM! (they still shook the earth, and dirt trickled in). WHAM!

It was over. The men jumped out to see if their buddies in the surrounding foxholes had been hit. The anti-aircraft still made a deafening racket. Grass fires were blazing. There was the pop-pop-pop of exploding ammunition in the burning airplanes on the ground. The reek of cordite. Overhead the Grummans dived with piercing screams. And the Jap bombers left smoke trails as they plummeted into [the] sea.

Kwajalein

"The entire island looked as if it had been picked up to 20,000 feet and then dropped."[1]

Peleliu

First Marines *Regimental Narrative* describes the terrain thus:

The ground of Peleliu's western peninsula was the worst ever encountered by the regiment in three Pacific campaigns. Along its center, the rocky spine was heaved up in a contorted mass of decayed coral, strewn with rubble, crags, ridges and gulches thrown together in a confusing maze. There were no roads, scarcely any

Source: Quoted in Crowl and Love, *Seizure of the Gilberts*, p. 232.

1. CINCPAC-CINCPOA Opns in POA, Feb 44, Annex A, p. 35; TF 51 Marshalls Rpt, Incl E, p. 11.

trails. The pock-marked surface offered no secure footing even in the few level places. It was impossible to dig in: the best the men could do was pile a little coral or wood debris around their positions. The jagged rock slashed their shoes and clothes, and tore their bodies every time they hit the deck for safety. Casualties were higher for the simple reason it was impossible to get under the ground away from the Japanese mortar barrages. Each blast hurled chunks of coral in all directions, multiplying many times the fragmentation effect of every shell. Into this the enemy dug and tunnelled like moles; and there they stayed to fight to the death.

General O. P. Smith adds:

Ravines, which on the map and photographs appeared to be steep-sided, actually had sheer cliffs for sides, some of them 50 to 100 feet high. With nothing else on your mind but to cover the distance between two points, walking was difficult. . . . There were dozens of caves and pillboxes worked into the noses of the ridges and up the ravines. It was very difficult to find blind spots as the caves and pillboxes were mutually supporting. . . . These caves and pillboxes housed riflemen, machine gunners, mortars, rockets, and field-pieces. The Japanese technique was to run the piece out of the cave, fire, then run the piece back in the cave before we could react.

Among the few civilian news correspondents who chose to share the fate of the Marines on shore was Robert ("Pepper") Martin, of *Time*, who furnished the following description of what it was like there:

Peleliu is a horrible place. The heat is stifling and rain falls intermittently—the muggy rain that brings no relief, only greater misery. The coral rocks soak up the heat during the day and it is only slightly cooler at night. Marines are in the finest possible physical condition, but they wilted on Peleliu. By the fourth day there were as many casualties from heat prostration as from wounds.

Peleliu is incomparably worse than Guam in its bloodiness, terror, climate and the incomprehensible tenacity of the Japs. For sheer brutality and fatigue, I think it surpasses anything yet seen in the Pacific, certainly from the standpoint of numbers of troops involved and the time taken to make the island secure.

SOURCE: Quoted in Frank O. Hough, *The Assault on Peleliu* (Marine Corps Monographs, 7) (Washington, 1950), pp. 77, 94.

LEYTE

GENERAL HEADQUARTERS
SOUTHWEST PACIFIC AREA
OFFICE OF THE COMMANDER-IN-CHIEF

PROCLAMATION

TO THE PEOPLE OF THE PHILIPPINES:

I have returned. By the grace of Almighty God our forces stand again on Philippine soil—soil consecrated in the blood of our two peoples. We have come, dedicated and committed, to the task of destroying every vestige of enemy control over your daily lives, and of restoring, upon a foundation of indestructible strength, the liberties of your people.

At my side is your President, Sergio Osmena, worthy successor of that great patriot, Manuel Quezon, with members of his cabinet. The seat of your government is now therefore firmly re-established on Philippine soil.

The hour of your redemption is here. Your patriots have demonstrated an unswerving and resolute devotion to the principles of freedom that challenges the best that is written on the pages of human history. I now call upon your supreme effort that the enemy may know from the temper of an aroused and outraged people within that he has a force there to contend with no less violent than is the force committed from without.

Rally to me. Let the indomitable spirit of Bataan and Corregidor lead on. As the lines of battle roll forward to bring you within the zone of operations, rise and strike. Strike at every favorable opportunity. For your homes and hearths, strike! For future generations of your sons and daughters, strike! In the name of your sacred dead, strike! Let no heart be faint. Let every arm be steeled. The guidance of divine God points the way. Follow in His Name to the Holy Grail of righteous victory!

DOUGLAS MacARTHUR.

SOURCE: Quoted in Cannon, *Leyte*, unpaged. Reprinted by permission of the Department of the Army.

The 29th was a day that will be long remembered. . . . Two more Nips were added to the unit's score; . . . the 49 Group's 500th victory. But more important at that time was the fact . . . [that] the . . . road between the strip and the camp collapsed under army traffic. . . . The already long hours were lengthened still more as pilots and men were forced to arise between three and four o'clock in the morning, make their way to the barge at Tacloban, cross to the strip by water and then sweat out the pre-dawn raids. At night, the planes landing at dusk had hardly hit the runway before . . . BOFORS [40-mm antiaircraft guns] went off and the lights went out. Then down to the end of the strip near the gas dumps, and another session of sweating beneath A/A [antiaircraft] awaiting the barge for the trip back to Tacloban and then to camp. Supper was served as late as 10 o'clock . . . a few brave individuals tried an alternate road to the south, swinging out east to White Beach above Dulag and then north along the beach to Tacloban Strip. Japanese snipers soon put a stop to this travel during the hours of darkness.

To add to the "big day"—29 October—the weather observers reported a 50 knot gale on the way. Working after dark, pilots and linemen minus the regular tie downs and using tent ropes and anything available secured the airplanes to jeeps, trucks, trailers and tractors. At night, in camp, the small typhoon hit and with it went three or four tents, occupants of which awoke to find themselves thoroughly drenched and at odds with the world, Leyte in particular.

At 1930 the Japanese launched their final concentrated attack against the airfields. They began to fire at the administration buildings of the Fifth Air Force, and some of the bullets went through the plywood walls of the house of Maj. Gen. Ennis C. Whitehead. "The General ducked a bullet, ordered someone to find out who the blankety-blank was responsible and that he'd blankety-blank better stop or think up a blankety-blank good reason."[1]

A staff officer immediately started to investigate the situation. He got Lt. Col. Paul V. Kaessner of the 8th Aviation Signal Battalion on the telephone. The following conversation is reported to have ensued:

1. Maj Herbert O. Johansen, "Banzai at Burauen," Air Force, Vol. 28, No. 3, March 1945, p. 7.

"Colonel," he said sternly, "you've got to stop that promiscuous firing down there immediately!"

"Like to, sir," answered the colonel, "but the Japs . . ."

"Japs," shouted the staff officer, "that can't be Japs. That fire is coming from our fifties."

"That's right . . . and the Japs are doing the shooting!"

"Where in the hell did the Japs get our machine guns?"

"How in hell should I know, sir?"

"The bullets are coming right through the general's quarters."

"Tell the general to get down on the floor. Incidentally, that yelling you hear is a Banzai raid on our mess hall."[2]

These bearded, mud caked soldiers came out of the mountains exhausted and hungry. Their feet were heavy, cheeks hollow, bodies emaciated, and eyes glazed. They had seen thirty-one comrades mortally wounded, watched fifty-five others lie suffering in muddy foxholes without adequate medical attention. Yet their morale had not changed. It was high when they went in and high when they came out. They were proud that they had rendered invaluable aid to the main forces fighting in ORMOC CORRIDOR by disrupting the Japanese supply lines and preventing strong reinforcements from passing up the ORMOC ROAD. They were proud that they had outfought the Emperor's toughest troops, troops that had been battle trained in Manchuria. They were certain they had killed at least 606 of the enemy and felt that their fire had accounted for many more. And they were proud that this had all been accomplished despite conditions of extreme hardship. Two hundred and forty-one of the battalion's officers and enlisted men were hospitalized for skin disorders, foot ulcers, battle fatigue, and sheer exhaustion.

GUAM

A Marine was already in the cave and had gone to sleep. It was an excellent shelter from the nightly mortar and artillery fire. The Japanese crawled in on top of him and he could not get out. He couldn't use his carbine because they were sitting on it. He stayed there with them all night without them discovering him.

SOURCE: Quoted in Cannon, Leyte, pp. 97–98, 225, 227, 304–305. Reprinted by permission of the Department of the Army.

2. Johansen, "Banzai," p. 7.

They must have thought, jammed against him in the darkness, that he was one of them. Just before daybreak the Japanese left the cave and the Marine got out and scrambled up the bank as the daylight fighting got well underway. I don't remember this Marine's name, but as I recall he had to be evacuated that day as a mental patient. The strain of spending the night packed into the cave with the Japanese drove him insane, at least temporarily.[1]

Iwo Jima

Between these fortifications and the sea lay a wilderness of rocky, cave-studded terrain. An excellent description of this area is contained in the division intelligence report of 5 March:

> . . . During the period the terrain not under our control to the Div's front was scrupulously observed and studied by D-2 observers from various Bn OP's, close inshore from an LCI(G), and from a VMO-4 OY-1. The volcanic, crevice lined area is a tangled conglomeration of torn trees and blasted rocks. Ground observation is restricted to small areas. While there are sundry ridges, depressions and irregularities, most of the crevices of any moment radiate from the direction of Hill 382 to fan out like spokes generally in a southeasterly direction providing a series of cross corridors to our advance and eminently suitable for the enemy's employment of mortars. The general debris caused by our supporting fires provides perfect concealment for snipers and mortar positions. From the air, caves and tracks are observed everywhere, but the enemy's camouflage discipline is flawless and it is the rarest occasion that an AO (Aerial Observer) can locate troops.[2]

As a result of a close study of the enemy's recent defensive action, aided by observation from OI's and air reconnaissance, the following explanation is suggested of the enemy's defense in this Div's Z of A. The enemy remains below ground in his maze of communicating tunnels throughout our preliminary arty fires. When the fire ceases he pushes OI's out of entrances not demolished by our fires. Then choosing a suitable exit he moves as many men and weapons to the surface as he can, depending on the cover

Source: Quoted in O. R. Lodge, *The Recapture of Guam* (Marine Corps Monographs, 12) (Washington, 1954), p. 85.

1. Ltr Col J. S. Letcher to CMC, 14 Mar 47.
2. 4th MarDiv D-2 Periodic Rpt No 62, 5 Mar 45.

and concealment of that area, often as close as 75 yards from our front. As our troops advance toward this point he delivers all the fire at his disposal, rifle, machine gun, and mortar. When he has inflicted sufficient casualties to pin down our advance he then withdraws through his underground tunnels most of his forces, possibly leaving a few machine gunners and mortars. Meanwhile our Bn CO has coordinated his direct support weapons and delivers a concentration of rockets, mortars and artillery. Our tanks then push in, supported by infantry. When the hot spot is overrun we find a handful of dead Japs and few if any enemy weapons. While this is happening, the enemy has repeated the process and another sector of our advance is engaged in a vicious fire fight, and the cycle continues. Supporting indications to these deductions are:

(1) When the hot spot is overrun we find far too few dead enemy to have delivered the fire encountered in overrunning the position;
(2) We find few if any enemy weapons in the position overrun but plenty of empty shell cases;
(3) We find many tunnel entrances, some caved in, all appearing deep and well prepared, some with electric light wires;
(4) During the cycle, close air and OP observation detects no enemy surface movement.[3]

In attacking these positions, no Japanese were to be seen, all being in caves or crevices in the rocks and so disposed as to give an all-around interlocking, ghost-like defense to each small compartment. Attacking troops were subjected to fire from flanks and rear more than from their front. It was always difficult and often impossible to locate exactly where defensive fires originated. The field of fire of the individual Japanese defender in his cave position was often limited to an arc of 10 degrees or less, conversely he was protected from fire except that coming back on this arc. The Japanese smokeless, flashless powder for small arms, always advantageous, was of particular usefulness here. When the position was overrun or threatened, the enemy retreated further into his caves

SOURCE: Quoted in William S. Bartley, *Iwo Jima: Amphibious Epic* (Marine Corps Monographs, 13), (Washington, 1954), pp. 150, 176–177, 190.

3. 4th MarDiv D-2 Periodic Rpt No 63, 6 Mar 45.

where he usually was safe from gunfire, only to pop out again as soon as the occasion warranted unless the cave was immediately blown.[4]

OKINAWA

If the supply problem was difficult before, it was a killer now. That 1,200-foot hill looked like Pike's Peak to the tired, sweaty men who started packing up ammunition and water on their backs. Practically everyone in the 1st Bn headquarters company grabbed as much ammunition as he could carry. A man would walk by carrying a five-gallon water can on his shoulder and the battalion commander would throw a couple of bandoleers of ammunition over the other! . . . The battalion commander, on his way up to the front lines to get a closer look at the situation, packed a water can on his way up. Stretchers also had to be carried up, and all hands coming down the hill were employed as stretcher bearers.

In the midst of the bitter struggle for the Shuri line the troops received almost unbelievable news. Early on 12 April word flashed through the bivouac areas and along the front lines on Okinawa that President Roosevelt had died. The enemy also heard the news, and attempted to capitalize on it. Shortly afterward a Japanese propaganda leaflet was found which stated:

> We must express our deep regret over the death of President Roosevelt. The "American Tragedy" is now raised here at Okinawa with his death. You must have seen 70% of your CV's and 73% of your B's sink or be damaged causing 150,000 casualties. Not only the late President but anyone else would die in the excess of worry to hear such an annihilative damage. The dreadful loss that led your late leader to death will make you orphans on this island. The Japanese special attack corps will sink your vessels to the last destroyer. You will witness it realized in the near future.

SOURCE: Quoted in Nichols and Shaw, *Okinawa*, p. 102; Roy E. Appleman, James M. Burns, Russell A. Gugeler, and John Stevens, *Okinawa: The Last Battle (United States Army in World War II: The War in the Pacific)* (Washington, 1948), pp. 125, 343. Reprinted by permission of the Department of the Army.

4. 5th Mar Div Intel Rpt, 27.

Some days later Tokyo Radio broadcast a message in English to the American troops on Okinawa:

Sugar Loaf Hill . . . Chocolate Drop . . . Strawberry Hill. Gee, those places sound wonderful! You can just see the candy houses with the white picket fences around them and the candy canes hanging from the trees, their red and white stripes glistening in the sun. But the only thing red about those places is the blood of Americans. Yes, sir, those are the names of hills in southern Okinawa where the fighting's so close that you get down to bayonets and sometimes your bare fists. Artillery and naval gunfire are all right when the enemy is far off but they don't do you any good when he's right in the same foxhole with you. I guess it's natural to idealize the worst places with pretty names to make them seem less awful. Why Sugar Loaf has changed hands so often it looks like Dante's Inferno. Yes, sir, Sugar Loaf Hill . . . Chocolate Drop . . . Strawberry Hill. They sound good, don't they? Only those who've been there know what they're really like.

h. Japanese Reactions

MARIANAS

MESSAGE OF LIEUTENANT GENERAL YOSHITSUGU SAITO
JULY 7, 1944

I am addressing the officers and men of the Imperial Army on Saipan.

For more than twenty days since the American Devils attacked, the officers, men, and civilian employees of the Imperial Army and Navy on this island have fought well and bravely. Everywhere they have demonstrated the honor and glory of the Imperial Forces. I expected that every man would do his duty.

Heaven has not given us an opportunity. We have not been able to utilize fully the terrain. We have fought in unison up to the present time but now we have no materials with which to fight and our artillery for attack has been completely destroyed. Our comrades have fallen one after another. Despite the bitterness of defeat, we pledge, "Seven lives to repay our country."

SOURCE: Quoted in Philip A. Crowl, *Campaign in The Marianas* (*United States Army in World War II: The War in the Pacific*) (Washington, 1960), pp. 257, 337. Reprinted by permission of the Department of the Army.

The barbarous attack of the enemy is being continued. Even though the enemy has occupied only a corner of Saipan, we are dying without avail under the violent shelling and bombing. Whether we attack or whether we stay where we are, there is only death. However, in death there is life. We must utilize this opportunity to exalt true Japanese manhood. I will advance with those who remain to deliver still another blow to the American Devils, and leave my bones on Saipan as a bulwark of the Pacific.

As it says in the "Senjinkum" (Battle Ethics), "I will never suffer the disgrace of being taken alive," and "I will offer up the courage of my soul and calmly rejoice in living by the eternal principle."

Here I pray with you for the eternal life of the Emperor and the welfare of the country and I advance to seek out the enemy.

Follow me!

Actually, General Saito was too feeble and sick to lead the charge in person. Shortly after issuing his final order he committed suicide. A captured Japanese officer who was with the general almost until the end described what probably took place: "Cleaning off a spot on the rock himself, Saito sat down. Facing the misty East saying 'Tenno heika! Banzai! (Long live the Emperor) . . . he drew his own blood first with his own sword and then his adjutant shot him in the head with a pistol."

But if their seishin was ebbing, the Japanese on Guam remained high in shiki—meaning morale in the sense of a willingness to die in combat. This spirit is reflected, with the usual rhetorical flourishes, in the diary of one enlisted man: "I will not lose my courage, but now is the time to prepare to die! If one desires to live, hope for death. Be prepared to die!

With this conviction one can never lose. . . . Look upon us! We have shortened our expectancy of 70 years of life to 25 in order to fight. What an honor it is to be born in this day and age."

LEYTE

Stories reached the War Ministry that Lt. Gen. Kuroda was devoting more time to his golf, reading and personal matters than to the execution of his official duties. It appeared that his control

SOURCE: Cannon, Leyte, pp. 50, 364, 367.

over staff officers and troops was not sufficiently strong and that there was a good deal of unfavorable criticism of his conduct among the troops. There was also indications that discipline was becoming very lax.

On 4 September 1944, I left Tokyo under orders . . . to investigate. As a result I obtained many statements substantiating the unfavorable stories in regard to Lt. Gen. Kuroda. The recommendations of all the staff was that Lt. Gen. Kuroda be relieved as soon as possible, and be replaced by Gen. Yamashita . . . who was a superb tactician and excellent leader.[1]

On the 25th of December, General Yamashita sent the following message to General Suzuki:

> Sixty days have already elapsed since the American forces invaded Leyte Island, during which period the *Thirty-fifth Army*, under the forceful leadership of its commander, has waged many a heroic battle against superior enemy forces and in the face of numerous difficulties. The Army gave a great blow to the enemy. Moreover, the *Thirty-fifth Army* by containing the opposing enemy for this long period of time deprived him of freedom of action for the coming operation, thereby facilitating the general conduct of our operations in this battle and rendering great services to our cause. I am deeply impressed particularly with the fact that the *Takachiho Unit* captured the hostile airfield at BURAUEN after the *Thirty-fifth Army*, despite its inferiority in equipment and number of men, and the stoppage of supply, made a timely and resolute attack against the enemy with the commander himself leading them. However, the enemy, who has increased his material power and war potential, now threatens, solely on the strength of his material superiority, to bear down on Luzon Island despite the heroic and desperate efforts of our sea and air forces as well as of the *Thirty-fifth Army*. In view of the sudden change in the situation, we shall seek and destroy our enemy on Luzon Island, thereby doing our part in the heroic struggle of the Army and avenging many a valiant warrior who fell before the enemy. As munitions have not been supplied adequately, I cannot keep back tears of remorse for tens of thousands of our officers and men fighting in Leyte Island. Nevertheless, I must impose a still harder task upon you. Please try to understand my intentions. They say it is harder to live than to die. You, officers and men, be patient enough to endure the hardships of life, and help guard and maintain the pros-

1. Statement of Lt. Col. Seiichi Yoshie, Circumstances Leading to the Relief of General Kuroda. 1 Oct. 51, copy in OCMH.

perity of the Imperial Throne through eternal resistance to the enemy, and be ready to meet your death calmly for our beloved country. I sincerely instruct you as above.

During his travels, General Suzuki composed two poems which he presented to his "dear brother Tomochika." One of these, entitled "A Farewell Poem," ran as follows:

> Every soldier must expect to sacrifice his life in War,
> Only then has his duty been done;
> Be thankful that you can die at the front,
> Rather than an inglorious death at home.

Iwo Jima

We must strive to disperse, conceal, and camouflage personnel, weapons, and materiel, and make use of installations to reduce damage during enemy bombing and shelling. In addition we will enhance the concealment of various positions by the construction of dummy positions to absorb the enemy shelling and bombing.

During the battle for the volcano, the district commander of the Mount Suribachi Sector sent the following message to General Kuribayashi:

> Enemy's bombardments from the air and sea and their assaults with explosions are very fierce and if we ever try to stay and defend our present position it will lead us to self-destruction. We should rather like to go out of our position and choose death by "banzai" charges.

General Kuribayashi's reply to this message is not available, if indeed he chose to reply. But the following exerpt from the enemy plan of battle seems to typify the doctrine employed in the defense of this fortress:

> Even if the enemy does capture our positions we will defend Suribachi Yama to the utmost and, . . . even though all positions fall into enemy hands and organized resistance becomes difficult, we will continue fighting fiercely to the last man and inflict heavy casualties on the enemy.

Source: Quoted in Bartley, *Iwo Jima*, pp. 12, 78, 146, 148, 191–192.

I am very sorry that I have let the enemy occupy one part of the Japanese territory, but I am taking comfort in giving heavy damages to the enemy.

In a dispatch to Tokyo on 10 March, General Kuribayashi summed up the Japanese situation in this manner:

> Although the attacks of the enemy against our Northern districts are continuing day and night, our troops are still fighting bravely and holding their positions thoroughly *** 200 or 300 American infantrymen with several tanks attacked "*Tenzan*" all day. The enemy's bombardments from one battleship (or cruiser), 11 destroyers, and aircraft are very severe, especially the bombing and machine-gun fire against Divisional Headquarters from 30 fighters and bombers are so fierce that I cannot express nor write here.

Then on the 21st Chichi Jima received a message from Iwo, "We have not eaten nor drunk for five days. But our fighting spirit is still running high. We are going to fight bravely till the last."

After a silence of almost three days Hori's radio crackled again and his operator brought him another message, "All officers and men of Chichi Jima, goodbye." This was the last word from the Japanese defenders on Iwo Jima.

OKINAWA

General Ushijima radioed his last message to Imperial Headquarters on the evening of 21 June. The impetuous General Cho made a last appeal for all units to fight to the utmost. He also prepared several messages which he hoped his secretary could eventually deliver in Japan. "Our strategy, tactics, and technics," he explained, "all were used to the utmost and we fought valiantly, but it was as nothing before the material strength of the enemy." Realizing that they could hold out no longer, Generals Ushijima and Cho made ready for death. Their cook prepared an especially large meal to be served shortly before midnight. When the meal was finished, the two generals and their staff drank numerous farewell toasts with the remaining bottles of Scotch whisky which had been carried from Shuri. The rest of the story is told by a prisoner

SOURCE: Quoted in Nichols and Shaw, *Okinawa*, pp. 470–471.

who learned the details of the death of Ushijima and Cho from other prisoners:

> Alas! The Stars of the Generals have fallen with the setting of the waning moon over Mabuni. . . .
>
> The pale moon shimmers bluish white over the waters of the southern sea, but on Hill 89 which juts abruptly from the reefs, the rocks and boulders are dyed crimson by the blood of the penetration unit which, with burning patriotism, rush the American positions for the last stand. The surrounding area displays a picture of concentrated fireworks; bursts of naval gun fire, flashes of mortar and artillery fire, to which is added the occasional chatter of machine guns. . . .
>
> Gathered around their section chiefs, members of each section bow in veneration toward the eastern sky and the cheer of "long live the Emperor" echoes among the boulders. . . . The faces of all are flushed with deep emotion and tears fall upon ragged uniforms, soiled with the dirt and grime of battle. . . .
>
> Four o'clock, the final hour of Hara-kiri; the Commanding General, dressed in full field uniform, and the Chief of Staff in a white kimono appeared. . . . The Chief of Staff says as he leaves the cave first, "Well, Commanding General Ushijima, as the way may be dark, I, Cho, will lead the way." The Commanding General replies, "Please do so, and I'll take along my fan since it is getting warm." Saying this he picked up his Okinawa-made Kuba fan and walked out quietly fanning himself. . . .
>
> The moon, which had been shining until now, sinks below the waves of the western sea. Dawn has not yet arrived and, at 0410, the generals appeared at the mouth of the cave. The American forces were only three meters away [sic]. Four meters away from the mouth of the cave a sheet of white cloth is placed on a quilt; this is the ritual place for the two Generals to commit Hara-kiri. The Commanding General and the Chief of Staff sit down on the quilt, bow in reverence towards the eastern sky, and Adjutant J. respectfully presents the sword. Finally, the time for the honored rites of Hara-kiri arrives. At this time several grenades were hurled near this solemn scene by the enemy troops who observed movements taking place beneath them. A simultaneous shout and a flash of a sword, then another repeated shout and a flash, and both Generals had nobly accomplished their last duty to their Emperor. . . .
>
> All is quiet after the cessation of gunfire and smoke; and the full moon is once again gleaming over the waves of the southern sea. Hill 89 of Mabuni will live in memory forever.

The death of General Ushijima and his Chief of Staff, General Cho, marked the end of the Okinawa campaign and the *32d Army*.

KAMIKAZE

The high-level background of these bizarre developments is delineated in the diary of Vice Admiral Kimpei Teraoka, who recorded events at headquarters in Manila from the time he turned over command of the First Air Fleet to Admiral Ohnishi until Ohnishi's return from Mabalacat.

18 October 1944: *Sho* Operation activated.

Time is against us. Available airplanes are limited in number. We are forced to take the most effective method to fight in this operation. The time has arrived for consideration of Admiral Ohnishi's proposal to employ crash-dive tactics. Various opinions were frankly expressed:

"Ordinary tactics are ineffective."

"We must be superhuman in order to win the war."

"Volunteers for suicide missions will have to be reported to Imperial Headquarters before their take-off, so that they will feel secure and composed."

"Should we speak directly to the young fliers, or through their group commanders?"

"It would be better for future actions to have their group commanders present the proposition."

"If the first suicide unit is organized by fighter pilot volunteers, other units will follow their example. If all air units do it, surface units will also be inclined to take part. And if there is a unanimous response by the Navy, the Army will follow suit."

After exchanging these opinions, we arrived at the conclusion that suicide tactics were the only possible salvation for the nation. It was decided to let the new commander, Ohnishi, organize the special units at his discretion.

Admiral Ohnishi summoned Captain Yamamoto, 201st Air Group commander at Mabalacat, and his flight officer, Commander Nakajima, to Manila. When they failed to arrive at the appointed time, Ohnishi set off for Clark Field at 1600, hoping to meet them on the way. (Sunset at 1830.)

Captain Yamamoto, however, arrived at Manila a little after 1700, having remained at Clark Field to send off the afternoon sortie unit.

SOURCE: Quoted in Rikihei Inoguchi, Tadashi Nakajima, Roger Pineau, *The Divine Wind: Japan's Kamikaze Force in World War II* (Annapolis, 1958), pp. 20–21, 148–149, 168, 200–203, 207–208. Reprinted by permission of Roger Pineau.

Yamamoto's executive officer, Commander Tamai, was on hand at Mabalacat to receive Admiral Ohnishi and to assure him of volunteers for suicide missions.

Twenty-four men volunteered for the first assignment, and the group was christened the *Shimpu* Special Attack Corps. It was divided into four units: *Shikishima, Yamato, Asahi,* and *Yamazakura.* These names were taken from the *waka* (poem) by Norinaga Motoori, a nationalistic scholar of the Tokugawa period. *Shikishima no Yamato-gokoro wo hito towaba Asahi ni niou Yamazakura-bama*—(The Japanese spirit is like mountain cherry blossoms, radiant in the morning sun).

Admiral Ohnishi was pleased to find that Lieutenant Yukio Seki, an Academy man, had jumped at the opportunity of leading the corps. The Admiral returned to Manila from Clark Field on the evening of 20 October. He was enthusiastic in telling about the Kamikaze Corps. "The fliers are eager, and have formed a good outfit. They asked permission to work out the organizational details by themselves, and I approved."

Ohnishi relieved me of command at 2000. I sincerely wished him good fortune with the new tactics, and he pledged his best efforts to achieve success. . . .

Around 16 June the enemy succeeded in penetrating the main defense positions of the Army in the south. General Ushijima rallied all his forces for a last offensive, and finally broke off communications with the following message:

With a burning desire to destroy the arrogant enemy, the men in my command have fought the invaders for almost three months. We have failed to crush the enemy, despite our death-defying resistance, and now we are doomed.

Since taking over this island our forces have, with the devoted support of the local population, exerted every effort to build up defenses. Since the enemy landing, our air and land forces, working in concert have done everything possible to defend the island.

To my great regret we are no longer able to continue the fight. For this failure I tender deepest apologies to the Emperor and the people of the homeland. We will make one final charge to kill as many of the enemy as possible. I pray for the souls of men killed in battle and for the prosperity of the Imperial Family.

Death will not quell the desire of my spirit to defend the homeland.

With deepest appreciation of the kindness and co-operation of my superiors and my colleagues in arms, I bid farewell to all of you forever.

Mitsuru Ushijima

There was a poetic postscript to his letter:

> *Green grass dies in the islands without waiting for fall,*
> *But it will be reborn verdant in the springtime of the homeland.*
> *Weapons exhausted, our blood will bathe the earth, but the*
>   *spirit will survive;*
> *Our spirits will return to protect the motherland.*

Four of these planes were forced down because of engine trouble. The others made their way to Okinawa. Endo maintained radio communication with the base and gave occasional reports on their progress. The last report contained a final message from Admiral Ugaki:

> I alone am to blame for our failure to defend the homeland and destroy the arrogant enemy. The valiant efforts of all officers and men of my command during the past six months have been greatly appreciated.
>
> I am going to make an attack at Okinawa where my men have fallen like cherry blossoms. There I will crash into and destroy the conceited enemy in the true spirit of *Bushido*, with firm conviction and faith in the eternity of Imperial Japan.
>
> I trust that the members of all units under my command will understand my motives, will overcome all hardships of the future, and will strive for the reconstruction of our great homeland that it may survive forever.
>
> Long live His Imperial Majesty the Emperor!

28 October 1944

Dear Parents:

Please congratulate me. I have been given a splendid opportunity to die. This is my last day. The destiny of our homeland hinges on the decisive battle in the seas to the south where I shall fall like a blossom from a radiant cherry tree.

I shall be a shield for His Majesty and die cleanly along with my squadron leader and other friends. I wish that I could be born seven times, each time to smite the enemy.

How I appreciate this chance to die like a man! I am grateful from the depths of my heart to the parents who have reared me with their constant prayers and tender love. And I am grateful as well to my squadron leader and superior officers who have looked after me as if I were their own son and given me such careful training.

Thank you, my parents, for the 23 years during which you have cared for me and inspired me. I hope that my present deed will in some small way repay what you have done for me. Think well of me and know that your Isao died for our country. This is my last wish, and there is nothing else that I desire.

I shall return in spirit and look forward to your visit at the Yasukuni Shrine. Please take good care of yourselves.

How glorious is the Special Attack Corps' Giretsu Unit whose *Suisei* bombers will attack the enemy. Our goal is to dive against the aircraft carriers of the enemy. Movie cameramen have been here to take our pictures. It is possible that you may see us in newsreels at the theater.

We are 16 warriors manning the bombers. May our death be as sudden and clean as the shattering of crystal.

Written at Manila on the eve of our sortie.

Isao

Soaring into the sky of the southern seas, it is our glorious mission to die as the shields of His Majesty. Cherry blossoms glisten as they open and fall.

Dear Father:

Spring seems to come early to southern Kyushu. Here the blossoms and flowers are all beautiful. There is a peace and tranquillity, and yet this place is really a battleground.

I slept well last night; didn't even dream. Today my head is clear and I am in excellent health.

It makes me feel good to know that we are on the same island at this time.

Please remember me when you go to the temple, and give my regards to all our friends.

Nobuo

I think of springtime in Japan while soaring to dash against the enemy.

22 February 1945

I am actually a member at last of the Kamikaze Special Attack Corps.

My life will be rounded out in the next thirty days. My chance will come! Death and I are waiting. The training and practice have been rigorous, but it is worthwhile if we can die beautifully and for a cause.

I shall die watching the pathetic struggle of our nation. My life will gallop in the next few weeks as my youth and life draw to a close. . . .

. . . The sortie has been scheduled for the next ten days.

I am a human being and hope to be neither saint nor scoundrel, hero nor fool—just a human being. As one who has spent his life in wistful longing and searching, I die resignedly in the hope that my life will serve as a "human document."

The world in which I lived was too full of discord. As a community of rational human beings it should be better composed. Lacking a single great conductor, everyone lets loose with his own sound, creating dissonance where there should be melody and harmony.

We shall serve the nation gladly in its present painful struggle. We shall plunge into enemy ships cherishing the conviction that Japan has been and will be a place where only lovely homes, brave women, and beautiful friendships are allowed to exist.

What is the duty today? It is to fight.

What is the duty tomorrow? It is to win.

What is the daily duty? It is to die.

We die in battle without complaint. I wonder if others, like scientists, who pursue the war effort on their own fronts, would die as we do without complaint. Only then will the unity of Japan be such that she can have any prospect of winning the war.

If, by some strange chance, Japan should suddenly win this war it would be a fatal misfortune for the future of the nation. It will be better for our nation and people if they are tempered through real ordeals which will serve to strengthen.

> Like cherry blossoms
> In the spring,
> Let us fall
> Clean and radiant.

i. Visitors at the Front

F.D.R. TO WILLIAM F. HALSEY ON MRS. ROOSEVELT'S VISIT

THE WHITE HOUSE,
AUG. 15, 1943

Dear Bill:

As you know, Mrs. Roosevelt is leaving for the Southwest Pacific and I am delighted that she will be able to see you. She is, of course, anxious to see everything, but I leave it wholly to your discretion as to where she should go and where she should not go. She is especially anxious to see Guadalcanal and at this moment it looks like a pretty safe place to visit.

I have told her that I am leaving the decision wholly up to the Area Commanders, not only in regard to Guadalcanal, but other places as well. I doubt, of course, at the present writing, whether she should go to New Georgia or to Funafuti.

Also, I would not have you let her go to any place which would interfere in any way with current military or naval operations—in other words, the war comes first.

I think that Mrs. Roosevelt's visit to places where we have military or naval personnel will help the general morale—because Mrs. Roosevelt has been visiting and will continue to visit the various hospitals in this country, especially on the West Coast where she meets returning sick or wounded personnel from the Southwest Pacific.

You have been doing a grand job and we are all proud of you.

Let her have any personal messages you would care to have her bring on her return.

All the good luck in the world.

Sincerely yours,

Mrs. Roosevelt's second wartime trip, made at the suggestion of F.D.R., covered New Zealand, Australia, New Caledonia, the Heb-

SOURCE: Franklin D. Roosevelt, *F.D.R., His Personal Letters*, ed. Elliott Roosevelt (New York, 1950), II: 1439–1440. Reprinted by permission of Hawthorn Books, Inc. William F. Halsey, *Admiral Halsey's Story* (New York, 1947), pp. 166–168. Reprinted by permission of William F. Halsey, III.

rides, Guadalcanal, and most of the small, isolated garrisons on islands which were serving us as steppingstones between Honolulu and the South Pacific. All in all, she covered twenty-three thousand miles. In this letter the President left the decision as to whether Mrs. Roosevelt should visit Guadalcanal to the on-the-spot commanders. In previous talks with representatives of the Australian and New Zealand governments, F.D.R. had said that he did not wish Mrs. Roosevelt to go to Guadalcanal under any circumstances. But Mrs. Roosevelt had been through several hospitals on the Pacific Coast filled with Marines from the Solomons, and she told the President she would never be able to face these men again if she were to be so near an island they had given so much to take and did not actually go to it. Mrs. Roosevelt did not learn, until she returned to Admiral Halsey's headquarters in Nouméa from New Zealand and Australia, that he had decided to let her go to Guadalcanal.

A fresh anxiety arose within a week. I was informed that Mrs. Roosevelt was making an air tour of the South and Southwest Pacific, and would reach Nouméa on the twenty-fifth. Among an area commander's worst problems are the politicians, admirals and generals, "special" correspondents, and "do-gooders" who present themselves in the assurance that their visit is a "morale factor," or that they are entitled to "see it from the inside." Mrs. Roosevelt I classed as a do-gooder, and I dreaded her arrival.

This opinion was strictly COMSOPAC's, not Bill Halsey's. I had known Mrs. Roosevelt for many years and had always liked and admired her; but I could find no excuse for her entering my area and monopolizing planes, crews, and fuel that were needed for military purposes. Secondly, large delegations from the Australian government and from General MacArthur insisted on coming over to give her an official welcome, and Nouméa had no accommodations for them. Thirdly, a series of contradictory messages were pouring into my headquarters, announcing, canceling, and changing her future itinerary, and it was impossible for me to arrange transportation for her until her schedule crystallized. Lastly, I'd have to wrench my attention from New Georgia, put on a necktie, and play the gracious, solicitous host. I had no time for such folderol, yet I'd have to take time.

She was wearing a Red Cross uniform when she stepped from her plane. I asked her at once if she would tell me her plans.

"What do you think I should do?" she asked.

"Mrs. Roosevelt," I said, "I've been married for thirty-odd years, and if those years have taught me one lesson, it is never to try to make up a woman's mind for her."

We decided she should stay in Nouméa for two days, then fly over to Australia, and spend two more days with us on her way home. I had begun to breathe more easily when she handed me a letter from the President, requesting permission for her to go to Guadalcanal, if I considered the trip feasible. That set me back on my heels. I told her rather curtly, "Guadalcanal is no place for you, Ma'am!"

"I'm perfectly willing to take my chances," she said. "I'll be entirely responsible for anything that happens to me."

I said, "I'm not worried about the responsibility, and I'm not worried about the chances you'd take. I know you'd take them gladly. What worries me is the battle going on in New Georgia at this very minute. I need every fighter plane I can put my hands on. If you fly to Guadalcanal, I'll have to provide a fighter escort for you, and I haven't got one to spare."

She looked so crestfallen that I found myself adding, "However, I'll postpone my final decision until your return. The situation may have clarified by then."

This cheered her up, and we drove into town.

I billeted her in Wicky-Wacky Lodge, where she would be more comfortable and would have more privacy than in our other quarters adjoining. Of course, we had a cordon of MP's around the house the whole time she was there. That night I gave a small reception and dinner for her (I put on a tie), and early next morning she started her rounds. Here is what she did in twelve hours: she inspected two Navy hospitals, took a boat to an officers' rest home and had lunch there, returned and inspected an Army hospital, reviewed the 2d Marine Raider Battalion (her son Jimmy had been its executive officer), made a speech at a service club, attended a reception, and was guest of honor at a dinner given by General Harmon.

When I say that she inspected those hospitals, I don't mean that she shook hands with the chief medical officer, glanced into a sunparlor, and left. I mean that she went into every ward, stopped at every bed, and spoke to every patient What was his name? How did he feel? Was there anything he needed? Could she take a message home for him? I marveled at her hardihood, both physical and mental; she walked for miles, and she saw patients who were grievously and gruesomely wounded. But I marveled most at their expressions as she leaned over them. It was a sight I will never forget. (At one hospital, I arranged for her to pin the Navy Cross and two Purple Hearts on my "one-man army," Lieutenant Miller of the *Strong*.)

The New Georgia campaign was finished by the time she returned from Australia, and I consented—though with misgivings— to her visiting Guadalcanal. When I saw her off, I told her that it was impossible for me to express my appreciation of what she had done, and was doing, for my men. I was ashamed of my original surliness. She alone had accomplished more good than any other person, or any group of civilians, who had passed through my area. In the nine months left to me as COMSOPAC, nothing caused me to modify this opinion.

Incidentally, my misgivings about her Guadalcanal trip were very nearly warranted. The night before her plane arrived, the enemy sent his first bombing attack against the island in two months, and sent another the night after her departure. I was there at the time, on a tour of our northern positions, and again I wondered if our team was the only one with code-breakers.

My reluctance to let Mrs. Roosevelt junket through my area at the expense of aviation fuel and a fighter escort reminds me of the similar trouble I had with correspondents. An essential part of their job is, of course, seeing the battle zone and describing it for their readers. I realized this, but I too had a job—to fight the war—and where my job conflicted with theirs, mine took precedence. The point of conflict was air transportation to the front. At one time during the Guadalcanal campaign we had only 3,500 gallons of aviation fuel on the island, or enough for only two ten-plane strikes. Ammunition was also low; so were bombs, torpedoes, food, and medicine. When the situation reached the stage where even a dribble of supplies was vital, we grounded all passengers, took over the transport planes, loaded them until they were bow-legged, and flew them up the line. (The combat pilots were glamor boys, but save a cheer for the transport pilots who hauled fuel and live ammunition in unarmed planes, without escort, and landed them under fire!)

CHARLES A. LINDBERGH

Tuesday, March 28
[1944]

Morning at home putting affairs in order. Family lunch. To Ford airport, Dearborn, in afternoon. Stopped at Edison Institute en route to leave a photograph of Grandfather and his old iron mortar, to be placed in the showcase with his gas furnace.

Wednesday, March 29

Phone call from Jack Horner. Authorization for my trip to the South Pacific has been received from Admiral Ramsey. I plan to leave here tomorrow night. First part of the morning spent on plans and putting affairs in shape. To Willow Run for a short conference with Bricker. Lunch with Bennett at the Rouge administration building. Henry Ford and Henry Ford II came in afterward to say good-by and wish me good luck on my trip. Home early and rest of afternoon putting affairs in order for leaving. Hour with the children before their bedtime. Supper in the library with Anne and Jon.

May 22, 1944

We are back at 10,000 feet again and circling directly over Rabaul. There are wrecks of ships in the harbor—victims of previous raids. All is quiet; no sign of life below on the streets or roads. Yet we know there are thousands of Japanese: hundreds of eyes looking at us, range finders keeping us in view, someone figuring out whether it is worth while to shoot at pursuit planes flying at our altitude. The Japanese are cut off from most of their shipping. Ammunition must be running low. Pursuit planes are difficult targets. Probably it is not worth while.

We circle over the airstrips. There are several of them around the harbor. Most are pock-marked with bomb craters. Three or

SOURCE: Charles A. Lindbergh, *The Wartime Journals of Charles A. Lindbergh* (New York, 1970), pp. 773, 816–818, 820–821, 839–840.

four are serviceable. I see a number of planes in revetments along the side of one field—probably unserviceable, or they would be better camouflaged. There has been no sign of air opposition during the last several strikes. We sweep over the harbor again. It is almost 11:00 and the end of our patrol. Four more fighters will be out to relieve us. We fly over the objectives we are to strafe before we start back to Green Island—two oblong buildings near the shore and surrounded by coconut palms. Gunfire was seen coming from them on one of the previous raids. I am to take the one nearest the beach, Major Armstrong the one a hundred yards inland. I reach down and purge my wing tanks and set controls for the dive.

We swing around into position. Major Armstrong noses down. Five seconds later I follow. The building is squarely in my sight; but Armstrong's plane is in the way—don't want to shoot so close to him. His tracers are striking his target and ricocheting back up off the ground. I am at 2,000 feet now, but he is still in the way. I keep the building in my sight and hold fire—roof, palm trees, and ground rushing up at me. No sign of life. Armstrong pulls up. I press the trigger. Long streams of tracers bury themselves in the roof and wall. Everything is still lifeless.

The ground is close. I level out over the tree tops. It was a short burst, but most of the bullets went home. I hope there was no one in that building except soldiers—no women, no children. I will never know. There is no time to think about it. Tree tops are twenty feet below, passing at 400 miles an hour. Armstrong is ahead, firing at some huts. I get another in my sight and give it a short burst—a dozen rounds; we are moving too fast for more. Still no sign of life on the ground. An airfield lies ahead. It is probably well defended with machine guns. We bank out toward the sea. The shore line flashes past. I hold low over the water.

We are to rendezvous over a small island off the coast. Here we are met by the other two planes of our patrol. They had been assigned a different target: similar buildings, two or three miles away. Everyone has ammunition left. We fly over to the Duke of York, an enemy-held island northeast of Rabaul containing a Japanese airstrip—apparently abandoned. Orders are to strafe everything in sight. We fly low over the palms and fire on huts and villages. The native inhabitants are reported to have gone to the hills in the interior long ago, and Japanese troops have been using their dwellings.

I get a line of a dozen huts in my sights and rake them from one end to the other—dust and fragments flying into the air—tracers bouncing up into the sky. I bank left, low along the coast, and then head in toward shore. I see the other Corsairs diving down on their targets. There is a hut much larger than the rest directly ahead of me. I rake it with fire as I approach. The tracers disappear inside. I keep shooting until within one hundred yards and pull up steeply to miss the hill and trees of the shore line, banking as I climb.

Another row of huts along the shore, but there is time only for a short burst. They were well hidden among the trees, and I was too close before I saw them. I circle back toward the airstrip. There is a larger building at ideal range ahead. I bank steeply and get it centered in the sight rings. I am about to pull the trigger when I see a steeple rising through the palms. I hold fire. Yes, a church. I flash thirty feet above it. Thank God I saw what it was in time. It is difficult to identify buildings when one is flying at tree-top level, and one is too good a target for machine guns at a higher altitude. In wartime one must be either very low or very high for safety. I find another group of huts and rake them with fire. My ammunition boxes are almost empty—only one gun still shooting. (I learned later in the day that even churches are fired on in this area; the Japanese are said to use them for their troops. However, I will leave churches for someone else to shoot at unless I see gunfire coming from their windows. I suppose our enemies say the same about our churches. It seems that both sides can find an excuse to shoot at anything in war.)

The patrol planes are rendezvousing off the coast. I join them, and we start back to Green Island. A radio message comes to sweep St. Georges Channel for a rubber boat. Apparently some plane is unaccounted for. We spread out 1,000 yards apart and fly 500 feet above the water, keeping a sharp lookout. We find nothing. Back into tight formation as we approach Green Island—in right echelon for landing breakup. On the ground at 12:20. Turn in equipment. Report what we saw during the patrol, and off to lunch. Other planes are getting ready to take off for a strike as we drive away.

Neither Major Armstrong nor I saw any antiaircraft fire near our planes. However, one of the pilots of the second unit reported that we were shot at over Rabaul—the burst being high and behind.

Met Lieutenant Colonel [Roger T.] Carleson, the C.O. of MAG-14, as I was walking along the path to my hut. He had been informed that I was going up on a patrol over Green Island, not the one over Rabaul. Nothing ever happens over Green Island. There hasn't been an enemy raid for weeks. He was much concerned when he learned that I was over Rabaul—one of the Marine officers told me that as we were driving from the airstrip to our quarters in the jeep. "It's so very irregular," the officer said. "You're on civilian status. If you'd had to land and the Japs caught you, you would have been shot." I replied that I didn't see it made much difference what status you were on if you were forced down on Jap territory, because according to reports they shot you anyway. (The Marine camps are full of stories about the torture and beheading of American pilots captured by the Japanese.)

"You didn't fire your guns, did you?" Colonel Carleson asked. I told him that I had fired my guns. "But you should never have done that. The Japs would shoot you if they caught you." The discussion continued while we went off for lunch together at the officers mess. "You have a right to observe combat as a technician, but not to fire guns."

"Of course, it would be all right for him to engage in target practice on the way home," another Marine officer put in. The tenseness began to ease up.

"Yes, he has a right to observe combat—and there's no reason he shouldn't observe it from an F4U any more than from a TBF or an SBD. We've had civilians observing from them, you know."

"Yes, he can observe from an F4U, and he can engage in target practice on the way home if he wants to; there's nothing wrong with that."

"Let's wait a day or so and see if anybody kicks up a fuss."

The more I see of the Marines the more I like them.

Stopped to talk to the maintenance crews of both Corsair squadrons. Then to see some of the Navy B-24s which are under repair. One of the B-24s exploded on take-off a few days ago—cause unknown. It crashed into the water not far from the end of the runway. No one is certain whether the explosion took place before or after the crash. All of the crew lost.

Wednesday, May 24

Arranged to go on a reconnaissance and strafing mission this afternoon along the northeast coast of New Ireland. To Intelligence hut for briefing at 1:00. There are to be four planes—no restrictions on targets. But weather is moving in toward the coast of New Ireland; possibly the ceiling will be too low. We are to take off and go on or turn back according to the conditions we encounter.

I get my chute and equipment, check code and radio signals, and start my plane—first cartridge this time. We are off at 13:55 and join up as we circle the field. Charge our guns and take up combat formation as soon as we are over the water. The New Ireland coast is clear—not enough low clouds to bother. The center of the storm is still north of us.

We fly along the coast at 2,000 or 3,000 feet at first, looking for signs of new Japanese activity. Then down 200 or 300 feet above the jungle, zooming up mountainsides, clearing the trees on top by less than our wing span, diving steeply down into the valley beyond, always just over the tree tops, watching for targets ahead or the telltale streaks of tracers from the ground.

We cut inland to avoid a Japanese airstrip where strong antiaircraft positions have been reported. "There are no targets in that vicinity worth the risk." There is a bridge below—bombed a few days back—hit squarely by a 500-pounder from a Corsair. A great gap shows in one end of the structure. Several Japanese are working on a scaffolding in an attempt to make repairs. We come on them too suddenly to shoot and are past like a flash. "We'll get them on the way back" (over the radio).

More miles over the tree tops, zooming up now and then for a few seconds to get a better look around, and then down again before there is time for someone to train a gun on us. Out to the coast line—four Corsairs abreast, racing over the water—I am the closest one to land. The trees pass, a streak of green; the beach a band of yellow on my left. Is it a post a mile ahead in the water, or a man standing? It moves toward shore. It is a man.

All Japanese or unfriendly natives on New Ireland—everything is a target—no restrictions—shoot whatever you see. I line up my sight. A mile takes ten seconds at our speed. At 1,000 yards my .50-calibers are deadly. I know just where they strike. I cannot miss.

Now he is out of the water, but he does not run. The beach is wide. He cannot make the cover of the trees. He is centered in my sight. My finger tightens on the trigger. A touch, and he will crumple on the coral sand.

But he disdains to run. He strides across the beach. Each step carries dignity and courage in its timing. He is not an ordinary man. The shot is too easy. His bearing, his stride, his dignity—there is something in them that has formed a bond between us. His life is worth more than the pressure of a trigger. I do not want to see him crumple on the beach. I release the trigger.

I ease back on the stick. He reaches the tree line, merges with the streak of green on my left. I am glad I have not killed him. I would never have forgotten him writhing on the beach. I will always remember his figure striding over the sand, the fearless dignity of his steps. I had his life balanced on a muscle's twitch. I gave it back to him, and thank God that I did so. I shall never know who he was—Jap or native. But I realize that the life of this unknown stranger—probably an enemy—is worth a thousand times more to me than his death. I should never quite have forgiven myself if I had shot him—naked, courageous, defenseless, yet so unmistakably man.

There is no more time to think about it. We turn inland again, skimming the palms of a coconut plantation, up and down more mountain sides. There is an antiaircraft position on our right—out of range; they do not shoot. We are over hills and jungle. There will be no antiaircraft here—too wild. We climb for altitude—to 4,000 feet. We have reached the limit of our patrol. . . .

Saturday, June 3

Off the strip at 7:00. Three Corsairs. Direct to Kavieng, but we pass over without bombing. Might as well keep the Japs uncertain about when they will be hit. We fly all around our patrol area at 10,000 feet; then return to Kavieng, and Lieutenant Gillespie drops one bomb. I dive down and strafe with my guns while it is being dropped—to divide the attention of the ground gunners. I see no antiaircraft fire. Either they are not using tracers or they are short of ammunition and holding what they have for better targets than pursuit planes. We fly around for another twenty minutes. Then I go in for my drop.

Climb to 12,000 feet and circle around over the city and airstrip, always making irregular turns to throw off the aim of the larger antiaircraft guns. Finally get my target lined up, drop my dive brakes, do a wing over, and line my sight up on the group of long, narrow buildings I have selected—Japanese supply houses.

It is a screaming dive—over 60°. I open up with my machine guns—the ground rushes up—mustn't get too low—the Kavieng gunners are deadly—three SBD's on the last strike. I stop firing—line up for the bomb—press the button—start the pull-out—lift the dive brakes—altimeter shows 5,000 feet.

I am blacking out—ease the stick forward slightly—the sky is clear again—I turn out over water—reverse turn—there are antiaircraft on the island below—I reverse again—and again. The island is behind—out of range. Where did the bomb hit? I look back at my target. There is a thin column of smoke on the ground. Is that all that 500 lbs. of high explosive does? It must be. Time passes, and there is no other mark to indicate a bomb hit. Then I overshot—still, it is among the buildings, I will know better how to aim next time.

I am back at 10,000 feet. I turn over the city. Even at this altitude I can see some Jap planes in revetments around the airstrip. How they must feel down there! They have not had a plane in the air for weeks, unless it is at night, and that is doubtful. We circle wherever we wish above them with no opposition except when we come within range of the ground guns. I spot some long buildings hidden among trees below not far from the airstrip. There are no bomb pits around them. Our pilots appear to have overlooked them in favor of more obvious objectives.

I dive down—almost vertical—and watch my tracers sink into the roofs. My recovery takes me over guns along the coast. I weave back and forth until I am far out over the water.

I climb again and dive on another objective. My guns must be almost empty—they hold only 400 rounds apiece—2,400 altogether. I must hold some for an emergency. We are not yet home. I join the planes of the first section. They have been circling at 10,000 feet. We finish our two-hour patrol and head back for Emirau.

j. Japanese: Move toward Peace

KASE DIARY

January 1, 1945

The year 1945 dawned to the shrieks of air-raid sirens. I find the following entry in my diary:

Monday, January 1—Fine weather. Early in the morning a small number of planes raided Tokyo area. Toward the direction of Ueno the sky was ablaze with fire. Poor helpless people rendered homeless on New Year's day!

This is the year of decision. This year will see the end of war both in Europe and Asia. Sad though it is, we must face realities squarely. We have lost the war.

Since last December the Germans have been attacking with vigor in the West and have made some advance. If this gives the appearance of German strength, it is deceptive. A local success of this character cannot alter the fundamental situation which is already past repair.

As for the Pacific war theater, our situation is extremely grave. We can no longer hold Leyte. The American forces landed successfully on Mindoro and are now pushing northward toward Luzon in great strength. In view of the rapid depletion of the sinews of war, it is impossible to improve the military situation which is bound to deteriorate daily. Defeat now stares us stark in the face. There is only one question left: how can we avert the chaos attendant upon a disastrous defeat and how shall we seek the reconstruction of Japan, so defeated?

The preservation of my fatherland, that is the paramount task assigned to me by fate. The hostile attack is developing so surprisingly swiftly that it may be diplomacy cannot intervene before it is too late. But that will surely mean the complete destruction of the nation. I shudder to think of such an eventuality. I must therefore redouble my efforts to expedite the restoration of peace. For that purpose I shall 1) cultivate closer contact with the lord privy seal and the jushin; 2) secure friends in the Army who will collaborate with me secretly; 3) enlighten public opinion through wider exchange of views with politicians, publicists, and press representatives. Chances are that the reorientation of our policy is yet feasible.

SOURCE: Kase, *Journey to the "Missouri,"* p. 99.

If so, the nation will escape annihilation. Even so, it will probably be accompanied by civil disturbances. Much blood will flow—and who knows that mine, too will not be spilt? I do not, of course, hesitate to sacrifice my life for the cause of the country. On the contrary, I consider it my privilege. But I do not like to die meaninglessly. I must hold on to my life tenaciously in order to exert my utmost efforts to save my country and people.

This, in short, is my New Year's day prayer.

KIDO MEMORANDUM

June 8, 1945

1. Okinawa seems now to be doomed, its fall being imminent.

2. The report on "The Present State of Material Power," which was submitted to the imperial conference, shows clearly that by the latter half of the year this country will lose practically all its ability to pursue the war.

3. It is easy for the enemy to overrun all our towns and villages one by one, depriving the nation of all food, clothing, and shelter. The destruction of these necessities of life will certainly cause widespread unrest among the people, who will be subjected to untold miseries by the advent of the cold season. It is feared that the situation, if left unchecked, will prove difficult to ameliorate. Therefore it is of paramount importance that a courageous step be taken at this critical juncture to terminate hostilities without delay.

4. As it is plain that the principal aim of the enemy powers is to bring about the downfall of the military clique, it is desirable that the Army should request peace and that the government should shape policies accordingly, in order to open diplomatic negotiations. But it is also plain that in the prevailing circumstances this is entirely out of the question. Should we, however, wait idly until an opportunity for action presents itself we would be too late and the maintenance of the imperial house and of our national structure would become altogether impossible. Consequently we must now appeal to the throne for guidance in ending the war quickly.

5. I propose therefore humbly to submit the following for the august consideration of the sovereign:

SOURCE: Kase, *Journey to the "Missouri,"* pp. 176–177.

A. An envoy should be dispatched to Moscow entrusted with a personal message from the Emperor. Since no direct negotiations with the United States and Great Britain are as yet feasible, it will be better to solicit the good offices of the Soviet government as a go-between.

B. The Imperial message will embody His Majesty's cherished desire to restore peace in the larger interests of humanity. Painful though it is for us to sue for peace, it has become necessary in order to save mankind from the miseries of prolonged warfare.

C. We should be content with the imposed terms of peace so long as they are compatible with the national honor. If the Pacific Ocean could be made really peaceful, true to its name, we should be satisfied with such terms as would secure the independence of our nation. Consequently,

1. we should be prepared to abandon established positions of influence over the people in the occupied regions;

2. we should voluntarily withdraw our overseas expeditionary forces;

3. we should be content with the minimum armaments sufficient for our national defense.

KIDO AFFIDAVIT AND KASE COMMENTS

June, 1945

With my [Kido] tentative peace plan being decided as shown above, I showed it to Chief Secretary Matsudaira the next day, that is, June 9, 1945, and had a full exchange of views with him on it. Prior to this I had been secretly in touch with Mr. Kase of the Foreign Office and Colonel Matsutani of the War Ministry through Chief Secretary Matsudaira in connection with peace moves or measures for terminating the war. If my tentative peace plan was to be put into practice, therefore, it was necessary to seek their views. So I asked Chief Secretary Matsudaira to get in touch with them immediately. At 1:30 PM the same day I had an audience with the Emperor at which I fully reported to His Majesty on my tentative peace plan and obtained imperial sanction to consult the prime minister, and the three ministers—war, navy, and foreign affairs—

SOURCE: Kase, *Journey to the "Missouri,"* pp. 180–181.

upon it. His Majesty, who was as deeply concerned as anybody else over the adverse developments of the war situation, was satisfied with my memorial, especially since His Majesty grieved that many medium and small towns were reduced to ashes by bombing attacks one after another in quick succession, with a large number of innocent people being rendered homeless. His Majesty commanded me to set my hand to the tentative peace plan immediately. My diary of June 9, 1945, states:

"June 9, 1945. At 11 AM I had a full exchange of views with Chief Secretary Matsudaira on the countermeasures against the pending national crisis. From 1:30 to 2 PM I had an audience with the Emperor at the Gobunko (library) when I fully reported to the throne on the measures for saving the national situation. His Majesty was pleased to tell me his intentions.

"The Diet happened to be in session, so that Prime Minister Suzuki and all other cabinet ministers were very busy. So I refrained from approaching them with the peace plan. It was on June 13, 1945, the day when the Diet was formally closed, that I had talks with Prime Minister Suzuki and Navy Minister Yonai about the peace plan."

After a few days I [Kase] offered my comments on the Kido memorandum. I said among other things:

1. Since it is likely that we will have to terminate hostilities by unconditional surrender, or on terms virtually similar to that, we must be prepared to accept this fact in embarking upon diplomatic negotiations and must take necessary measures on the home front in anticipation of the worst. Consequently "the peace with honor" envisaged by the lord privy seal is too optimistic, being incompatible with the grim realities.

2. We may conduct diplomatic negotiations either directly with the enemy powers or through neutral countries. Logically speaking, the direct course is simpler, but the Army will not countenance it, as it will involve a loss of face on its part. On the other hand the minor neutral countries are of limited influence. Therefore Moscow seems to offer a convenient channel. However, to rely on the Soviet Union at this critical juncture, when the very fate of our nation hangs by a thread, may, as some point out, be liable to cause later complications by introducing subversive influences into the highly complex and combustible situation. It is in a sense like crossing a dangerous bridge. But as there is no other way we are obliged to risk it. Only it seems wiser to approach Great Britain and the United States also at a later stage in a propitious moment in

order to counterbalance the Soviet influence by conducting a parallel negotiation.

SUPREME WAR COUNCIL SECRET AGREEMENT

June 18, 1945

After consultations with Kido Togo succeeded in impressing upon Suzuki the necessity of convening the six original members of the Supreme War Council at once in order to adjust the views of the government and the Supreme Command. The council met on June 18 in utmost secrecy and agreed that

Although we have no choice but to continue the war so long as the enemy insists upon unconditional surrender, we deem it advisable, while we still possess considerable power of resistance, to propose peace through neutral powers, especially the Soviet Union, and to obtain terms which will at least ensure the preservation of our monarchy.

With that in mind, we entrust it to the foreign minister to ascertain the Soviet attitude by the beginning of July with a view to terminating the war if possible by September.

k. Unofficial Peace Feeler through Switzerland

MEMORANDUM BY THE DIRECTOR OF THE OFFICE OF STRATEGIC SERVICES
DONOVAN TO THE SECRETARY OF STATE

WASHINGTON, 16 July, 1945

The following information, a sequel to a memorandum dated 13 July concerning a new Japanese attempt to approach Allied authorities through OSS representatives in Switzerland, has been received from Mr. Allen Dulles in Wiesbaden. The information was supplied by the source of the reference memorandum, Per Jacobsson, a Swedish national and economic adviser to the Bank for International Settlements in Basel. Jacobsson had asked to see Mr. Dulles

SOURCE: Kase, *Journey to the "Missouri,"* p. 184.
SOURCE: *Foreign Relations* (1945), VI: 489–491.

and was brought to Wiesbaden for that purpose on 15 July, returning immediately to Basel.

Jacobsson reports that between 10 and 13 July he had a series of
conferences with Yoshimura, a Japanese official attached to the
Bank for International Settlements, and Kojiro Kitamura, a director of the Bank, representative of the Yokohama Specie Bank,
and former financial attaché in Berlin. Yoshimura and Kitamura
claim to be acting in consultation with the Japanese Minister to
Switzerland, Shunichi Kase, and Brigadier General Kiyotomi Okamoto, former Japanese military attaché in Bern, who now is believed to be chief of Japanese Intelligence in Europe. Yoshimura
and Kitamura claim further that Kase and Okamoto have direct
and secret means of communicating with the Japanese Chief of
Staff. Yoshimura also claims that the peace group which he repre
sents includes General Yoshijiro Umezu, Army Chief of Staff;
Admiral Mitsumasa Yonai, Minister of Navy, and Shigenori Togo,
Foreign Minister.

Yoshimura and Kitamura appeared to Jacobsson no longer to
question the principle of unconditional surrender, though at one
point they asked whether unconditional military and naval surrender might not be sufficient. On his own initiative, Jacobsson
replied that such a proposal would not be acceptable to the Allies
but would be considered merely a quibble. Both Japanese officials
raised the question of maintaining Japanese territorial integrity,
but they apparently did not mean to include Manchukuo, Korea or
Formosa.

Throughout discussion with Jacobsson, the Japanese officials
stressed only two points: (a) the preservation of the Emperor, and
(b) the possibility of returning to the constitution promulgated in
1889. Kitamura prepared and presented to Jacobsson a memorandum asking him to sound out Mr. Dulles' opinion on the two
points.

(Mr. Dulles feels that these two Japanese are insisting on the
retention of the Emperor because they feel that he alone can take
effective action with respect to surrender and that some hope of
survival must be held out to him in order to gain his support for
unconditional surrender.)

Later Yoshimura and Kitamura prepared a second memorandum
in which they asked how, if Tokyo were ready to proceed, conversa-

tions could be arranged with Allied representatives and what form of authorization would be required.

Jacobsson is personally convinced that these approaches are serious and that the Japanese group in Switzerland is in constant cable contact with Tokyo. This conviction appears to be based on impressions only, since his two Japanese contacts never stated precisely that they had received instructions from any authorized agency in Tokyo.

(Mr. Dulles, in carefully guarded statements, pointed out to Jacobsson that:

(1. Mr. Grew's statement of 10 July covered the situation. As yet these approaches which Jacobsson described, in the absence of conclusive evidence that they emanated from a fully-empowered official, fall squarely into the category of "peace feelers" described by Mr. Grew.

(2. If competent Japanese authorities accepted unconditional surrender, appropriate Allied authorities would determine how such a surrender should be effected.

(3. He (Mr. Dulles) had no comments to make with regard to dynastic and constitutional questions.

(4. Prompt unconditional surrender appears to be the only way to save anything out of the wreckage.

(Mr. Dulles agrees with Jacobsson that the Japanese have taken to heart the consequences which Germany has suffered, including extensive physical destruction and the collapse of all German authority, because it prolonged a futile struggle many months after its hopelessness was wholly apparent. Jacobsson feels therefore that a tendency is growing in certain Japanese circles to try to terminate the war at any cost, provided that non-militaristic Japanese governmental institutions can be preserved in the Japanese home islands.

(Mr. Dulles expects within a few days to obtain some evidence as to whether these approaches by Yoshimura and Kitamura have any serious backing or represent merely an effort by the Japanese group in Switzerland to start something on their own initiative.)

WILLIAM J. DONOVAN

1. *Japanese Peace Feelers through Soviet Russia*

THE JAPANESE MINISTER OF FOREIGN AFFAIRS TOGO TO
THE JAPANESE
AMBASSADOR IN THE SOVIET UNION SATO

VERY SECRET   TOKYO, July 11, 1945—3 PM
URGENT

890. Re my telegram No. 884.

The foreign and domestic situation for the Empire is very serious, and even the termination of the war is now being considered privately. Therefore the conversations mentioned in my telegram No. 852 are not being limited solely to the objective of closer relations between Japan and the U. S. S. R., but we are also sounding out the extent to which we might employ the U. S. S. R. in connection with the termination of the war.

Our readiness to promise long-term mutual support for the maintenance of peace, as mentioned in our proposal, was also intended for the purpose of sounding out the Soviet attitude toward Japan with reference to the above. The Soviet Union should be interested in, and probably will greet with much satisfaction, an abandonment of our fishery rights as an amendment to the Treaty of Portsmouth. With reference to the other items, the manner of answering the arguments would be to meet fully the demands of the Soviets according to my telegram No. 885. Therefore, although we of course wish the completion of an agreement from the Malik–Hirota negotiations, on the other hand, sounding out the Soviets as to the manner in which they might be used to terminate the war is also desired. We would like to learn quickly the intentions of the Soviet Government regarding the above. As this point is a matter with which the Imperial Court is also greatly concerned, meet with Molotov immediately whether or not T. V. Soong is present in the U. S. S. R. With the circumstances of the earlier part of this telegram in mind, ascertain as best you can their intentions and please answer by telegram immediately.

SOURCE: *Foreign Relations, The Conference of Berlin (The Potsdam Conference) 1945*, I: 874–878, II: 1250–1251.

As you are skilled in matters such as this, I need not mention this, but in your meetings with the Soviets on this matter please bear in mind not to give them the impression that we wish to use the Soviet Union to terminate the war.

THE JAPANESE MINISTER OF FOREIGN AFFAIRS TOGO TO
THE JAPANESE AMBASSADOR IN THE SOVIET UNION SATO

SECRET   TOKYO, July 11, 1945—7 PM
URGENT

891. As it has been recognized as appropriate to make clear to Russia our general attitude concerning the termination of the international war despite the last paragraph in my telegram No. 890, please explain our attitude as follows, together with the substance of the above telegram, and let me know of your progress with Molotov by telegram as soon as possible:

> "We consider the maintenance of peace in Asia as one aspect of maintaining world peace. We have no intention of annexing or taking possession of the areas which we have been occupying as a result of the war; we hope to terminate the war with a view to establishing and maintaining lasting world peace."

Please confer with Mr. M. within a day or two.

THE JAPANESE MINISTER OF FOREIGN AFFAIRS TOGO TO
THE JAPANESE AMBASSADOR IN THE SOVIET UNION SATO

SECRET   TOKYO, July 12, 1945—8:50 PM
URGENT

893. Re telegram No. 891 and others.

Not having seen the telegram regarding the meeting with Molotov, I feel as though I am sending troops out without sufficient reconnaissance. Much as I dislike doing so, I find that I must proceed at this time and would like to have you convey to the Soviet side before the Three-Power Conference begins the matter concerning the Imperial wishes for the termination of the war. The substance of the following should be borne in mind as appropriate in your direct explanation to Molotov:

> "His Majesty the Emperor is greatly concerned over the daily increasing calamities and sacrifices faced by the citizens of the various belligerent countries in this present war, and it is His Majesty's

heart's desire to see the swift termination of the war. In the Greater East Asia War, however, as long as America and England insist on unconditional surrender, our country has no alternative but to see it through in an all-out effort for the sake of survival and the honor of the homeland. The resulting enormous bloodshed of the citizens of the belligerent powers would indeed be contrary to His Majesty's desires, and so it is His Majesty's earnest hope that peace may be restored as speedily as possible for the welfare of mankind.

"The above Imperial wishes are rooted not only in His Majesty's benevolence toward his subjects but in his sincere desire for the happiness of mankind, and he intends to dispatch Prince Fumimaro Konoye as special envoy to the Soviet Union, bearing his personal letter. You are directed, therefore, to convey this to Molotov, and promptly obtain from the Soviet Government admission into that country for the special envoy and his suite. (The list of members of the special envoy's suite will be cabled later.) Furthermore, though it is not possible for the special envoy to reach Moscow before the Russian authorities leave there for the Three-Power Conference, arrangements must be made so that the special envoy may meet them as soon as they return to Moscow. It is desired, therefore, that the special envoy and his suite make the trip by plane. You will request the Soviet Government to send an airplane for them as far as Manchouli or Tsitsihar."

THE JAPANESE MINISTER OF FOREIGN AFFAIRS TOGO TO THE JAPANESE AMBASSADOR IN THE SOVIET UNION SATO

VERY SECRET   TOKYO, July 12, 1945—2:20 AM [sic]
URGENT

894. Re my telegram No. 893.

When you convey this matter to them, please make it understood that the subject should be treated as absolutely secret. I realize that I am being presumptuous in saying this; I mention it merely to be sure.

THE JAPANESE AMBASSADOR IN THE SOVIET UNION SATO TO THE JAPANESE MINISTER OF FOREIGN AFFAIRS TOGO

VERY SECRET   Moscow, July 12, 1945—11:25 PM
URGENT

1. Your telegrams No. 890 and 891 were received on the 12th immediately after my reply No. 1381 was sent. I take it that the purpose of your telegram was to sound out the possibilities of uti-

lizing the Soviet Union in connection with the termination of the war.

In the unreserved opinion of this envoy and on the basis of your telegram No. 885, I believe it no exaggeration to say that the possibility of getting the Soviet Union to join our side and go along with our reasoning is next to nothing. That would run directly counter to the foreign policy of this country as explained in my frequent telegrams to you. It goes without saying that the objectives cannot be successfully attained by sounding out the possibilities of using the Soviet Union to terminate the war on the above basis. This is clearly indicated in the progress of the conferences as reported in my telegram no. 1379.

Moreover, the manner of your explanation in your telegram No. 891—"We consider the maintenance of peace in Asia as one aspect of maintaining world peace"—is nothing but academic theory. For England and America are planning to take the right of maintaining peace in East Asia away from Japan, and the actual situation is now such that the mainland of Japan itself is in peril. Japan is no longer in a position to be responsible for the maintenance of peace in all of East Asia, no matter how you look at it.

2. Although the Empire and its commanders have said, "We have no intention of annexing or taking possession of the areas which we have been occupying," what kind of reaction can we expect when in fact we have already lost or are about to lose Burma, the Philippines, and even a portion of our mainland in the form of Okinawa?

As you already know, the thinking of the Soviet authorities is realistic. It is difficult to move them with abstractions, to say nothing about the futility of trying to get them to consent to persuasion with phrases beautiful but somewhat remote from the facts and empty in content. In fact, with reference to your proposal in telegram No. 853, Molotov does not show the least interest. And again in his refusal he gave a very similar answer. If indeed our country is pressed by the necessity of terminating the war, we ourselves must first of all firmly resolve to terminate the war. Without this resolution an attempt to sound out the intentions of the Soviet Union will result in no benefit. In these days, with the enemy air raids accelerated and intensified, is there any meaning in showing that our country has reserve strength for a war of resistance, or in sacrificing the lives of hundreds of thousands of conscripts and millions of other innocent residents of cities and metropolitan areas?

Concerning these important matters, we here do not have appropriate or accurate information relative to our present armament production and therefore are not in a position to judge matters correctly. To say nothing about the fact that it was only by chance hearsay what we learned of the Imperial Conference which began in early June, at which it was resolved to take positive steps. And, if worse comes to worst and the progress of the war following the conference turns extremely disadvantageous for our side, it would behoove the Government in this situation to carry out that important resolution. Under these circumstances, the Soviet Government might be moved, and the desire to have it mediate will not be an impossibility. However, in the above situation, the immediate result facing us would be that there will be no room for doubt that it will very closely approximate unconditional surrender.

I have expressed my extremely unreserved opinion in the foregoing and I beg your pardon for such frank statements at this time. I have also heard that at the Imperial Court His Majesty is greatly concerned. I find these dreadful and heartbreaking thoughts unbearable. However, in international relations there is no mercy, and facing reality is unavoidable. I have transmitted the foregoing to you in all frankness, just as I see it, for I firmly believe it to be my primary responsibility to put an end to any loose thinking which gets away from reality. I beg for your understanding.

THE JAPANESE AMBASSADOR IN THE SOVIET UNION
SATO TO THE JAPANESE MINISTER OF FOREIGN
AFFAIRS TOGO

VERY SECRET   Moscow, July 19, 1945—2:30 PM
URGENT

1417. Re my telegram No. 1385

On the evening of the 18th I received a confidential note from Lozovsky which reads as follows:

"Moscow, July 18, 1945

"His Excellency Naotake Sato, Envoy Extraordinary and Ambassador Plenipotentiary to the Soviet Union

"Excellency:

"I have the honor to confirm that I am in receipt of your note dated July 13, and the message from His Majesty the Emperor of Japan.

"By order of the Government of the USSR, I have the honor to call your attention to the fact that the Imperial views stated in the message of the Emperor of Japan are general in form and contain no concrete proposal. The mission of Prince Konoye, special envoy, is also not clear to the Government of the USSR.

"The Government of the USSR, accordingly, is unable to give any definite reply either as to the message of the Emperor of Japan or to the dispatch of Prince Konoye as special envoy mentioned in your note of July 13.

"I avail myself of this opportunity to express to you my highest esteem.   S. A. Lozovsky"[.]

The Japanese Ambassador in the Soviet Union Sato to the Japanese Minister of Foreign Affairs Togo

VERY SECRET   Moscow, July 19, 1945—4:42 PM
URGENT

1418. Re my telegram No. 1417.

Concerning the matter of the dispatch of the special envoy, the Soviet Government has declined to accept such an envoy for the time being on the grounds that the mission is not specific. The above is indeed regrettable but just as I said in my humble opinion in my telegrams Nos. 1386 and 1392, and as again demonstrated this time, there is no way other than to present a concrete proposal when dealing with this government. Although your opinion expressed in your telegram No. 913–2 [913–1] has its point from the Japanese side, it does not at all conform to the atmosphere here. That you cannot achieve your objective of having them act in accordance with your hopes can almost be inferred from their attitude in rejecting the special envoy at this time.

m. Potsdam Proclamation

THE SECRETARY OF WAR STIMSON TO THE PRESIDENT

TOP SECRET   BABELSBERG, 16 July 1945

THE CONDUCT OF THE WAR WITH JAPAN

With the great needs of rehabilitation both domestically and abroad facing us, we still find ourselves engaged in war with a major Pacific power. The length and limitation upon our lines of communications to the Pacific combat areas aggravate the strains upon our resources which the wastes of war always impose. The Japanese soldier has proved himself capable of a suicidal, last ditch defense; and will no doubt continue to display such a defense on his homeland. Yet we have enormous factors in our favor and any step which can be taken to translate those advantages into a prompt and successful conclusion of the war should be taken. I have already indicated in my memorandum to you of 2 July 1945, the reasons which impel me to urge that warnings be delivered to Japan, designed to bring about her capitulation as quickly as possible. While that war is going on, it will be most difficult politically and economically to make substantial contributions to the reestablishment of stable conditions abroad. The longer that war progresses, the smaller will our surpluses become, and the more our over-all resources will be strained.

It seems to me that we are at the psychological moment to commence our warnings to Japan. The great marshalling of our new air and land forces in the combat area in the midst of the ever greater blows she is receiving from the naval and already established Army forces, is bound to provoke thought even among their military leaders. Added to this is the effect induced by this Conference and the impending threat of Russia's participation, which it accentuates.

Moreover, the recent news of attempted approaches on the part of Japan to Russia, impels me to urge prompt delivery of our warning. I would therefore urge that we formulate a warning to

SOURCE: *Foreign Relations, The Conference of Berlin (The Potsdam Conference) 1945*, II: 1265–1267.

Japan to be delivered during the course of this Conference, and rather earlier than later, along the lines of the draft prepared by the War Department and now approved, I understand, by both the State and Navy Departments. In the meantime our tactical plans should continue to operate without let up, and if the Japanese persist, the full force of our newer weapons should be brought to bear in the course of which a renewed and even heavier warning, backed by the power of the new forces and possibly the actual entrance of the Russians in the war, should be delivered.

Whether the Russians are to be notified of our intentions in advance in this regard, would depend upon whether an agreement satisfactory to us had been reached with the Russians on the terms of their entry into the Japanese war.

HENRY L. STIMSON

POTSDAM PROCLAMATION

PROCLAMATION BY THE HEADS OF GOVERNMENTS, UNITED STATES, CHINA AND THE UNITED KINGDOM

(1) We, the President of the United States, the President of the National Government of the Republic of China and the Prime Minister of Great Britain, representing the hundreds of millions of our countrymen, have conferred and agree that Japan shall be given an opportunity to end this war.

(2) The prodigious land, sea and air forces of the United States, the British Empire and of China, many times reinforced by their armies and air fleets from the west are poised to strike the final blows upon Japan. This military power is sustained and inspired by the determination of all the allied nations to prosecute the war against Japan until she ceases to resist.

(3) The result of the futile and senseless German resistance to the might of the aroused free peoples of the world stands forth in awful clarity as an example to the people of Japan. The might that now converges on Japan is immeasurably greater than that which, when applied to the resisting Nazis, necessarily laid waste to the

SOURCE: *Foreign Relations, The Conference of Berlin (The Potsdam Conference) 1945*, II: 1474–1476.

lands, the industry and the method of life of the whole German people. The full application of our military power, backed by our resolve, *will* mean the inevitable and complete destruction of the Japanese armed forces and just as inevitably the utter devastation of the Japanese homeland.

(4) The time has come for Japan to decide whether she will continue to be controlled by those self-willed milita[r]istic advisers whose unintelligent calculations have brought the Empire of Japan to the threshold of annihilation, or whether she will follow the path of reason.

(5) Following are our terms. We will not deviate from them. There are no alternatives. We shall brook no delay.

(6) There must be eliminated for all time the authority and influence of those who have deceived and misled the people of Japan into embarking on world conquest, for we insist that a new order of peace, security and justice will be impossible until irresponsible militarism is driven from the world.

(7) Until such a new order is established *and* until there is convincing proof that Japan's war-making power is destroyed, points in Japanese territory to be designated by the Allies shall be occupied to secure the achievement of the basic objectives we are here setting forth.

(8) The terms of the Cairo Declaration shall be carried out and Japanese sovereignty shall be limited to the islands of Honshu, Hokkaido, Kyushu, Shikoku and such minor islands as we determine.

(9) The Japanese military forces, after being completely disarmed, shall be permitted to return to their homes with the opportunity to lead peaceful and productive lives.

(10) We do not intend that the Japanese shall be enslaved as a race or destroyed as [a] nation, but stern justice shall be meted out to all war criminals, including those who have visited cruelties upon our prisoners. The Japanese government shall remove all obstacles to the revival and strength[en]ing of democratic tendencies among the Japanese people. Freedom of speech, of religion, and of thought, as well as respect for the fundamental human rights shall be established.

(11) Japan shall be permitted to maintain such industries as will sustain her economy and permit the exaction of just repara-

tions in kind, but not those industries which would enable her to re-arm for war. To this end, access to, as distinguished from control of raw materials shall be permitted. Eventual Japanese participation in world trade relations shall be permitted.

(12) The occupying forces of the Allies shall be withdrawn from Japan as soon as these objectives have been accomplished and there has been established in accordance with the freely expressed will of the Japanese people a peacefully inclined and responsible government.

(13) We call upon the Government of Japan to proclaim now the unconditional surrender of all the Japanese armed forces, and to provide proper and adequate assurances of their good faith in such action. The alternative for Japan is prompt and utter destruction.

POTSDAM July 26, 1945

> HARRY S. TRUMAN
> WINSTON CHURCHILL
> by H. S. T.
> PRESIDENT OF CHINA
> by wire

PRESS CONFERENCE BY PRIME MINISTER SUZUKI

TOKYO, July 28, 1945

Premier Suzuki, at his press conference held at his Official Residence at 3 PM July 28, which lasted about an hour, answered questions on various government policies taken at this decisive stage of the war and expressed strong conviction of sure Japanese victory.

Question: "What is the Premier's view regarding the Joint Proclamation by the three countries?"

Answer: "I believe the Joint Proclamation by the three countries is nothing but a rehash of the Cairo Declaration. As for the Government, it does not find any important value in it, and there is no other recourse but to ignore it entirely and resolutely fight for the successful conclusion of this war."

SOURCE: *Foreign Relations, The Conference of Berlin (The Potsdam Conference) 1945,* II: 1293.

MEMORANDUM OF CONVERSATION, BY MR. MAX W. BISHOP
OF THE OFFICE OF THE POLITICAL ADVISER
IN JAPAN

TOKYO, November 9, 1945

Participants: Mr. Sakomizu Hisatsune, Former Chief Secretary of
the Suzuki Cabinet (April 7 to August 15, 1941);
Mr. Kubo;
Mr. Bishop

Mr. Sakomizu said that at Mr. Kubo's suggestion he had come to tell Mr. Bishop the details of developments in Japan leading up to the surrender which was announced on August 15. In order that the relationship of personal friendship and close association between the Emperor and Suzuki would be clear, he explained that Prime Minister Suzuki had been the Emperor's Aide-de-Camp from 1930 to 1936; that Suzuki had been assaulted and wounded in the military revolt or "incident" on February 26, 1936; and that Suzuki had later in 1936 upon his recovery been made Vice President of the Privy Council, and in 1940 had become President. He said that the relationship between such Prime Ministers as Tojo and Koiso and the Emperor had been an official one, and that, therefore, with the appointment of Suzuki as Prime Minister, the Emperor was able for the first time since the outbreak of war to express his true feelings through the Prime Minister. Following is Mr. Sakomizu's narrative:

The first question to be taken up by the Suzuki Cabinet was a complete re-examination of the real situation of the war. The Navy Minister, Admiral Yonai, and Prime Minister Suzuki, working closely together and in complete secrecy from the Army, reached the conclusion that to continue the war could mean utter destruction of Japan and the Japanese people, and would also, each day it continued, be further destructive of world civilization.

During the last ten days of June, the Emperor of his own will and without official advice from anyone, although it was undoubtedly true that he had discussed the matter with the Prime Minister, called an Imperial Conference (*Gozenkai*). Six persons attended this Conference before the Emperor—the Prime Minis-

SOURCE: *Foreign Relations* (1945), VI: 702–708.

ter, the War Minister, the Navy Minister, the Foreign Minister, the Chief of Staff for the Army and the Chief of Staff for the Navy. At this meeting the Emperor asked that steps be taken to bring about an end to the war.

In the discussion which followed it was decided that there were two ways in which the Emperor's wishes could be met:

> 1) To open direct communications with the Allied nations, or
> 2) To approach the Allies indirectly and through the mediation of a third party or neutral country.

It was decided in the first part of July, around the 10th actually, to make an approach to the Allies through Russia. (It has been learned from another source that Foreign Minister Togo was principally responsible for this decision.) A message was sent to the Japanese Ambassador in Moscow asking Russia to accept a special envoy from Japan. The Russians replied by asking for a full explanation of the purposes of sending such an envoy and of the powers which it was proposed to give to the special envoy. The Japanese replied that they desired to send a special envoy for two purposes:

> 1) To improve Russo-Japanese relations, and
> 2) To discuss the use of Russia's good offices in bringing about an end to the war.

The fundamental purpose was, of course, to seek Russia's good offices in terminating the hostilities. It was decided that Prince Konoye would be the special envoy. (As an explanation of the selection of Prince Konoye, Mr. Sakomizu stated that when Prince Konoye had resigned as Prime Minister in October of 1941, he had promised the Emperor that if he were needed at any time thereafter, he would do whatever he could. Mr. Sakomizu explained that selection of Konoye was rather difficult to explain as it involved a personal promise made by Konoye to the Emperor.)

Before any reply to the Japanese message was made, Mr. Stalin and Mr. Molotov had to leave Moscow for the Potsdam Conference. It was stated that the Soviet reply would be forthcoming upon their return. Although it seemed apparent to the Japanese that obtaining of Soviet Russia's good offices was hopeless, the Japanese Government nevertheless continued to press Ambassador Sato for an answer.

On July 26, the Potsdam Declaration was issued and was carefully scrutinized by the Japanese Cabinet which came to the conclusion that this Declaration constituted an acceptable basis for Japanese surrender. Although the Army itself had lost confidence in its ability to continue the war, the force of militarism and the momentum which was carrying the war along were like a "bicycle rolling down hill without brakes": there was no way to stop it and the Army itself did not know how to give up. It was therefore necessary for the Cabinet to discover some development or event on which to capitalize in order to force the militarists to halt and to bring about surrender. At this juncture the atomic bomb was dropped on Hiroshima. The Cabinet felt that it had found a suitable peg on which to pin its surrender movement; but the Army asserted that the explosion at Hiroshima was not really an atomic bomb but was merely a super-bomb using already known explosives. To settle this argument a scientific staff of experts was sent to Hiroshima. On August 9 the scientists submitted proof that it was actually an atomic bomb. Early on the same morning Russia entered the war.

Prime Minister Suzuki decided that the war must be stopped immediately and that the atomic bomb and Russia's entry were sufficient "excuse" devices. He went to the Emperor about 8:00 AM. The Emperor agreed that the war should be brought to an end and on the basis of the Potsdam Declaration. After leaving the palace, the Prime Minister gathered together at 9:30 AM the same six men who had attended the Imperial Conference in the latter part of June. (This meeting in the morning of August 9 was not an Imperial Conference). At this time it was decided that:

(a) The Potsdam Declaration could be accepted with the understanding that it does not include abolishing the Emperor, or
(b) That it could be accepted with two conditions:
1) That Allied troops not occupy Japan;
2) That Japan be allowed to call back all its soldiers from abroad under its own orders and that surrender not be effected abroad.

The Prime Minister, the Navy Minister and the Foreign Minister favored the acceptance of the Potsdam Declaration with the understanding that the Emperor not be abolished. The War Minister and the Chief of Staff of the Army and the Chief of Staff of the Navy favored acceptance of the Potsdam Declaration only with the above two conditions. There was a Cabinet meeting called the same afternoon, August 9, about two o'clock. The consensus expressed was in agreement with the views of the Prime Minister, the Navy Minister, and the Foreign Minister. However, some ministers were not "big enough" to express clearly their own individual opinions and to accept responsibility for those opinions; they merely stated that they would agree with the Prime Minister. No clear decision was reached at the Cabinet meeting and the Prime Minister then went to the Emperor and an Imperial Conference was called at eleven o'clock the night of August 9.

The same six key men and the President of the Privy Council, Baron Hiranuma Kiichiro, and Mr. Sakomizu were present. Baron Hiranuma joined with the Prime Minister and his group making the vote four to three. The Emperor was then told that, as he could see, it was impossible for an agreement to be reached by the conference, that they could not make a decision and that it was therefore necessary for them to follow whatever the Emperor decided. The Emperor then expressed his concurrence with Baron Hiranuma, the Prime Minister and the Navy and Foreign Ministers. Always before it had been the custom for a Conference to reach a decision without directly involving the Emperor—one side or the other yielding so that an agreement could be reached. *But, in this instance neither side would yield until the Emperor spoke.*

(Mr. Sakomizu described the extreme tension and emotion at this important meeting.) Everyone present was impressed with the feeling that the "curtain" which had heretofore hung between the Emperor and the people was drawn aside, and that for the first time since the Meiji Restoration, the Emperor actually stepped from behind this "curtain" and came directly and personally before the people and on the side of the people. The experience was so intensely emotional that "tears flowed freely." All present sensed the "great historic importance" of the occasion. By using the figure of a "curtain" between the Emperor and the people, Mr. Sakomizu had reference to the fact that it had been customary for someone or a group to stand between the Emperor and any important action or decision and for that person or group to accept responsibility for the decision or act.

The Emperor went on to give his reasons for his decision (Mr. Sakomizu said that because of the emotion of the moment, he could not remember every word as it had been uttered by the Emperor, but that three points were especially clear.) The Emperor said:

1) That from the very start of the war, the plans and information of the military had been far removed from the facts of the true situation;

2) that to continue the war would mean the destruction of the Japanese people and the country and would also be disastrous to world civilization; and

3) that although it was sad and moving to recall the sacrifices which had been made and the suffering which had been endured, nevertheless the termination of the war in this manner and at this time was in accordance with the will of God and the destiny of the world.

(Speaking parenthetically and as an example of the real feeling of the Emperor, Mr. Sakomizu pointed out that in the original draft of the Imperial Rescript at the beginning of the war, there had been a period after the statement that war with the United States and Great Britain had become inevitable, but that the Emperor had himself inserted the phrase "How far this is removed from my true wishes!")

The Imperial Conference closed at 3:00 AM on August 10 and a telegram to the Allied Nations was dispatched at 7:00 AM the same morning. On August 13 at 5:00 AM the reply was received from the Allied Nations in which it was stated that the ultimate form of government in Japan would depend upon the freely expressed will of the Japanese people. This reply was hotly debated— certain Japanese insisting that it was only the Emperor himself who could decide the ultimate form of government in Japan, other Japanese insisting that the Emperor's will and the people's will were the same thing, and that the Emperor's will encompassed the people's will and vice versa. The latter group urged immediate acceptance of the Allied reply.

Mr. Sakomizu himself advised the Prime Minister to follow this course. The Prime Minister already had the same view and at once urged Japan's immediate surrender. The War Minister and the militarists were unalterably opposed. The Navy was divided with the Navy Minister, Admiral Yonai, on the side of the Prime Minister. Failure of these officials to reach an agreement among themselves made it necessary to hold another Imperial Conference. However, to petition for an Imperial Conference required the signature of three persons; the Prime Minister, the Chief of Staff of the Army and the Chief of Staff of the Navy. The Navy Chief of Staff, Admiral Toyoda, and the Army Chief of Staff refused to sign and it was therefore required that some extra-ordinary means of circumventing their refusal be found. (Ordinarily a signed petition to call an Imperial Conference is submitted to the Emperor before such action is taken.) Prime Minister Suzuki then consulted the Emperor, and the Emperor on his own initiative, summoned the six key officials and all other members of the Cabinet to an Imperial Conference on August 14, at 10:30 AM.

The War Minister, the Chiefs of Staff of the Army and Navy expressed the view that the Allied reply should not be accepted unless Japanese conditions were met. The Emperor thereupon addressed the Conference and stated that he would express at that point his opinion and that he would require all to agree with his views. He said that his opinion was in no way different from that which he expressed at the Imperial Conference on August 9, that in the future, Japan would entirely be separated from the means to wage war and would be without any arms or armament, and that Japan would in this way enjoy true eternal peace, completely separated from any form of militarism and would thus contribute to world peace as a country enjoying peace not maintained by arms. The Emperor thereupon ordered the Cabinet immediately to draft an Imperial Rescript terminating the war.

Since August 10, Mr. Sakomizu had been working on a draft for such an Imperial Rescript, following the general outline of the Emperor's remarks at the Imperial Conference on August 9–10. It was therefore necessary merely to insert the additional ideas which the Emperor had set forth at the meeting on the 14th.

(Mr. Sakomizu at this point said he wanted to emphasize two especially important phrases in the Imperial Rescript terminating the war. They were: "Our wish to bring into realization great peace for the benefit of all future generations" and "We are always together with our good and loyal subjects." He went on to point out that there had been some criticism in the foreign press for the reason that in the first Imperial Rescript there had been no use of the word "surrender." He said that in drafting he had consciously avoided using the word. He added it should not be difficult to understand the intense emotional feeling under which he and all Japanese were laboring at that time. This depth of emotion made it impossible to use specifically the word surrender which he believed would have detracted from the solemnity and dignity of the document and therefore would have lessened its powerful effect on all Japanese. He was consciously attempting to put as much dignity and force into the document as he could. He added that on September 2, at the time of the signing of the surrender, the word "surrender" was used in the Imperial Rescript and that the Japanese people by then had come to understand the true situation and were prepared for the use of the word "surrender." In the first rescript he felt that the two words "extra-ordinary measure" actually meant surrender and had so intended.)

The first Imperial Rescript was completed and approved at 11:00 PM August 14. The Emperor himself made the decision to broadcast directly to the people.

At this time there was great fear that the Army would attempt some sort of *coup d'état*. Every effort was therefore made to deceive the rabid militarists. General Anami, the War Minister, also did all in his power to prevent an incident. However, he alone could not have forestalled action by the militarists, and all who favored peace worked strenuously during the week before surrender. (Mr. Sakomizu described his efforts as being like those of a skilled fisherman who plays the fish until it is exhausted.) There were only minor disturbances. From midnight of August 15 until 8:00 in the morning, the Army placed soldiers in the front of all entrances to the Palace and prevented anyone from going in or coming out, in an effort to forestall the broadcast of the Emperor. General Tanaka of the Eastern Defense Command finally went to the gates and personally persuaded the soldiers to depart. Other groups of militarists attacked the Prime Minister's residence with machine guns. Prime Minister Suzuki's and Baron Hiranuma's homes were burned by the militarists.

On August 15 at 4:00 AM the War Minister committed suicide. (Mr. Sakomizu gave a rather interesting explanation of this suicide. He stated that the War Minister personally had no confidence in continuing the war and wanted it to stop, but because of loyalty to the Army the War Minister felt that he had to be on the militarists' side and could find no way to put an end to the force of militarism which, as Mr. Sakomizu had said earlier, was like a "bicycle rolling down hill without brakes." The War Minister therefore felt that in order to "apologize" to the militarists, he had to commit suicide. Mr. Sakomizu added that the War Minister was the only one who truly followed the *Samurai* tradition of suicide.)

Prime Minister Suzuki who was in poor health and exhausted, desired release from the Cabinet. He felt that it would not be advisable for a Cabinet to sign the surrender and then immediately resign. In view of his health which would not allow him to continue in office for any length of time, Prime Minister Suzuki seized upon the occasion of the suicide of the War Minister as a good opportunity to present his resignation. (It would have been necessary for him to obtain a new War Minister and re-organize his Cabinet had he continued as Prime Minister.) Accordingly on August 15 at 3:00 PM the Suzuki Cabinet submitted its resignation to the Emperor.

Note: The following were important members in the government during this period:

Prime Minister .... Suzuki Kantaro
Foreign Minister .... Togo Shigenori
Navy Minister .... Yonai Mitsumasa
Army Minister .... Anami Korechika
Chief Secretary .... Sakomizu Hisatsune
President of Privy Council .... Baron Hiranuma Kiichiro
Chief of Staff of the Army .... General Umezu Yoshijiro
Chief of Staff of the Navy .... Admiral Toyoda Soemu

MAX W. BISHOP

THE ACTING SECRETARY OF STATE TO REPRESENTATIVE
BERTRAND W. GEARHART OF CALIFORNIA

WASHINGTON, December 18, 1945

MY DEAR MR. GEARHART: I have your letter of December 9, 1945 in which, with reference to previous correspondence, you inquire if search of the Department's records has revealed anything that could be said to have thrown light on the origin of the report of a Japanese peace offer prior to August 10, 1945. You ask whether or

SOURCE: *Foreign Relations, 1945*, VI: 496–497.

not any peace offer or any statement looking toward peace was transmitted to the President by the Japanese prior to August 10, 1945 and whether President Truman carried something with him to Potsdam which might be regarded as a Japanese peace offer.

Since my letter of October 1, 1945 was addressed to you, a thorough search of the Department's records has been instituted and inquiries have been made in all directions. As the result of these investigations I feel fully satisfied that there is no evidence of any peace offer or of any statement looking toward peace transmitted to this Government prior to August 10, 1945 from official Japanese sources or from any person authorized to act as an agent for the Japanese Government. I narrow the definition only for the reason that we obviously cannot account for all the expressions of the desire for peace communicated to this Government or to individuals in this Government by unofficial Japanese persons. The statement in my previous letter to you that the Department received no official Japanese peace offer prior to August 10, 1945 still stands without qualification.

In view of the foregoing, I hardly need to add that President Truman did not carry with him to Potsdam anything which might be regarded as a Japanese peace offer.

Sincerely yours,

DEAN ACHESON

n. War's End

GRÄSSLI TO BYRNES

August 10, 1945

THE HONORABLE
JAMES F. BYRNES
    Secretary of State

SIR:

I have the honor to inform you that the Japanese Minister to Switzerland, upon instructions received from his Government, has requested the Swiss Political Department to advise the Government of the United States of America of the following:

SOURCE: U.S. State Department (Far Eastern Series 17), *Occupation of Japan: Policy and Progress* (Washington, 1946), pp. 56–60.

"In obedience to the gracious command of His Majesty the Emperor who, ever anxious to enhance the cause of world peace, desires earnestly to bring about a speedy termination of hostilities with a view to saving mankind from the calamities to be imposed upon them by further continuation of the war, the Japanese Government several weeks ago asked the Soviet Government, with which neutral relations then prevailed, to render good offices in restoring peace vis a vis the enemy powers. Unfortunately, these efforts in the interest of peace having failed, the Japanese Government in conformity with the august wish of His Majesty to restore the general peace and desiring to put an end to the untold sufferings entailed by war as quickly as possible, have decided upon the following.

"The Japanese Government are ready to accept the terms enumerated in the joint declaration which was issued at Potsdam on July 26th, 1945, by the heads of the Governments of the United States, Great Britain, and China, and later subscribed by the Soviet Government, with the understanding that the said declaration does not comprise any demand which prejudices the prerogatives of His Majesty as a Sovereign Ruler.

"The Japanese Government sincerely hope that this understanding is warranted and desire keenly that an explicit indication to that effect will be speedily forthcoming."

In transmitting the above message the Japanese minister added that his Government begs the Government of the United States to forward its answer through the intermediary of Switzerland. Similar requests are being transmitted to the Governments of Great Britain and the Union of Soviet Socialist Republics through the intermediary of Sweden, as well as to the Government of China through the intermediary of Switzerland. The Chinese Minister at Berne has already been informed of the foregoing through the channel of the Swiss Political Departments.

Please be assured that I am at your disposal at any time to accept for and forward to my Government the reply of the Government of the United States.

GRÄSSLI
Chargé d'Affaires ad interim
of Switzerland.

BYRNES TO GRÄSSLI

August 11, 1945

MR. MAX GRÄSSLI
  Chargé d'Affaires ad interim
    of Switzerland

SIR:

I have the honor to acknowledge receipt of your note of August 10, and in reply to inform you that the President of the United States has directed me to send to you for transmission by your Government to the Japanese Government the following message on behalf of the Governments of the United States, the United Kingdom, the Union of Soviet Socialist Republics, and China:

"With regard to the Japanese Government's message accepting the terms of the Potsdam proclamation but containing the statement, 'with the understanding that the said declaration does not comprise any demand which prejudices the prerogatives of His Majesty as a sovereign ruler,' our position is as follows:

"From the moment of surrender the authority of the Emperor and the Japanese Government to rule the state shall be subject to the Supreme Commander of the Allied powers who will take such steps as he deems proper to effectuate the surrender terms.

"The Emperor will be required to authorize and ensure the signature by the Government of Japan and the Japanese Imperial General Headquarters of the surrender terms necessary to carry out the provisions of the Potsdam Declaration, and shall issue his commands to all the Japanese military, naval and air authorities and to all the forces under their control wherever located to cease active operations and to surrender their arms, and to issue such other orders as the Supreme Commander may require to give effect to the surrender terms.

"Immediately upon the surrender the Japanese Government shall transport prisoners of war and civilian internees to places of safety, as directed, where they can quickly be placed aboard Allied transports.

"The ultimate form of government of Japan shall, in accordance with the Potsdam Declaration, be established by the freely expressed will of the Japanese people.

"The armed forces of the Allied Powers will remain in Japan until the purposes set forth in the Potsdam Declaration are achieved."

JAMES F. BYRNES
Secretary of State

TRUMAN STATEMENT

August 14, 1945

I have received this afternoon a message from the Japanese Government in reply to the message forwarded to that Government by the Secretary of State on August 11. I deem this reply a full acceptance of the Potsdam Declaration which specifies the unconditional surrender of Japan. In the reply there is no qualification.

Arrangements are now being made for the formal signing of surrender terms at the earliest possible moment.

General Douglas MacArthur has been appointed the Supreme Allied Commander to receive the Japanese surrender. Great Britain, Russia, and China will be represented by high-ranking officers.

Meantime, the Allied armed forces have been ordered to suspend offensive action.

The proclamation of V-J Day must wait upon the formal signing of the surrender terms by Japan.

Following is the Japanese Government's message accepting our terms:

"Communication of the Japanese Government of August 14, 1945, addressed to the Governments of the United States, Great Britain, the Soviet Union, and China:

"With reference to the Japanese Government's note of August 10 regarding their acceptance of the provisions of the Potsdam declaration and the reply of the Governments of the United States, Great Britain, the Soviet Union, and China sent by American Secretary of State Byrnes under the date of August 11, the Japanese Government have the honor to communicate to the Governments of the four powers as follows:

"1. His Majesty the Emperor has issued an Imperial rescript regarding Japan's acceptance of the provisions of the Potsdam declaration.

"2. His Majesty the Emperor is prepared to authorize and ensure the signature by his government and the Imperial General Headquarters of the necessary terms for carrying out the provisions of the Potsdam declaration. His Majesty is also prepared to issue his commands to all the military, naval, and air authorities of Japan and all the forces under their control wherever located to cease active operations, to surrender arms and to issue such other orders as may be required by the Supreme Commander of the Allied Forces for the execution of the above-mentioned terms."

JAPANESE EMPEROR'S STATEMENT

To Our good and loyal subjects:

After pondering deeply the general trends of the world and the actual conditions obtaining in Our Empire today, We have decided to effect a settlement of the present situation by resorting to an extraordinary measure.

We have ordered Our Government to communicate to the Governments of the United States, Great Britain, China and the Soviet Union that Our Empire accepts the provisions of their Joint Declaration.

To strive for the common prosperity and happiness of all nations as well as the security and well-being of Our subjects is the solemn obligation which has been handed down by Our Imperial Ancestors, and which We lay close to heart. Indeed, We declared war on America and Britain out of Our sincere desire to ensure Japan's self preservation and the stabilization of East Asia, it being far from Our thought either to infringe upon the sovereignty of other nations or to embark upon territorial aggrandizement. But now the war has lasted for nearly four years. Despite the best that has been done by everyone—the gallant fighting of military and naval forces, the diligence and assiduity of Our servants of the State and the devoted service of Our one hundred million people, the war situation has developed not necessarily to Japan's advantage, while the general trends of the world have all turned against her interest. Moreover, the enemy has begun to employ a new and most cruel bomb, the power of which to do damage is indeed incalculable, taking the toll of many innocent lives. Should We continue to

SOURCE: *Oriental Economist*, XII (July–August, 1945), 254. Reprinted by permission of *Oriental Economist*.

fight, it would not only result in an ultimate collapse and obliteration of the Japanese nation, but also it would lead to the total extinction of human civilization. Such being the case, how are We to save the millions of Our subjects; or to atone Ourselves before the hallowed spirits of Our Imperial Ancestors? This is the reason why We have ordered the acceptance of the provisions of the Joint Declaration of the Powers.

We cannot but express the deepest sense of regret to our Allied nations of East Asia, who have consistently cooperated with the Empire towards the emancipation of East Asia. The thought of those officers and men as well as others who have fallen in the fields of battle, those who died at their posts of duty, or those who met with untimely death and all their bereaved families, pains Our heart night and day. The welfare of the wounded and the war-sufferers, and of those who have lost their homes and livelihood, are the objects of Our profound solicitude. The hardships and sufferings to which Our nation is to be subjected hereafter will be certainly great. We are keenly aware of the inmost feelings of all ye, Our subjects. However, it is according to the dictate of time and fate that We have resolved to pave the way for a grand peace for all the generations to come by enduring the unendurable and suffering what is insufferable.

Having been able to safeguard and maintain the structure of the Imperial State, We are always with ye, Our good and loyal subjects, relying upon your sincerity and integrity. Beware most strictly of any outbursts of emotion which may engender needless complications, or any fraternal contention and strife which may create confusion, lead ye astray and cause ye to lose the confidence of the world. Let the entire nation continue as one family from generation to generation, ever firm in its faith of the imperishableness of its divine land, and mindful of its heavy burden of responsibilities, and the long road before it. Unite your total strength to be devoted to the construction for the future. Cultivate the ways of rectitude; foster nobility of spirit; and work with resolution so as ye may enhance the innate glory of the Imperial State and keep pace with the progress of the world.

The 14th day of the 8th month
of the 20th year of Showa.

o. Atomic Bomb

STIMSON

On August 6, 1945, an atomic bomb was dropped by an American Army airplane on the Japanese city of Hiroshima. There was thus awfully announced to the world man's mastery of a force vastly more deadly, and potentially more beneficial too, than any other in human history. In the months that followed, as Americans considered in mingled pride and fear the extraordinary achievement of the free world's scientists in combination with American engineers and industry, there was much discussion of the Hiroshima attack. As one of those largely concerned in this decision, Stimson at length concluded that it would be useful "to record for all who may be interested my understanding of the events which led up to the attack." The paper which he published in February, 1947, in *Harper's Magazine*, contains a careful record of his personal connection with this issue to which only occasional comments need be added.

"It was in the fall of 1941 that the question of atomic energy was first brought directly to my attention. At that time President Roosevelt appointed a committee consisting of Vice President Wallace, General Marshall, Dr. Vannevar Bush, Dr. James B. Conant, and myself. The function of this committee was to advise the President on questions of policy relating to the study of nuclear fission which was then proceeding both in this country and in Great Britain. For nearly four years thereafter I was directly connected with all major decisions of policy on the development and use of atomic energy, and from May 1, 1943, until my resignation as Secretary of War on September 21, 1945, I was directly responsible to the President for the administration of the entire undertaking; my chief advisers in this period were General Marshall, Dr. Bush, Dr. Conant, and Major General Leslie R. Groves, the officer

SOURCE: Henry L. Stimson and McGeorge Bundy, *On Active Service in Peace and War* (New York, 1947), pp. 612, 613, 630. Copyright, 1947 by Henry L. Stimson. Reprinted by permission of Harper & Row, Publishers, Inc.

in charge of the project. At the same time I was the President's senior adviser on the military employment of atomic energy.

"The policy adopted and steadily pursued by President Roosevelt and his advisers was a simple one. It was to spare no effort in securing the earliest possible successful development of an atomic weapon. The reasons for this policy were equally simple. The original experimental achievement of atomic fission had occurred in Germany in 1938, and it was known that the Germans had continued their experiments. In 1941 and 1942 they were believed to be ahead of us, and it was vital that they should not be the first to bring atomic weapons into the field of battle. Furthermore, if we should be the first to develop the weapon, we should have a great new instrument for shortening the war and minimizing destruction. At no time, from 1941 to 1945, did I ever hear it suggested by the President, or by any other responsible member of the government, that atomic energy should not be used in the war. All of us of course understood the terrible responsibility involved in our attempt to unlock the doors to such a devastating weapon; President Roosevelt particularly spoke to me many times of his own awareness of the catastrophic potentialities of our work. But we were at war, and the work must be done. I therefore emphasize that it was our common objective, throughout the war, to be the first to produce an atomic weapon and use it. The possible atomic weapon was considered to be a new and tremendously powerful explosive, as legitimate as any other of the deadly explosive weapons of modern war. The entire purpose was the production of a military weapon; on no other ground could the wartime expenditure of so much time and money have been justified. The exact circumstances in which that weapon might be used were unknown to any of us until the middle of 1945, and when that time came, as we shall presently see, the military use of atomic energy was connected with larger questions of national policy." . . .

"The two atomic bombs which we had dropped were the only ones we had ready, and our rate of production at the time was very small. Had the war continued until the projected invasion on November 1, additional fire raids of B-29s would have been more destructive of life and property than the very limited number of atomic raids which we could have executed in the same period. But the atomic bomb was more than a weapon of terrible destruction;

it was a psychological weapon. In March, 1945, our Air Forces had launched the first great incendiary raid on the Tokyo area. In this raid more damage was done and more casualties were inflicted than was the case at Hiroshima. Hundreds of bombers took part and hundreds of tons of incendiaries were dropped. Similar successive raids burned out a great part of the urban area of Japan, but the Japanese fought on. On August 6 one B-29 dropped a single atomic bomb on Hiroshima. Three days later a second bomb was dropped on Nagasaki and the war was over. So far as the Japanese could know, our ability to execute atomic attacks, if necessary by many planes at a time, was unlimited. As Dr. Karl Compton has said, 'it was not one atomic bomb, or two, which brought surrender; it was the experience of what an atomic bomb will actually do to a community, *plus the dread of many more*, that was effective.'

"The bomb thus served exactly the purpose we intended. The peace party was able to take the path of surrender, and the whole weight of the Emperor's prestige was exerted in favor of peace. When the Emperor ordered surrender, and the small but dangerous group of fanatics who opposed him were brought under control, the Japanese became so subdued that the great undertaking of occupation and disarmament was completed with unprecedented ease."

BYRNES

I do not remember just when it was that President Roosevelt told me about the atomic bomb. I do remember that it was a hot summer afternoon and the two of us were sitting alone in his oval office discussing certain phases of the war mobilization program. Suddenly, and for no apparent reason, he began to tell me the awesome story of the Manhattan Project.

I confess I thought the story fantastic. I was sure the President was exaggerating the possibilities just to watch my amazed reaction. I didn't disappoint him. And, as he noted my amazement,

SOURCE: James F. Byrnes, *Speaking Frankly* (New York, 1947), pp. 257–259. Copyright, 1947 by Donald S. Russell, Trustee of the James F. Byrnes Foundation. Reprinted by permission of Harper & Row, Publishers, Inc.

he proceeded with obvious pleasure to astound me with the scientists' prediction of what atomic energy would do. He told me that, prior to 1939, the Germans had made some progress with their experiments and he knew they were continuing their efforts. It was a race between us, he said, to see who could develop the first bomb.

At that time, which I believe was the summer of 1943, the President thought the Germans were ahead of us in the atomic race. It was evident that the information on which he based his belief contained more speculation than fact. Our Intelligence agents necessarily were restricted in securing accurate information on such a highly technical matter. From what we learned after the war, it was clear that the President had overestimated the progress of the Germans in this respect. Nevertheless, such reports served to stimulate the extraordinary efforts put forth on the Manhattan Project.

After the first discussion, neither the President nor I mentioned the atomic project to each other for many months. In fact, no one ever talked about it unless it was absolutely necessary. I remember once mentioning it to Secretary of War Stimson who, from its very inception, personally supervised the Manhattan Project. His reaction indicated surprise that I knew about it.

Even if the President had not told me about the project, as Director of War Mobilization I could not have avoided noting certain aspects of an enterprise as colossal as this. It, of course, held a top priority both for men and materiel. With manpower one of our most critical shortages, a project that at its peak claimed the labor of 125,000 men could not escape my notice, particularly since so many of the workers were highly skilled technicians.

However, I was not directly concerned with the project and was too busy to be curious. Thus it was not until December 1944, when another aspect of the labor situation brought me into the picture, that I learned definitely of the great progress we had been making.

An effort was being made to organize the workers at the Oak Ridge plant; controversies over the jurisdiction of the labor organizations involved had arisen and these had been referred to the National Labor Relations Board. The public hearing required under the circumstances had been postponed four times at the War Department's request; no further postponement was possible.

Under Secretary of War Robert Patterson and Major General

Leslie R. Groves came over to the White House to discuss the problem with me. General Groves pointed out that the hearing would require the presentation of evidence on such things as the number of workers employed, the number to be employed, the relationship of a particular unit to the project as a whole, and so on. Such evidence, General Groves was convinced, would necessitate disclosures that would seriously jeopardize the security of the project. They thought it would be helpful if I would arrange a meeting at the White House for the three of us and the leaders of the labor organizations involved. I agreed.

During our discussions, Mr. Patterson said that the War Department would know by April 1, 1945, whether or not they could develop the bomb. Both he and General Groves thought the effort would succeed, and they were confident they would know one way or the other by that date. It was the first time I had heard anyone venture to name a date.

The conference was arranged for the morning of December 5. The union officials were Mr. Joseph P. Clark of the International Brotherhood of Firemen and Oilers and Mr. Al Wegener of the International Brotherhood of Electrical Workers.

We took these men into our confidence. We told them that few people knew about the project. At that time, I believe, only four members of Congress had been given any concrete information. We asked the labor officials to waive their rights under the Wagner Act and to co-operate with General Groves in protecting the security of the project. They were good and patriotic men. They agreed to help and left immediately to do so. They were given authority to explain the situation to the presidents of their respective unions, Mr. John F. McNamara and Mr. Edward J. Brown; both of these leaders likewise promised their full co-operation. Their promise involved sacrificing rights given them by the law, but they kept it. They convinced the local union leaders, and the secret was protected for the duration of the war.

As a matter of fact, it was always amazing to me that the project did not become more generally known. It also was surprising that the Congress was willing to appropriate approximately two billion dollars without demanding more information on the use to which it was being put. It is a great tribute to those few congressional leaders who did have some idea of the nature of the project that they resisted the temptation to tell their colleagues and thus share the great responsibility.

The April 1 deadline came, but the result of the gigantic effort still was in doubt. Secretary Stimson, however, was confident of success. He instilled his confidence in the President. I am glad he did. But I have always regretted that President Roosevelt died without knowing definitely that the project was a success: It had been undertaken and carried to a conclusion solely because of his vision and courage in the days when the effort seemed hopeless.

Shortly after President Roosevelt's death, Secretary Stimson told President Truman that the scientists and others who had been working under his direction felt confident they would produce an atomic bomb within a very short time. He suggested the appointment of an Interim Committee to consider and make recommendations to the President on such important questions of policy as the test of the bomb, its use in the war, and the postwar use of atomic energy.

President Truman approved Mr. Stimson's suggestion and asked him to serve as chairman. The President requested me to act as his representative on the committee. The committee also included Under Secretary of the Navy Ralph Bard; Assistant Secretary of State William L. Clayton; Dr. Vannevar Bush, Director of the Office of Scientific Research and Development; Dr. James B. Conant, President of Harvard University; Dr. Karl T. Compton, President of the Massachusetts Institute of Technology; and Mr. George L. Harrison, President of the New York Life Insurance Company and special consultant to Secretary Stimson. Mr. Harrison served as chairman in Secretary Stimson's absence. We were assisted in our work by a group of scientists who had been connected with the project. They were Dr. Arthur H. Compton, Dr. Enrico Fermi, Dr. E. O. Lawrence, and Dr. J. Robert Oppenheimer.

CORRESPONDENCE

THE ACTING CHAIRMAN OF THE INTERIM COMMITTEE HARRISON TO THE SECRETARY OF WAR STIMSON

TOP SECRET   WASHINGTON, 21 July 1945

URGENT

WAR 35987. Secretary of WAR EYES ONLY TopSec from Harrison.

All your local military advisors engaged in preparation definitely favor your pet city[1] and would like to feel free to use it as first choice if those on the ride select it out of four possible spots in the light of local conditions at the time.

THE SECRETARY OF WAR STIMSON TO THE ACTING CHAIRMAN OF THE INTERIM COMMITTEE HARRISON

TOP SECRET   BABELSBERG, 21 July, 1945

URGENT

VICTORY 189. Reference WAR 35987 from Stimson to Pasco for Harrison's EYES ONLY. Message begins: Aware of no factors to change my decision. On the contrary new factors here tend to confirm it. End.

THE ACTING CHAIRMAN OF THE INTERIM COMMITTEE HARRISON TO THE SECRETARY OF WAR STIMSON

TOP SECRET   WASHINGTON, 21 July [19]45

URGENT

WAR–35988. Secretary of War EYES ONLY top secret from Harrison.

Patient progressing rapidly and will be ready for final operation first good break in August. Complicated preparations for use are proceeding so fast we should know not later that July 25 if any change in plans.

SOURCE: *Foreign Relations, The Conference of Berlin (The Potsdam Conference) 1945*, II: 1372–1375.

1. The reference is to the selection of Kyoto as a possible target for atomic attack. See Stimson and Bundy, *On Active Service in Peace and War*, p. 625.

The Secretary of War Stimson to the Acting Chairman of the Interim Committee Harrison

TOP SECRET   BABELSBERG, 23 July 1945
URGENT

VICTORY 218. To AGWar from Stimson to Pasco for Harrison[']s EYES ONLY. Reference your number WAR 35988. We are greatly pleased with apparent improvement in timing of patient[']s progress. We assume operation may be any time after the first of August. Whenever it is possible to give us a more definite date please immediately advise us here where information is greatly needed. Also give name of place or alternate places, always excluding the particular place against which I have decided. My decision has been confirmed by highest authority.

The Acting Chairman of the Interim Committee Harrison to the Secretary of War Stimson

TOP SECRET   WASHINGTON, 23 July 1945
URGENT

WAR 36791. Top secret Secretary of War EYES ONLY from Harrison.

Reference my WAR 35987 and your VICTORY 218 Hiroshima, Kokura, Niigata in [is?] order of choice here.

The Acting Chairman of the Interim Committee Harrison to the Secretary of War Stimson

TOP SECRET   WASHINGTON, 23 July 1945
OPERATIONAL PRIORITY

WAR 36792. Secretary of War EYES ONLY top secret from Harrison.

Operation may be possible any time from August 1 depending on state of preparation of patient and condition of atmosphere. From point of view of patient only, some chance August 1 to 3, good chance August 4 to 5 and barring unexpected relapse almost certain before August 10.

The Secretary of War Stimson to the President

TOP SECRET   WASHINGTON, 30 July 1945
URGENT

WAR 41011. To the President from the Secretary of War.

The time schedule on Groves' project is progressing so rapidly that it is now essential that statement for release by you be available not later than Wednesday, 1 August. I have revised draft of statement, which I previously presented to you, in light of

(a) Your recent ultimatum,

(b) Dramatic results of test and

(c) Certain minor suggestions made by British of which Byrnes is aware.

While I am planning to start a copy by special courier tomorrow in the hope you can be reached, nevertheless in the event he does not reach you in time, I will appreciate having your authority to have White House release revised statement as soon as necessary.

Sorry circumstances seem to require this emergency action.

Prime Minister Attlee to President Truman

BERLIN, August 1, 1945

DEAR MR. PRESIDENT: Thank you so much for your letter of to-day about the new weapon to be used on Japan. If it is quite convenient to you, I will come to see you for a few minutes after the Plenary Session this afternoon.

I am deeply touched by the very kind words you use about me and I, too, have been greatly encouraged by the unity which exists between our two countries on policies for world peace. I shall work with all my strength to maintain this unity unimpaired during the difficult years which lie before us.

May I also thank you warmly for the great personal consideration and kindness which you have shown to me and which has been such a help, especially during these last few days.

Yours sincerely

C. R. ATTLEE

The United States and World War II
Military and Diplomatic Documents

Printed by offset lithography by Halliday Lithograph Corporation on 55# Warren's University Text. This acid-free paper, noted for its longevity, has been watermarked with the University of South Carolina Press colophon. Binding by Halliday Lithograph Corporation in Scott Graphics' Corinthian Kivar 9.